EDITION DE LUXE

:::   :::   **ESSAYS OF**   :::   :::

JOSEPH ADDISON

CHOSEN AND EDITED BY

JOHN RICHARD GREEN, M. A., LL. D.

HONORARY FELLOW OF JESUS COLLEGE, OXFORD

THE ROGER DE COVERLEY CLUB

LONDON   AND   NEW YORK

EDITION DE LUXE

This Edition of Addison's Essays is limited to One Thousand
copies, printed for subscribers only

CONTENTS

CONTENTS.

INTRODUCTION.

WE commonly regard the Age of the Revolution as an age of military exploits and political changes, an age whose warlike glories loom dimly through the smoke of Blenheim or of Ramillies, and the greatness of whose political issues still impresses us, though we track them with difficulty through a chaos of treasons and cabals. But to the men who lived in it the age was far more than this. To them the Revolution was more than a merely political revolution; it was the recognition not only of a change in the relations of the nation to its rulers, but of changes almost as great in English society and in English intelligence. If it was the age of the Bill of Rights, it was the age also of the Spectator. If Marlborough and Somers had their share in shaping the new England that came of 1688, so also had Addison and Steele. And to the bulk of people it may be doubted whether the change that passed over literature was not more startling and more interesting than the change that passed over politics. Few changes, indeed, have ever been so radical and complete. Literature suddenly doffed its stately garb of folio or octavo, and stepped abroad in the light and easy dress of pamphlet and essay. Its long arguments and cumbrous sentences condensed themselves into the quick reasoning and terse easy phrases of ordinary conversation. Its tone lost the

pedantry of the scholar, the brutality of the contro-
versialist, and aimed at being unpretentious, polite,
urbane. The writer aimed at teaching, but at teaching in pleasant and familiar ways; he strove to make
evil unreasonable and ridiculous; to shame men by
wit and irony out of grossness and bad manners; to
draw the world to piety and virtue by teaching piety
and virtue themselves to smile. And the change of
subject was as remarkable as the change of form.
Letters found a new interest in the scenes and characters of the common life around them, in the chat of
the coffee-house, the loungers of the Mall, the humors
of the street, the pathos of the fireside. Every one
has felt the change that passed in this way over our
literature; but we commonly talk as if the change
had been a change in the writers of the time, as if
the intelligence which produces books had suddenly
taken of itself a new form, as if men like Addison had
conceived the Essay and their readers had adapted
themselves to this new mode of writing. The truth
lies precisely the other way. In no department of
human life does the law of supply and demand operate
so powerfully as in literature. Writers and readers
are not two different classes of men: both are products
of the same social and mental conditions: and the
thoughts of the one will be commonly of the same
order and kind as the thoughts of the other. Even
in the form which a writer gives to his thought, there
will be the same compelling pressure from the world
about him; he will unconsciously comply with what
he feels to be the needs of his readers; he will write
so as best to be read. And thus it is that if we seek
a key to this great literary change of the Age of the
Revolution, we must look for it not in the writers of

the Revolution so much as in the public for whom they wrote.

I restrict myself here, however, to a single feature of this change. " As a bashful and not forward boy," says the novelist Richardson, " I was an early favorite with all the young women of taste and reading in the neighborhood. Half-a-dozen of them, when met to work with their needles, used, when they got a book they liked and thought I should, to borrow me to read to them, the mothers sometimes with them, and both mothers and daughters used to be pleased with the observations they put me on making." The close of this bit of boyish autobiography is amusingly characteristic; and there are still, I trust, readers of Richardson to whom this little group of Englishwomen, "met to work with their needles," may have its interest, as the first of a series of such groups which gathered round the honest printer throughout his life, and out of which, half-a-century later, the one great imaginative achievement of the age of the Georges, the story of Clarissa, was to spring. But it is not for Richardson's sake, or for Clarissa's, that I quote it here. I quote it because it is one of the earliest instances that I can recall of the social revolution of which I spoke, in its influence on letters. Till now English letters had almost exclusively addressed themselves to men. As books had been written by men, so—it was assumed—they would be read by men; and not only was this true of the philosophical and theological works of the time, but even its more popular literature, the novelettes—for instance—of Greene and his fellow-Elizabethans, bear on the face of them that they were written to amuse not women but men. The most popular branch of letters, in fact, the drama, so ex-

clusively addressed itself to male ears that up to the
Restoration no woman filled even a woman's part on
the boards, nor could a decent woman appear in a
theater without a mask. Even the great uprooting of
every political, social, and religious belief in the Civil
Wars left this conception of literature almost un-
touched. The social position of woman indeed profited
little by the Great Rebellion. If she appeared as a
preacher among the earlier Quakers, no feature of
the Quaker movement gave greater scandal among
Englishmen at large; and Milton's cry for Divorce
was founded not on any notion of woman's equality,
but on the most arrogant assertion ever made of her
inferiority to man. It is a remarkable fact that amidst
the countless schemes of political reform which the age
produced, schemes of every possible order of novelty
and extravagance, I do not remember a single one
which proposed that even the least share of political
power should be given to women. And yet it is from
the time of the Great Rebellion that the change in
woman's position really dates. The new dignity given
to her by the self-restraint which Puritanism imposed
on human life, by the spiritual rank which she shared
equally with husband or son as one of "the elect of
God," by the deepening and concentration of the affections within the circle of the home, which was one
of the results of its withdrawal of the "godly" from the
general converse and amusements of the outer world,
told quickly on the social position of woman. And it
told as quickly on her relations to literature. It is now
that, shyly and sporadically, and sometimes under odd
forms, we hear of women as writers; of the Duchess
of Newcastle, of Aphra Behn, of Mrs. Hutchinson.
And it is now for the first time that we hear of women,

not exceptional women such as Lady Jane Grey, but
common English mothers and English maidens, as fur-
nishing a new world of readers. In groups such as
Richardson sketches for us literature finds a new world
opening before it, a world not of men only but of
women, of wives and daughters as well as husbands
and sons, a world not of the street or the study but of
the home.

It is in this new relation of writers to the world of
women that we find the key to the Essayists. It was
because these little circles of mothers and girls were
quickened by a new curiosity, by a new interest in the
world about them, because readers of this new sort
were eager to read, that we find ourselves in presence
of a new literature, of a literature more really popular
than England had ever seen, a literature not only of
the street, the pulpit, the tavern, and the stage, but
which had penetrated within the very precincts of the
home. Steele has the merit of having been the first
to feel the new intellectual cravings of his day and to
furnish what proved to be the means of meeting them.
His "Tatler" was a periodical of pamphlet form, in
which news was to be varied by short essays of criticism and gossip. But his grasp of the new literature
was a feeble grasp. His sense of the fitting form for
it, of its fitting tone, of the range and choice of its
subjects, were alike inadequate. He seized indeed by
a happy instinct on letter-writing and conversation as
the two molds to which the Essay must adapt itself ;
he seized with the same happy instinct on humor as
the pervading temper of his work and on " manners " as
its destined sphere. But his notion of " manners " was
limited not only to the external aspects of life and
society, but to those aspects as they present themselves

in towns; while his humor remained pert and superficial. The "Tatler," however, had hardly been started when it was taken in hand by a greater than Steele. "It was raised," as he frankly confessed, "to a greater thing than I intended," by the co-operation of Joseph Addison. As men smiled over the humors of Tom Folio and the Political Upholsterer, over the proceedings of the Court of Honor or the Adventures of a Shilling, they recognized the promise of a deeper and subtler vein of social observation and portraiture than any English prose writer had ever shown before. And the promise was soon fulfilled. The life of the "Tatler" lasted through the years 1709 and 1710; the two next years saw it surpassed by the Essays of the "Spectator," and this was followed in 1713 by the "Guardian," in 1714 by a fresh series of "Spectators," in 1715 by the "Freeholder." In all these successive periodicals what was really vital and important was the work of Addison. Addison grasped the idea of popularizing knowledge as frankly as Steele. He addressed as directly the new world of the home. "It was said of Socrates," he tells us, "that he brought philosophy down from heaven to inhabit among men; and I shall be ambitious to have it said of me that I have brought philosophy out of closets and libraries, schools and colleges, to dwell in clubs and assemblies, at tea-tables and in coffee-houses. I would therefore," he ends with a smile, "recommend these my speculations to all well-regulated assemblies that set apart one hour in every morning for tea and bread and butter, and would heartily advise them for their good to order this paper to be punctually served up, and to be looked upon as part of the tea-equipage." But in Addison's hands this popular writing became a part of literature. While it preserved the free movement of the letter-writer, the gaiety and briskness of chat, it obeyed the laws of literary art, and was shaped and guided by a sense of literary beauty. Its humor too became a subtler and more exquisite thing. Instead of the mere wit of the coffee-house, men found themselves smiling with a humorist who came nearer than any man before or since to the humor of Shakespeare.

It was thus that Addison became the typical representative of the revolution which passed in his day over English literature. His life and temper indeed equally fitted him to represent it. The training of his very boyhood had linked the sense of literature with the pieties of a home. Addison was the son of a country parson, who in later years came to be an archdeacon and a dean, but whose earlier career had been a checkered and eventful one, who had wandered as a minister of the fallen Church of England from country-house to country-house at the close of the Rebellion, had been chaplain to the garrison of Dunkirk and chaplain to the garrison of Tangier, and had only returned after years of this banishment among Flammands and Moors to a quiet parsonage in England. Throughout his life something of this old-home-atmosphere of the parsonage lingers about Addison; though he refuses to take orders and enlists among the wits, he never loses hold of the pieties of his early training; his instinctive love and reverence is for things that are pure and honest and of good report; he preaches all the more simply and naturally for the not being " strangled in his bands." His freedom from the bigotry and narrowness of view which so commonly go with the virtues of such a home may have been partly due to the wider experience of men and religions which his father had gained from a career among Papists and Mussulmans ; as his literary tendencies must have dated from the boyish years in which he saw Dr. Lancelot intent on his works about the religion of Barbary or the learning of the Hebrews. A love of letters and of religion such as he carried with him from his father's parsonage to Oxford might easily —as Oxford was then—have begotten but a pedant and a bigot. But ten years of Oxford life left Addison free whether from pedantry or from bigotry. At the moment, indeed, when he became a student at the University, the very loyalty to the Church which he had brought with him swayed him to a love of political and religious liberty with which the Church had commonly little sympathy. He entered at Queen's when Oxford was for once in opposition to the Crown, when the Church was in fact waging a war for existence with the tyranny of James the Second ; and his years as a demy of Magdalen were years during which Magdalen was still proud of the stand she had made against the worst of the Stuart kings. He became, as one who had seen such a struggle could hardly help becoming, a devoted adherent of the Revolution ; and he remained an adherent of it to the last. But firm as was his Whiggism, it had nothing in common with the faction and violence which disgraced the political temper of the time. While men were wrangling and intriguing and denouncing and betraying one another through the ten years that followed 1688, Addison was steeping himself in the Latin poets and tagging Latin verses under the elms of Magdalen ; and on the eve of the last great struggle with France, from the summer of 1699 to the close of 1703, he was traversing Europe in the leisurely fashion of the day, a fashion that suffered men to come into real contact with the

society of the land which they traversed, sauntering
through France and through Italy, or wandering with
a pupil over Switzerland, Germany, and the Low
Countries. The "practical" man may well be impatient of so desultory and unpractical a prelude to life as
this; but to Addison at least it seemed no small gain
that in an age of tumult and faction his converse should
have been with literature, with the "humanities" as
men called them then, in their highest and serenest
form, and that this converse with books should have
been quickened and enlarged by a liberal contact with
men.

When he returned at last to England it was to take
his place at once among the wits; and after a few
months of quiet poverty to enjoy a strange success. A
poem on Blenheim lifted him into fame : in a couple of
years he was Under-Secretary of State: by 1708 he
had a seat in Parliament, was rich enough to lend
Steele a thousand pounds, and became Chief Secretary
for Ireland. His career of dignity and good fortune
went on with hardly a check till, eleven years later,
his body was laid in that sacred resting-place of poets
and heroes, where he had so often mused amidst the
memories of the past on "that great day when we
shall all be contemporaries together." But it was not
as statesman or man of fortune that England honored
him with that grave in Westminster Abbey. True as
he was to his party he was yet truer to letters ; and
the years that saw him rise so suddenly into a Minister
of State saw him as suddenly take his rank as the
greatest of the Essayists.

I do not propose here to dwell on the characteristics
of Addison's genius, or the peculiar turn of his humor
or of his style. I would rather say briefly why in this

little book I have attempted to select from his Works what seemed to me the most fitted to give readers of to-day a sense of the grace and ease of the one, and of the indefinable sunshiny charm of the other. If selection is proper in the work of any great writer, it is proper in the work of Addison. Merely to gather what is his work together, indeed, an editor has to do a work of selection. As it has come down to us in " Tatlers " and " Spectators " and the like, it is mixed up with a huge mass of inferior matter from the pens of other men. Time has shown how high Addison rises above his fellow essayists; but when he actually wrote he wrote as one of a group of journalists, and the bulk of these journalists were very poor writers indeed. Steele, indeed, has a real vein of gayety and pathos—if not a very rich one—but who can read now-a-days the work of the Tickells or the Budgells! To reprint the " Tatler," or the " Guardian," or the " Spectator," that we may enjoy the essays of Addison seems to me much as if we were to reprint the "London Magazine " in order to enjoy the essays of Elia, or the " Morning Post " in order to enjoy the essays of Coleridge. It is only by selection then that we can read Addison at all. But even a selection from this mass of rubbish which gives us Addison alone hardly does justice to Addison. The needs of periodical literature are in some ways, no doubt, helps to a really great writer : the demand for " copy," the printer's devil waiting in the hall, often give the needful stimulus for production. But such necessities are hindrances as well as helps ; and if the printer's devil wrings good work out of a well stored brain, we cannot always reckon on his wringing the best work. Even with the greatest writers periodical work must have its inequalities; and Addison's

work is sometimes unequal. When he is humorous he
is always at his best: I do not know a single instance
where his humor loses its distinguishing delicacy and
refinement. But in his more serious papers we can
detect now and then the pressure of the printer. His
morality is sometimes dull, his criticism sometimes
commonplace, his wit—here and there—is a little ver-
bal and thin.

Most of my readers will probably grant that in passing by papers of this sort I am only taking out of their
path what are hindrances in any real appreciation of
Addison. But these are far from being the most serious obstacles to an appreciation of his work by readers
of to-day. A greater difficulty arises from the very
width of his range. Addison aimed at popularizing a
far wider world of thoughts and things than Steele
would have ventured on. He takes the whole range
of human thought and human action for the Essayist's
province. He chats with the little group around the
tea-table over the last new play or the last new head-
dress; but he chats with them too over poetry and
literature and politics and morals and religion. In his
hand the Essay is not the mere man of wit and fashion
who mingles with the crowd to amuse it with sprightly
talk and with passing allusions to deeper things; it is
the critic who quits his desk, and the statesman his
office, and the philosopher his study, and the preacher
his pulpit, to chat as freely as the wit himself with the
men and women about them. Such a range of subjects
gave a variety which is still one of the charms of the
"Spectator"; and to any inquirer into the thought of
the time it is perhaps the most valuable feature of
Addison's work. But viewed, as we are viewing them
here, from a purely literary stand-point, it must be

owned that a large number of these Essays have lost
all freshness and interest now. Addison's political
speculations, for instance, cannot fail to seem shallow
to readers who are children of a revolution far wider
and deeper than the Revolution of 1688. To him, as
to the wisest political thinkers of his day, to Locke or
to Somers, that "glorious revolution" marked a final
settlement and ordering of the national life, and the
establishment of relations between the people and its
rulers which were as nearly perfect as any human
relations could be. The struggle of centuries was
over; liberty—political, social, intellectual alike, was
secured; and what remained for the political philosopher to do was simply to expound the constitution of
things which had thus come into being, to bring home
its perfections to the devotees of a vanished past, and
to make wiser folk understand the true workings and
balance of this wonderful order. The change was
really so great, the improvement that had been wrought
so vast and important, that we can understand this
attitude of rest, of acquiescence, of simple contempla-
tive enjoyment. But we can do no more than understand it. A modern reader turns from Addison's
patient and methodical expositions of the Constitution
of 1688 with a mingled sense of boredom and amusement, as a railway traveler turns from an exposition
of the merits and arrangement of a stage-coach. And,
again, if we pass from his political to his literary
speculations, the amusement vanishes, while I fear the
boredom remains. As landmarks in the intellectual
history of Englishmen such papers as those on Paradise Lost and Chevy Chase will always have their
value. In reading them we cannot but feel how far
Addison was in advance of the critical feeling of his

age, by what a surprising effort he rose above its
canons of judgment, with what a freshness of mind he
felt forward towards a world of poetic feeling which
he never was fated absolutely to touch. But here
again the interest of such papers is historical rather
than literary. As an actual criticism of literature this
work has become dead to us; no one of our day, I
suppose, ever got help towards a right judgment of
Chevy Chase or Paradise Lost from Addison's essays
on them.

In this little book therefore I have given no selections from Addison's political or critical essays, even
though this rule forced me to omit such an exquisite
bit of writing as his character of Lord Somers. My
aim has been to give what was still living in his work,
and, whatever their interest may be to readers of tastes
like my own, I feel that to the bulk of readers his
politics and his criticisms are dead. And for the same
reason, but at still greater risk of censure, I have
given none of his moral or theological essays. It is
not that I share the common scorn of the morality or
theology of the last century, nor that I am blind to
the peculiar interest of Addison's position, or of the
work which he did. As the first of our lay-preachers,
Addison marks the expansion of a thirst for moral and
religious improvement beyond the circle of the clergy.
He is thus the ancestor of Howard and Wilberforce,
as he is the ancestor of Mr. Matthew Arnold. For a
whole century the Spectator had greater weight on
moral and religious opinions than all the charges of
the bishops. And on the moral side, at least, it deserved to have such a weight. Addison was not only
a moralist: he had what so few have had in the world's
history, an enthusiasm for conduct. "The great aim

of these my speculations," he says emphatically, "is to
banish vice and ignorance out of the territories of
Great Britain." It was this enthusiasm for morality
which enabled him to discern, to sympathize with, to
give shape to, the moral energy of his day. We hear
sometimes that the last century is "repulsive": but
what is it that repels us in it? Is it the age itself, or
the picture of itself which the age so fearlessly presents? There is no historic ground for thinking the
eighteenth century a coarser or a more brutal age than
the centuries that had gone before; rather there is
ground for thinking it a less coarse and a less brutal
age. The features which repel us in it are no features
of its own production. There were brutalized colliers
at Ringwood before Wesley; there were brutal squires
before Western; there were brutal mobs before the
Gordon riots. Vile as our prisons were when Howard
visited them, they were yet viler in the days of Elizabeth. Parliamentary corruption was a child of the
Restoration; the immorality of the upper classes was
as great under the Tudors as under the Georges. What
makes the Georgian age seem repulsive is simply that
it is the first age which felt these evils to be evils, which
dragged them, in its effort to amend them, into the
light of day. It is in fact the moral effort of the
time which makes it seem so immoral. Till now
social evil had passed unnoted, uncensured, because,
save by the directly religious world, it was unfelt. It
was a sudden and general zeal for better things which
made the eighteenth century note, describe, satirize
the evil of society. Then, as now, the bulk of Englishmen were honest and right-minded. "Between the
mud at the bottom and the scum of its surface," says
Mons. Taine fairly enough, "rolled on the great

current of the national life." Widely as it had parted from the theological and political doctrines of Puritanism, the moral conceptions of Puritanism lived on in the nation at large. The popular book of the upper and middle classes, the book that was in every lady's closet, was "The Whole Duty of Man." But then, for the first time, this moral temper of the individual Englishman quickened into a passion for moral reform in the whole structure of English society. The moral preaching which bores the reader of to-day was the popular literature of the eighteenth century. Not only can the essayist make conduct the groundwork of his essays, but the novelist takes it as the groundwork of his novels, the playwright as the basis of his plays. The Beggars' Opera, in which Gay quizzes political corruption, is played amidst thunders of applause. Everybody reads Pope's Satires. Whatever in fact men put their hands to takes somehow this shape of moral reform. "Give us some models of letters for servant-maids to write to their homes," said the publishers to Richardson; and Richardson, honestly striving to produce a Complete Letter-writer, gave them "Pamela."

What Addison did for this general impulse was to give it guidance, to stamp it with a larger, a more liberal, a more harmonious character, than it might otherwise have had. While Puritanism aimed at the culture of "the best," the Essayists aimed at the culture of all. Puritanism again had concentrated itself on the development of the religious side of man, as the Renascence had spent itself on the development of his intellectual, his artistic, his physical side. But what Addison aimed at was the development of man as a whole. He would have had men love God as

Cromwell loved him, and freedom better than Cromwell loved it, but he would have had liberty and religion associate themselves with all that was human; he would have had no "horseplay" at the singing of the king's death-warrant. And it is only fair to remember that what he aimed at, he in no small measure actually brought about. The men who sneered in our fathers' day at the preaching of the Essayists were the men whom that preaching had formed. Formal and external as the moral drill of the eighteenth century seems to us, it wrought a revolution in social manners. We smile perhaps at the minuteness of the drill, as when Chesterfield bids his son never pare his nails in society; but even in these minute matters it has succeeded. And its success is just as great in the greater matters. It is no small triumph to have dissociated learning from pedantry, courage from the quarrelsomeness of the bravo; to have got rid of the brutalities and brutal pleasures of that older life, of its "grinning matches" and bull-baitings, its drunkenness and oaths, its rakes and its mohawks; to have no more Parson Trullibers, to have superseded the Squire Westerns by the Squire All-worthys, and to have made Lovelace impossible. No doubt a thousand influences had been telling on English society through these hundred years to produce such a change as this; but Addison was certainly one of these influences, and he was not the one that told least, for through the whole of those years men and women alike were reading and smiling, and chatting and thinking, over the Essays of the Spectator. And yet, as I have said, I cannot feel that there is anything living, anything that really helps or interests us to-day, in the speculations of Addison. His religion

is not our religion, for it starts from assumptions
which we cannot grant; its conceptions, whether of
God or man, strike us as inadequate and poor; its ideal
of life has lost its charm. We do not care "to be easy
here and happy afterwards." And grateful as we
must be to Addison's morality, yet here again we can
but feel that his work is dead. It was far from being
commonplace to men who had left behind them ages
in which morals had been lost in theology, and to
whom the very notion of conduct was a new and fas-
cinating thing; it has become commonplace to us just
through its very success, through the charm it exercised
over men for a hundred years; but still it has become
commonplace. Graceful and earnest as such speculations may be, it is hard to read them without a
yawn.

When these then have been deducted, when we cease
to study Addison as a statesman or a critic, or a
theologian or a moralist, what of him remains? Well,
I think we may fairly answer, all that is individually
and distinctively Addison. There remains his light
and playful fancy. There remains his incomparable
humor. There remains, pervading all, his large and
generous humanity. I know no writer whose moral
temper so perfectly reflects itself in his work. His
style, with its free, unaffected, movement, its clear
distinctness, its graceful transitions, its delicate har-
monies, its appropriateness of tone; the temperance
and moderation of his treatment, the effortless self-
mastery, the sense of quiet power, the absence of ex-
aggeration or extravagance, the perfect keeping with
which he deals with his subjects; or again the exquisite reserve, the subtle tenderness, the geniality,
the pathos of his humor—what are these but the

literary reflection of Addison himself, of that temper
so pure and lofty yet so sympathetic, so strong yet so
lovable? In the midst of that explosion of individu-
ality, of individual energy and force, which marked
the eighteenth century, Addison stands out individual,
full of force, but of a force harmonious, self-controlled,
instinct with the sense of measure, of good taste, good
humor, culture, urbanity. It seems natural to him
that this temper should find its expression in the
highest literature. "The greatest wits I have conversed with," he says, "were men eminent for their
humanity;" and it is this for which he is himself so
eminent as a wit, he is humane. Man is the one interesting thing to him; he is never weary of tracking
out human character into its shyest recesses, of studying human conduct, of watching the play of human
thought and feeling, and of contrasting man's infinite
capacities of greatness with his infinite capacities of
littleness. But the sight stirs in him not only interest,
but sympathy; he looks on it with eyes as keen as
those of Swift, but with a calmer and juster intelligence; and as he looks it moves him not to the " saeva
indignatio " of the Dean, but to that mingled smile
and tear, that blending of "how wonderful a thing is
man," with, " but oh! the pity of it!" which had
found equal utterance but once before in Shakespeare.
It was the sense of this that won him so wide a love
in his own day; and it is the sense of this that still
makes his memory so dear to Englishmen. " To Addison," says Lord Macaulay, "we are bound by a sentiment as much like affection as any sentiment can be,
which is inspired by one who has been sleeping a
hundred and twenty years in Westminster Abbey."
It is because I have felt this affection from my own boy-

hood, when I read my Spectator beneath the shadows of the trees in " Addison's Walk," that I have attempted in these Selections to bring Addison home to readers of to-day.

SIR ROGER DE COVERLEY.

[In his general account of the Spectator Club, Addison gives us a vignette of Sir Roger, which may serve as preface to his papers.]

THE first of our society is a gentleman of Worcestershire, of ancient descent, a baronet, his name Sir Roger de Coverley. His great grandfather was inventor of that famous country-dance which is called after him. All who know that shire are very well acquainted with the parts and merits of Sir Roger. He is a gentleman that is very singular in his behavior, but his singularities proceed from his good sense, and are contradictions to the manners of the world, only as he thinks the world is in the wrong. However, this humor creates him no enemies, for he does nothing with sourness or obstinacy; and his being unconfined to modes and forms, makes him but the readier and more capable to please and oblige all who know him. When he is in town, he lives in Soho Square. It is said, he keeps himself a bachelor, by reason he was crossed in love by a perverse beautiful widow of the next county to him. Before this disappointment, Sir Roger was what you call a fine gentleman, had often supped with my Lord Rochester and Sir George Etherege, fought a duel upon his first coming to town, and kicked Bully Dawson, in a public coffeehouse, for calling him youngster. But, being ill used by the above mentioned widow, he was very serious for a year and a half; and though, his temper being naturally jovial, he at last got over it, he grew careless of himself, and never dressed afterwards. He continues to wear a coat and doublet of the same cut, that were in fashion at the time of his repulse, which, in his merry humors, he tells us, has been in and out twelve times since he first wore it. He is now in his fifty-sixth year, cheerful, gay, and hearty; keeps a good house both in town and country; a great lover of mankind; but there is such a mirthful cast in his behavior, that he is rather beloved than esteemed. His tenants grow rich, his servants look satisfied, all the young women profess love to him, and the young men are glad of his company; when he comes into a house, he calls the servants by their names, and talks all the way up-stairs to a visit. I must not omit, that Sir Roger is a justice of the *quorum;* that he fills the chair at a quarter-session with great abilities, and three months ago, gained universal applause, by explaining a passage in the game-act.

ESSAYS OF JOSEPH ADDISON.

SIR ROGER AT HOME.

HAVING often received an invitation from my friend
Sir Roger de Coverley to pass away a month with him
in the country, I last week accompanied him thither,
and am settled with him for some time at his country-
house, where I intend to form several of my ensuing
speculations. Sir Roger, who is very well acquainted
with my humor, lets me rise and go to bed when I
please; dine at his own table, or in my chamber, as I
think fit; sit still, and say nothing, without bidding me
be merry. When the gentlemen of the country come
to see him, he only shows me at a distance. As I have
been walking in his fields, I have observed them stealing a sight of me over an hedge, and have heard the
knight desiring them not to let me see them, for that I
hated to be stared at.

I am the more at ease in Sir Roger's family, because
it consists of sober and staid persons; for as the knight
is the best master in the world, he seldom changes his
servants; and as he is beloved by all about him, his servants never care for leaving him: by this means his
domestics are all in years, and grown old with their
master. You would take his valet de chambre for his
brother; his butler is gray-headed; his groom is one of
the gravest men that I have ever seen; and his coach-

1

man has the looks of a privy-councilor. You see the goodness of the master even in the old house-dog ; and in a gray pad, that is kept in the stable with great care and tenderness out of regard to his past services, though he has been useless for several years.

I could not but observe with a great deal of pleasure, the joy that appeared in the countenances of these ancient domestics upon my friend's arrival at his country-seat. Some of them could not refrain from tears at the sight of their old master ; every one of them pressed forward to do something for him, and seemed discouraged if they were not employed. At the same time the good old knight, with a mixture of the father and the master of the family, tempered the inquiries after his own affairs with several kind questions relating to themselves. This humanity and good-nature engages everybody to him, so that when he is pleasant upon any of them, all his family are in good humor, and none so much as the person whom he diverts himself with : on the contrary, if he coughs, or betrays any infirmity of old age, it is easy for a stander-by to observe a secret concern in the looks of all his servants.

My worthy friend has put me under the particular care of his butler, who is a very prudent man, and, as well as the rest of his fellow-servants, wonderfully desirous of pleasing me, because they have often heard their master talk of me as of his particular friend.

My chief companion, when Sir Roger is diverting himself in the woods or the fields, is a very venerable man, who is ever with Sir Roger, and has lived at his house in the nature of a chaplain above thirty years. This gentleman is a person of good sense, and some learning, of a very regular life, and obliging conversation : he heartily loves Sir Roger, and knows that he is very much in the old knight's esteem ; so that he lives in the family rather as a relation than a dependent.

I have observed in several of my papers, that my friend Sir Roger, amidst all his good qualities, is something of an humorist ; and that his virtues, as well as imperfections, are, as it were, tinged by a certain extravagance, which makes them particularly his, and distinguishes them from those of other men. This cast of mind, as it is generally very innocent in itself, so it renders his conversation highly agreeable, and more delightful than the same degree of sense and virtue would appear in their common and ordinary colors. As I was walking with him last night, he asked me how I liked the good man whom I have just now mentioned ; and, without staying for my answer, told me, that he was afraid of being insulted with Latin and Greek at his own table ; for which reason, he desired a particular friend of his at the University, to find him out a clergyman rather of plain sense than much learning, of a good aspect, a clear voice, a sociable temper, and, if possible, a man that understood a little of backgammon. My friend (says Sir Roger) found me out this gentleman, who, besides the endowments required of him, is, they tell me, a good scholar, though he does not show it. I have given him the parsonage of the parish ; and because I know his value, have settled upon him a good annuity for life. If he outlives me, he shall find that he was higher in my esteem than perhaps he thinks he is. He has now been with me thirty years ; and, though he does not know I have taken notice of it, has never in all that time asked anything of me for himself, though he is every day soliciting me for something in behalf of one or other of my

tenants, his parishioners. There has not been a law-
suit in the parish since he has lived among them : if
any dispute arises, they apply themselves to him for
the decision ; if they do not acquiesce in his judgment,
which I think never happened above once, or twice
at most, they appeal to me. At his first settling with
me, I made him a present of all the good sermons which
have been printed in English, and only begged of him
that every Sunday he would pronounce one of them
in the pulpit. Accordingly, he has digested them into
such a series, that they follow one another naturally,
and make a continued system of practical divinity.

As Sir Roger was going on in his story, the gentleman we were talking of came up to us; and upon the
knight's asking him who preached to-morrow (for it
was Saturday night), told us, the Bishop of St. Asaph
in the morning, and Dr. South in the afternoon. He
then showed us his list of preachers for the whole year,
where I saw with a great deal of pleasure, Archbishop
Tillotson, Bishop Saunderson, Doctor Barrow, Doctor
Calamy, with several living authors who have published
discourses of practical divinity. I no sooner saw this
venerable man in the pulpit, but I very much approved
of my friend's insisting upon the qualifications of a good
aspect and a clear voice ; for I was so charmed with
the gracefulness of his figure and delivery, as well as
the discourses he pronounced, that I think I never
passed any time more to my satisfaction. A sermon
repeated after this manner, is like the composition of
a poet in the mouth of a graceful actor.

I could heartily wish that more of our country
clergy would follow this example, and, instead of
wasting their spirits in laborious compositions of their
own, would endeavor after a handsome elocution,

and all those other talents that are proper to enforce
what has been penned by greater masters. This
would not only be more easy to themselves, but more
edifying to the people.

SIR ROGER AND WILL. WIMBLE.

As I was yesterday morning walking with Sir Roger before his house, a country fellow brought him a huge fish, which, he told him, Mr. William Wimble had caught that very morning; and that he presented it with his service to him, and intended to come and dine with him. At the same time he delivered a letter, which my friend read to me as soon as the messenger left him.

"Sir ROGER,

"I desire you to accept of a Jack, which is the best I have caught this season. I intend to come and stay with you a week, and see how the Perch bite in the Black river. I observed with some concern, the last time I saw you upon the Bowling-green, that your whip wanted a lash to it: I will bring half a dozen with me that I twisted last week which I hope will serve you all the time you are in the country. I have not been out of the saddle for six days last past, having been at Eaton with Sir John's eldest son. He takes to his learning hugely.

"I am, Sir, your humble Servant,
"WILL. WIMBLE."

This extraordinary letter, and message that accompanied it, made me very curious to know the character and quality of the gentleman who sent them; which I found to be as follows. Will. Wimble is younger brother to a baronet, and descended of the ancient family of the Wimbles. He is now between forty and

6

fifty; but being bred to no business, and born to no estate, he generally lives with his elder brother as superintendent of his game. He hunts a pack of dogs better than any man in the country, and is very famous for finding out a hare. He is extremely well versed in all the little handicrafts of an idle man: he makes a May-fly to a miracle; and furnishes the whole country with angle-rods. As he is a good-natured, officious fellow, and very much esteemed upon account of his family, he is a welcome guest at every house, and keeps up a good correspondence among all the gentlemen about him. He carries a tulip root in his pocket from one to another, or exchanges a puppy between a couple of friends that live perhaps in the opposite sides of the county. Will. is a particular favorite of all the young heirs, whom he frequently obliges with a net that he has weaved, or a setting-dog that he has *made* himself; he now and then presents a pair of garters of his own knitting to their mothers or sisters; and raises a great deal of mirth among them, by inquiring, as often as he meets them, "how they wear?" These gentleman-like manufactures, and obliging little humors, make Will. the darling of the country.

Sir Roger was proceeding in the character of him, when he saw him make up to us with two or three hazel-twigs in his hand, that he had cut in Sir Roger's woods, as he came through them in his way to the house. I was very much pleased to observe on one side the hearty and sincere welcome with which Sir Roger received him, and on the other, the secret joy which his guest discovered at sight of the good old knight. After the first salutes were over, Will. desired Sir Roger to lend him one of his servants to carry a set of shuttle-cocks, he had with him in a little box, to a lady that lived about a mile off, to whom it seems he had promised such a present for above this half-year. Sir Roger's back was no sooner turned, but honest Will. began to tell me of a large cock pheasant that he had sprung in one of the neighboring woods, with two or three other adventures of the same nature. Odd and uncommon characters are the game that I look for, and most delight in; for which reason I was as much pleased with the novelty of the person that talked to me, as he could be for his life with the springing of a pheasant, and therefore listened to him with more than ordinary attention.

In the midst of his discourse the bell rung to dinner, where the gentleman I have been speaking of had the pleasure of seeing the huge Jack, he had caught, served up for the first dish in a most sumptuous manner. Upon our sitting down to it, he gave us a long account how he had hooked it, played with it, foiled it, and at length drew it out upon the bank, with several other particulars, that lasted all the first course. A dish of wild fowl, that came afterwards, furnished conversation for the rest of the dinner, which concluded with a late invention of Will.'s for improving the quail-pipe.

Upon withdrawing into my room after dinner, I was secretly touched with compassion towards the honest gentleman that had dined with us; and could not but consider, with a great deal of concern, how so good an heart, and such busy hands, were wholly employed in trifles; that so much humanity should be so little beneficial to others, and so much industry so little advantageous to himself. The same temper of mind, and application to affairs, might have recommended

him to the public esteem, and have raised his fortune
in another station of life. What good to his country,
or himself, might not a trader or merchant have done
with such useful, though ordinary, qualifications ?

Will. Wimble's is the case of many a younger
brother of a great family, who had rather see their
children starve like gentlemen, than thrive in a trade
or profession that is beneath their quality. This
humor fills several parts of Europe with pride and
beggary. It is the happiness of a trading nation, like
ours, that the younger sons, though incapable of any
liberal art or profession, may be placed in such a way
of life, as may perhaps enable them to vie with the
best of their family : accordingly, we find several
citizens that were launched into the world with narrow
fortunes, rising by an honest industry to greater
estates than those of their elder brothers. It is not
improbable but Will. was formerly tried at divinity,
law, or physic ; and that finding his genius did not lie
that way, his parents gave him up at length to his
own inventions. But certainly, however improper he
might have been for studies of a higher nature, he
was perfectly well turned for the occupations of trade
and commerce.

SIR ROGER AT CHURCH.

I AM always very well pleased with a country Sunday; and think, if keeping holy the seventh day were only a human institution, it would be the best method that could have been thought of for the polishing and civilizing of mankind. It is certain the country-people would soon degenerate into a kind of savages and barbarians, were there not such frequent returns of a stated time, in which the whole village meet together with their best faces, and in their cleanliest habits, to converse with one another upon indifferent subjects, hear their duties explained to them, and join together in adoration of the Supreme Being. Sunday clears away the rust of the whole week, not only as it refreshes in their minds the notions of religion, but as it puts both the sexes upon appearing in their most agreeable forms, and exerting all such qualities as are apt to give them a figure in the eye of the village. A country-fellow distinguishes himself as much in the churchyard as a citizen does upon the Change, the whole parish-politics being generally discussed in that place either after sermon or before the bell rings.

My friend Sir Roger, being a good churchman, has beautified the inside of his church with several texts of his own choosing; he has likewise given a handsome pulpit-cloth, and railed in the communion-table at his own expense. He has often told me, that at

10

his coming to his estate he found his parishioners very irregular; and that in order to make them kneel and join in the responses, he gave every one of them a hassoc and a Common Prayer Book; and at the same time employed an itinerant singing-master, who goes about the country for that purpose, to instruct them rightly in the tunes of the psalms; upon which they now very much value themselves, and indeed out-do most of the country churches that I have ever heard.

As Sir Roger is landlord to the whole congregation, he keeps them in very good order, and will suffer nobody to sleep in it besides himself; for if by chance he has been surprised into a short nap at sermon, upon recovering out of it he stands up and looks about him, and if he sees anybody else nodding, either wakes them himself, or sends his servant to them. Several other of the old knight's particularities break out upon these occasions; sometimes he will be lengthening out a verse in the singing-psalms, half a minute after the rest of the congregation have done with it; sometimes, when he is pleased with the matter of his devotion, he pronounces Amen three or four times to the same prayer; and sometimes stands up when everybody else is upon their knees, to count the congregation, or see if any of his tenants are missing.

I was yesterday very much surprised to hear my old friend, in the midst of the service, calling out to one John Matthews to mind what he was about, and not disturb the congregation. This John Matthews, it seems, is remarkable for being an idle fellow, and at that time was kicking his heels for his diversion. This authority of the knight, though exerted in that odd manner which accompanies him in all circumstances of life, has a very good effect upon the parish, who are not polite enough to see anything ridiculous in his behavior ; besides that the general good sense and worthiness of his character, make his friends observe these little singularities as foils that rather set off than blemish his good qualities.

As soon as the sermon is finished, nobody presumes to stir till Sir Roger is gone out of the church. The knight walks down from his seat in the chancel between a double row of his tenants, that stand bowing to him on each side ; and every now and then he inquires how such an one's wife, or mother, or son, or father do, whom he does not see at church ; which is understood as a secret reprimand to the person that is absent.

The chaplain has often told me, that upon a catechizing-day, when Sir Roger has been pleased with a boy that answers well, he has ordered a Bible to be given him next day for his encouragement ; and sometimes accompanies it with a flitch of bacon to his mother. Sir Roger has likewise added five pounds a year to the clerk's place ; and that he may encourage the young fellows to make themselves perfect in the church-service, has promised, upon the death of the present incumbent, who is very old, to bestow it according to merit.

The fair understanding between Sir Roger and his chaplain, and their mutual concurrence in doing good, is the more remarkable, because the very next village is famous for the differences and contentions that rise between the parson and the 'squire, who live in a perpetual state of war. The parson is always at the 'squire, and the 'squire, to be revenged on the parson, never comes to church. The 'squire has made all his tenants atheists and tithe-stealers ; while the parson instructs them every Sunday in the dignity of his order, and insinuates to them, almost in every sermon, that he is a better man than his patron. In short, matters are come to such an extremity, that the 'squire has not said his prayers either in public or private this half year; and that the parson threatens him, if he does not mend his manners, to pray for him in the face of the whole congregation.

Feuds of this nature, though too frequent in the country, are very fatal to the ordinary people; who are so used to be dazzled with riches, that they pay as much deference to the understanding of a man of an estate, as of a man of learning; and are very hardly brought to regard any truth, how important soever it may be, that is preached to them, when they know there are several men of five hundred a year who do not believe it.

SIR ROGER AND THE WITCHES.

THERE are some opinions in which a man should stand neuter, without engaging his assent to one side or the other. Such a hovering faith as this, which refuses to settle upon any determination, is absolutely necessary in a mind that is careful to avoid errors and prepossessions. When the arguments press equally on both sides in matters that are indifferent to us, the safest method is to give up ourselves to neither.

It is with this temper of mind that I consider the subject of witchcraft. When I hear the relations that are made from all parts of the world, not only from Norway and Lapland, from the East and West Indies, but from every particular nation in Europe, I cannot forbear thinking that there is such an intercourse and commerce with evil spirits, as that which we express by the name of witchcraft. But when I consider that the ignorant and credulous parts of the world abound most in these relations, and that the persons among us who are supposed to engage in such an infernal commerce, are people of a weak understanding and crazed imagination, and at the same time reflect upon the many impostures and delusions of this nature that have been detected in all ages, I endeavor to suspend my belief, till I hear more certain accounts than any which have yet come to my knowledge. In short, when I consider the question, whether there are such persons in the world as those we call witches? my

14

mind is divided between two opposite opinions; or
rather (to speak my thoughts freely) I believe in general that there is, and has been, such a thing as witchcraft; but at the same time can give no credit to any
particular instance of it.

I am engaged in this speculation, by some occurrences that I met with yesterday, which I shall give
my reader an account of at large. As I was walking
with my friend Sir Roger, by the side of one of his
woods, an old woman applied herself to me for my
charity. Her dress and figure put me in mind of the
following description in Otway:

In a close lane, as I pursued my journey,
I spied a wrinkled hag, with age grown double,
Picking dry sticks, and mumbling to herself.
Her eyes with scalding rheum were galled and red ;
Cold palsy shook her head ; her hands seemed withered ;
And on her crooked shoulders had she wrapped
The tattered remnants of an old stripped hanging,
Which served to keep her carcass from the cold,
So there was nothing of a piece about her,
Her lower weeds were all o'er coarsely patched
With different colored rags, black, red, white, yellow,
And seemed to speak variety of wretchedness.

As I was musing on this description, and comparing
it with the object before me, the knight told me, that
this very old woman had the reputation of a witch all
over the country, that her lips were observed to be
always in motion, and that there was not a switch
about her house which her neighbors did not believe
had carried her several hundreds of miles. If she
chanced to stumble, they always found sticks or straws
that lay in the figure of a cross before her. If she

made any mistake at church, and cried Amen in a wrong place, they never failed to conclude that she was saying her prayers backwards. There was not a maid in the parish that would take a pin of her, though she should offer a bag of money with it. She goes by the name of Moll White, and has made the country ring with several imaginary exploits which are palmed upon her. If the dairy-maid does not make her butter to come so soon as she would have it, Moll White is at the bottom of the churn. If a horse sweats in the stable, Moll White has been upon his back. If a hare makes an unexpected escape from the hounds, the huntsman curses Moll White. Nay, (says Sir Roger,) I have known the master of the pack, upon such an occasion, send one of his servants to see if Moll White had been out that morning.

This account raised my curiosity so far, that I begged my friend Sir Roger to go with me into her hovel, which stood in a solitary corner under the side of the wood. Upon our first entering, Sir Roger winked to me, and pointed to something that stood behind the door, which, upon looking that way, I found to be an old broom-staff. At the same time he whispered me in the ear, to take notice of a tabby cat that sat in the chimney-corner, which, as the knight told me, lay under as bad a report as Moll White herself; for besides that Moll is said often to accompany her in the same shape, the cat is reported to have spoken twice or thrice in her life, and to have played several pranks above the capacity of an ordinary cat.

I was secretly concerned to see human nature in so much wretchedness and disgrace, but at the same time could not forbear smiling to hear Sir Roger, who is a little puzzled about the old woman, advising her, as a justice of peace, to avoid all communication with the devil, and never to hurt any of her neighbors' cattle. We concluded our visit with a bounty, which was very acceptable.

In our return home, Sir Roger told me that old Moll had been often brought before him for making children spit pins, and giving maids the nightmare; and that the country people would be tossing her into a pond, and trying experiments with her every day, if it was not for him and his chaplain.

I have since found, upon inquiry, that Sir Roger was several times staggered with the reports that had been brought him concerning this old woman, and would frequently have bound her over to the county sessions, had not his chaplain with much ado persuaded him to the contrary.

I have been the more particular in this account, because I hear there is scarce a village in England that has not a Moll White in it. When an old woman begins to dote, and grow chargeable to a parish, she is generally turned into a witch, and fills the whole country with extravagant fancies, imaginary distempers, and terrifying dreams. In the meantime the poor wretch that is the innocent occasion of so many evils, begins to be frighted at herself, and sometimes confesses secret commerces and familiarities that her imagination forms in a delirious old age. This frequently cuts off charity from the greatest objects of compassion, and inspires people with a malevolence towards those poor decrepit parts of our species in whom human nature is defaced by infirmity and dotage.

2

SIR ROGER AT THE ASSIZES.

A MAN's first care should be to avoid the reproaches of his own heart; his next, to escape the censures of the world: if the last interferes with the former, it ought to be entirely neglected; but otherwise there cannot be a greater satisfaction to an honest mind, than to see those approbations which it gives itself seconded by the applauses of the public: a man is more sure of his conduct, when the verdict which he passes upon his own behavior is thus warranted and confirmed by the opinion of all that know him.

My worthy friend Sir Roger is one of those who is not only at peace within himself, but beloved and esteemed by all about him. He receives a suitable tribute for his universal benevolence to mankind, in the returns of affection and good-will which are paid him by every one that lives within his neighborhood. I lately met with two or three odd instances of that general respect which is shown to the good old knight. He would needs carry Will. Wimble and myself with him to the country assizes: as we were upon the road, Will. Wimble joined a couple of plain men who rid before us, and conversed with them for some time; during which my friend Sir Roger acquainted me with their characters.

The first of them, says he, that hath a spaniel by his side, is a yeoman of about a hundred pounds a year, an honest man: he is just within the game act, and qualified to kill an hare or a pheasant: he knocks

down a dinner with his gun twice or thrice a week;
and by that means lives much cheaper than those who
have not so good an estate as himself. He would be a
good neighbor if he did not destroy so many part-
ridges : in short, he is a very sensible man; shoots flying; and has been several times foreman of the petty-
jury.

The other that rides with him is Tom Touchy, a
fellow famous for taking the law of everybody. There
is not one in the town where he lives that he has not
sued at a quarter-sessions. The rogue had once the
impudence to go to law with the widow. His head is
full of costs, damages, and ejectments : he plagued a
couple of honest gentlemen so long for a trespass in
breaking one of his hedges, till he was forced to sell
the ground it enclosed to defray the charges of the
prosecution. His father left him fourscore pounds a
year; but he has cast and been cast so often, that he
·is not now worth thirty. I suppose he is going upon
the old business of the willow-tree.

As Sir Roger was giving me this account of Tom
Touchy, Will. Wimble and his two companions stopped
short till we came up to them. After having paid their
respects to Sir Roger, Will. told him that Mr. Touchy
and he must appeal to him upon a dispute that arose
between them. Will. it seems, had been giving his
fellow-travelers an account of his angling one day in
such a hole; when Tom Touchy, instead of hearing
out his story, told him, that Mr. such an one, if he
pleased, might take the law of him for fishing in that
part of the river. My friend Sir Roger heard them
both, upon a round trot, and after having paused some
time, told them, with an air of a man who would not
give his judgment rashly, that much might be said on

both sides. They were neither of them dissatisfied
with the knight's determination, because neither of
them found himself in the wrong by it: upon which
we made the best of our way to the assizes.

The court was sat before Sir Roger came, but notwithstanding all the justices had taken their places
upon the bench, they made room for the old knight at
the head of them; who, for his reputation in the
country, took occasion to whisper in the judge's ear,
that he was glad his lordship had met with so much
good weather in his circuit. I was listening to the
proceedings of the court with much attention, and infinitely pleased with that great appearance of solemnity
which so properly accompanies such a public adminis-
tration of our laws; when, after about an hour's sitting, I observed, to my great surprise, in the midst of
a trial, that my friend Sir Roger was getting up to
speak. I was in some pain for him, till I found he had
acquitted himself of two or three sentences, with a look
of much business and great intrepidity.

Upon his first rising the court was hushed, and a
general whisper ran among the country people that
Sir Roger was up. The speech he made was so little
to the purpose, that I shall not trouble my readers
with an account of it ; and I believe was not so much
designed by the knight himself to inform the court, as
to give him a figure in my eye, and keep up his credit
in the country.

I was highly delighted, when the court rose, to see
the gentlemen of the country gathering about my old
friend, and striving who should compliment him most;
at the same time that the ordinary people gazed upon
him at a distance, not a little admiring his courage,
that was not afraid to speak to the judge.

In our return home we met with a very odd accident; which I cannot forbear relating, because it shows how desirous all who know Sir Roger are of giving him marks of their esteem. When we were arrived upon the verge of his estate, we stopped at a little inn to rest ourselves and our horses. The man of the house had, it seems, been formerly a servant in the knight's family; and to do honor to his old master, had some time since, unknown to Sir Roger, put him up in a sign-post before the door ; so that The Knight's Head had hung out upon the road about a week before he himself knew anything of the matter. As soon as Sir Roger was acquainted with it, finding that his servant's indiscretion proceeded wholly from affection and good-will, he only told him that he had made him too high a compliment: and when the fellow seemed to think that could hardly be, added with a more decisive look, that it was too great an honor for any man under a duke; but told him at the same time, that it might be altered with a very few touches, and that he himself would be at the charge of it. Accordingly they got a painter by the knight's directions to add a pair of whiskers to the face, and by a little aggravation of the features to change it into the Saracen's Head. I should not have known this story, had not the innkeeper, upon Sir Roger's alighting, told him in my hearing that his Honor's head was brought back last night, with the alterations that he had ordered to be made in it. Upon this my friend, with his usual cheerfulness, related the particulars above-mentioned, and ordered the head to be brought into the room. I could not forbear discovering greater expressions of mirth than ordinary upon the appearance of this monstrous face, under which, notwithstanding it was made to frown and stare in the most extraordinary manner, I could still discover a distant resemblance of my old friend.   Sir Roger, upon seeing me laugh, desired me to tell him truly if I thought it possible for people to know him in that disguise.   I at first kept my usual silence; but upon the knight's conjuring me to tell him whether it was not still more like himself than a Saracen, I composed my countenance in the best manner I could, and replied, " That much might be said on both sides."

These several adventures, with the knight's behavior in them, gave me as pleasant a day as ever I met with in any of my travels.

SIR ROGER AND THE GIPSIES.

As I was yesterday riding out in the fields with my friend Sir Roger, we saw at a little distance from us a troop of gipsies. Upon the first discovery of them, my friend was in some doubt whether he should not exert the justice of peace upon such a band of lawless vagrants: but not having his clerk with him, who is a necessary counselor on these occasions, and fearing that his poultry might fare the worse for it, he let the thought drop. But at the same time gave me a particular account of the mischiefs they do in the country, in stealing people's goods, and spoiling their servants. "If a stray piece of linen hangs upon an hedge (says Sir Roger), they are sure to have it; if a hog loses his way in the fields, it is ten to one but he becomes their prey: our geese cannot live in peace for them. If a man prosecutes them with severity, his hen-roost is sure to pay for it. They generally straggle into these parts about this time of the year; and set the heads of our servant-maids so agog for husbands, that we do not expect to have any business done, as it should be, whilst they are in the country. I have an honest dairy-maid who crosses their hands with a piece of silver every summer; and never fails being promised the handsomest young fellow in the parish for her pains. Your friend the butler has been fool enough to be seduced by them; and though he is sure to lose a knife, a fork, or a spoon every time his fortune is told him, generally

shuts himself up in the pantry with an old gipsy for
about half an hour once in a twelvemonth. Sweet-
hearts are the things they live upon, which they bestow
very plentifully upon all those that apply themselves to
them. You see now and then some handsome young
jades among them : the sluts have very often white
teeth and black eyes."

Sir Roger observing that I listened with great attention to his account of a people who were so entirely
new to me, told me, that if I would, they should tell
us our fortunes. As I was very well pleased with the
knight's proposal, we rid up and communicated our
hands to them. A Cassandra of the crew, after having
examined my lines very diligently, told me that I loved
a pretty maid in a corner, that I was a good woman's
man, with some other particulars which I do not think
proper to relate. My friend Sir Roger alighted from
his horse, and exposing his palm to two or three that
stood by him, they crumpled it into all shapes, and
diligently scanned every wrinkle that could be made in
it ; when one of them, who was older and more sun-
burnt than the rest, told him that he had a widow in
his line of life : upon which the knight cried, " Go, go,
you are an idle baggage ; " and at the same time smiled
upon me. The gipsy, finding he was not displeased in
his heart, told him, after a further inquiry into his hand,
that his true love was constant, and that she should
dream of him to-night. My old friend cried pish,
and bid her go on. The gipsy told him that he was
a bachelor, but would not be so long ; and that he
was dearer to somebody than he thought. The knight
still repeated, she was an idle baggage, and bid her go
on. " Ah, master, (says the gipsy,) that roguish leer
of yours makes a pretty woman's heart ache ; you

ha'n't that simper about the mouth for nothing." The
uncouth gibberish with which all this was uttered, like
the darkness of an oracle, made us the more attentive
to it. To be short, the knight left the money with her
that he had crossed her hand with, and got up again
on his horse.

As we were riding away, Sir Roger told me, that he
knew several sensible people who believed these gipsies
now and then foretold very strange things; and for
half an hour together appeared more jocund than ordinary. In the height of this good humor, meeting a
common beggar upon the road who was no conjurer,
as he went to relieve him, he found his pocket was
picked! that being a kind of palmistry at which this
race of vermin are very dexterous.

I might here entertain my reader with historical
remarks on this idle, profligate people, who infest all
the countries of Europe, and live in the midst of governments in a kind of commonwealth by themselves.
But, instead of entering into observations of this nature, I shall fill the remaining part of my paper with
a story which is still fresh in Holland, and was printed
in one of our monthly accounts about twenty years
ago. "As the Trekschuyt, or Hackney-boat, which
carries passengers from Leyden to Amsterdam, was
putting off, a boy running along the side of the canal
desired to be taken in; which the master of the boat
refused, because the lad had not quite money enough
to pay the usual fare. An eminent merchant being
pleased with the looks of the boy, and secretly touched
with compassion towards him, paid the money for
him, and ordered him to be taken on board. Upon
talking with him afterwards, he found that he could
speak readily in three or four languages, and learned

upon further examination, that he had been stolen
away when he was a child by a gipsy, and had rambled
ever since with a gang of those strollers up and down
several parts of Europe. It happened that the merchant, whose heart seems to have inclined towards the
boy by a secret kind of instinct, had himself lost a
child some years before. The parents, after a long
search for him, gave him for drowned in one of the
canals with which that country abounds; and the
mother was so afflicted at the loss of a fine boy, who
was her only son, that she died for grief of it. Upon
laying together all particulars, and examining the
several moles and marks by which the mother used
to describe the child when he was first missing, the
boy proved to be the son of the merchant, whose heart
had so unaccountably melted at the sight of him. The
lad was very well pleased to find a father who was so
rich, and likely to leave him a good estate : the father,
on the other hand, was not a little delighted to see a
son return to him, whom he had given for lost, with
such a strength of constitution, sharpness of understanding, and skill in languages." Here the printed
story leaves off; but if I may give credit to reports,
our linguist having received such extraordinary rudi-
ments towards a good education, was afterwards
trained up in everything that becomes a gentleman ;
wearing off, by little and little, all the vicious habits
and practises that he had been used to in the course
of his peregrinations: nay, it is said, that he has since
been employed in foreign courts upon national business, with great reputation to himself, and honor to
those who sent him, and that he has visited several
countries as a public minister, in which he formerly
wandered as a gipsy.

SIR ROGER IN TOWN.

I was this morning surprised with a great knocking at the door, when my landlady's daughter came up to me and told me there was a man below desired to speak with me. Upon my asking her who it was, she told me it was a very grave elderly person, but that she did not know his name. I immediately went down to him, and found him to be the coachman of my worthy friend Sir Roger de Coverley. He told me that his master came to town last night, and would be glad to take a turn with me in Grays-Inn walks. As I was wondering in myself what had brought Sir Roger to town, not having lately received any letter from him, he told me that his master was come up to get a sight of Prince Eugene, and that he desired I would immediately meet him.

I was not a little pleased with the curiosity of the old knight, though I did not much wonder at it, having heard him say more than once in private discourse, that he looked upon Prince Eugenio (for so the knight always calls him) to be a greater man than Scanderbeg.

I was no sooner come into Grays-Inn walks, but I heard my friend upon the terrace hemming twice or thrice to himself with great vigor, for he loves to clear his pipes in good air (to make use of his own phrase), and is not a little pleased with any one who takes notice of the strength which he still exerts in his morning hems.

27

I was touched with a secret joy at the sight of the good old man, who before he saw me was engaged in conversation with a beggar-man that had asked an alms of him. I could hear my friend chide him for not finding out some work ; but at the same time saw him put his hand in his pocket and give him six-pence.

Our salutations were very hearty on both sides, con-sisting of many kind shakes of the hand, and several affectionate looks which we cast upon one another. After which the knight told me my good friend his chaplain was very well, and much at my service, and that the Sunday before he had made a most incom-parable sermon out of Doctor Barrow. "I have left," says he, "all my affairs in his hands, and being willing to lay an obligation upon him, have deposited with him thirty marks, to be distributed among his poor parishioners."

He then proceeded to acquaint me with the welfare of Will. Wimble. Upon which he put his hand into his fob, and presented me in his name with a tobacco stopper, telling me that Will. had been busy all the beginning of the winter in turning great quantities of them ; and that he made a present of one to every gentleman in the country who has good principles, and smokes. He added, that poor Will. was at present under great tribulation, for that Tom Touchy had taken the law of him for cutting some hazel sticks out of one of his hedges.

Among other pieces of news which the knight brought from his country seat, he informed me that Moll White was dead ; and that about a month after her death the wind was so very high that it blew down the end of one of his barns. "But for my part," says

Sir Roger, "I do not think that the old woman had any hand in it."

He afterwards fell into an account of the diversions which had passed in his house during the holidays, for Sir Roger, after the laudable custom of his ancestors, always keeps open house at Christmas. I learned from him, that he had killed eight fat hogs for this season, that he had dealt about his chines very liberally amongst his neighbors, and that in particular he had sent a string of hog's puddings with a pack of cards to every poor family in the parish. "I have often thought," says Sir Roger, " it happens very well that Christmas should fall out in the middle of the winter. It is the most dead, uncomfortable time of the year, when the poor people would suffer very much from their poverty and cold, if they had not good cheer, warm fires, and Christmas gambols to support them. I love to rejoice their poor hearts at this season, and to see the whole village merry in my great hall. I allow a double quantity of malt to my small beer, and set it a running for twelve days to every one that calls for it. I have always a piece of cold beef and a mince-pie upon the table, and am wonderfully pleased to see my tenants pass away a whole evening in playing their innocent tricks, and smutting one another. Our friend Will. Wimble is as merry as any of them, and shows a thousand roguish tricks upon these occasions."

I was very much delighted with the reflection of my old friend, which carried so much goodness in it. He then launched out into the praise of the late act of parliament for securing the Church of England, and told me with great satisfaction, that he believed it already began to take effect; for that a rigid dissenter, who chanced to dine at his house on Christmas day, had been observed to eat very plentifully of his plum-porridge.

After having despatched all our country matters, Sir Roger made several inquiries concerning the club, and particularly of his old antagonist Sir Andrew Freeport. He asked me, with a kind of smile, whether Sir Andrew had not taken the advantage of his absence, to vent among them some of his republican doctrines ; but soon after gathering up his countenance into a more than ordinary seriousness, " Tell me truly," says he, " don't you think Sir Andrew had a hand in the pope's procession "—but without giving me time to answer him, " Well, well," says he, " I know you are a wary man, and do not care to talk of public matters."

The knight then asked me, if I had seen Prince Eugene ; and made me promise to get him a stand in some convenient place where he might have a full sight of that extraordinary man, whose presence does so much honor to the British nation. He dwelt very long on the praises of this great general, and I found that since I was with him in the country, he had drawn many observations together out of his reading in Baker's Chronicle, and other authors, who always lie in his hall window, which very much redound to the honor of this prince.

Having passed away the greatest part of the morning in hearing the knight's reflections, which were partly private and partly political, he asked me if I would smoke a pipe with him over a dish of coffee at Squire's. As I love the old man, I take a delight in complying with everything that is agreeable to him, and accordingly waited on him to the coffee-house, where his venerable figure drew upon us the eyes of the whole room. He had no sooner seated himself at the upper end of the high table, but he called for a clean pipe, a paper of tobacco, a dish of coffee, a wax candle, and the Supplement, with such an air of cheerfulness and good humor, that all the boys in the coffee-room (who seemed to take pleasure in serving him) were at once employed on his several errands, insomuch that nobody else could come at a dish of tea, till the knight had got all his conveniences about him.

SIR ROGER IN WESTMINSTER ABBEY.

My friend Sir Roger de Coverley told me the other
night, that he had been reading my paper upon Westminster Abbey, in which, says he, there are a great
many ingenious fancies. He told me at the same time,
that he observed I had promised another paper upon
the tombs, and that he should be glad to go and see
them with me, not having visited them since he had
read history. I could not at first imagine how this
came into the knight's head, till I recollected that he
had been very busy all last summer upon Baker's
Chronicle, which he has quoted several times in his
dispute with Sir Andrew Freeport, since his last coming to town. Accordingly I called upon him the next
morning, that we might go together to the Abbey.

I found the knight under his butler's hands, who always shaves him. He was no sooner dressed, than he
called for a glass of the widow Trueby's water, which
he told me he always drank before he went abroad.
He recommended to me a dram of it at the same time,
with so much heartiness, that I could not forbear drinking it. As soon as I had got it down, I found it very
unpalatable; upon which the knight observing that I
had made several wry faces, told me that he knew I
should not like it at first, but that it was the best thing
in the world against the stone or gravel.

I could have wished, indeed, that he had acquainted
me with the virtues of it sooner; but it was too late to

complain, and I knew what he had done was out of good-will. Sir Roger told me further, that he looked upon it to be very good for a man whilst he staid in town, to keep off infection, and that he got together a quantity of it upon the first news of the sickness being at Dantzic : when of a sudden turning short to one of his servants, who stood behind him, he bid him call a hackney coach, and take care it was an elderly man that drove it.

He then resumed his discourse upon Mrs. Trueby's water, telling me that the widow Trueby was one who did more good than all the doctors and apothecaries in the county : that she distilled every poppy that grew within five miles of her, that she distributed her water gratis among all sorts of people ; to which the knight added that she had a very great jointure, and that the whole country would fain have it a match between him and her ; " and truly," says Sir Roger, " if I had not been engaged, perhaps I could not have done better."

His discourse was broken off by his man's telling him he had called a coach. Upon our going to it, after having cast his eye upon the wheels, he asked the coachman if his axletree was good ; upon the fellow's telling him he would warrant it, the knight turned to me, told me he looked like an honest man, and went in without further ceremony.

We had not gone far, when Sir Roger, popping out his head, called the coachman down from his box, and upon his presenting himself at the window, asked him if he smoked ; as I was considering what this would end in, he bid him stop by the way at any good tobacconist's, and take in a roll of their best Virginia. Nothing material happened in the remaining part of

3

our journey, till we were set down at the west end of the Abbey.

As we went up the body of the church the knight pointed at the trophies upon one of the new monuments, and cried out, " A brave man I warrant him ! " Passing afterwards by Sir Cloudsly Shovel, he flung his hand that way, and cried, " Sir Cloudsly Shovel ! a very gallant man ! " As we stood before Busby's tomb, the knight uttered himself again after the same manner, " Dr. Busby, a great man ! he whipped my grandfather ; a very great man ! I should have gone to him myself, if I had not been a blockhead ; a very great man ! "

We were immediately conducted into the little chapel on the right hand. Sir Roger planting himself at our historian's elbow, was very attentive to everything he said, particularly to the account he gave us of the lord who had cut off the king of Morocco's head. Among several other figures, he was very well pleased to see the statesman Cecil upon his knees ; and, concluding them all to be great men, was conducted to the figure which represents that martyr to good housewifery, who died by the prick of a needle. Upon our interpreter's telling us, that she was a maid of honor to Queen Elizabeth, the knight was very inquisitive into her name and family ; and after having regarded her finger for some time, " I wonder, (says he,) that Sir Richard Baker has said nothing of her in his Chronicle."

We were then conveyed to the two coronation-chairs, where my old friend, after having heard that the stone underneath the most ancient of them, which was brought from Scotland, was called Jacob's Pillow, sat himself down in the chair ; and looking like the figure of an old Gothic king, asked our interpreter, what

authority they had to say that Jacob had ever been in
Scotland? The fellow, instead of returning him an
answer, told him, that he hoped his Honor would pay
his forfeit. I could observe Sir Roger a little ruffled
upon being thus trepanned; but our guide not insisting
upon his demand, the knight soon recovered his good
humor, and whispered in my ear, that if Will. Wimble
were with us, and saw those two chairs, it would go
hard but he would get a tobacco-stopper out of one or
t' other of them.

Sir Roger, in the next place, laid his hand upon
Edward the Third's sword, and leaning upon the
pummel of it, gave us the whole history of the Black
Prince; concluding, that in Sir Richard Baker's opinion, Edward the Third was one of the greatest princes
that ever sat upon the English throne.

We were then shown Edward the Confessor's tomb;
upon which Sir Roger acquainted us, that he was the
first that touched for the Evil; and afterwards Henry
the Fourth's, upon which he shook his head, and told
us, there was fine reading of the casualties of that
reign.

Our conductor then pointed to that monument where
there is the figure of one of our English kings without
an head; and upon giving us to know, that the head,
which was of beaten silver, had been stolen away
several years since: "Some Whig, I'll warrant you,
(says Sir Roger;) you ought to lock up your kings
better; they will carry off the body too, if you do not
take care."

The glorious names of Henry the Fifth and Queen
Elizabeth gave the knight great opportunities of shining, and of doing justice to Sir Richard Baker, who, as
our knight observed with some surprise, had a great

many kings in him, whose monuments he had not seen in the Abbey.

For my own part, I could not but be pleased to see the knight show such an honest passion for the glory of his country, and such a respectful gratitude to the memory of its princes.

I must not omit, that the benevolence of my good old friend, which flows out towards every one he converses with, made him very kind to our interpreter, whom he looked upon as an extraordinary man; for which reason he shook him by the hand at parting, telling him, that he should be very glad to see him at his lodgings in Norfolk-buildings, and talk over these matters with him more at leisure.

SIR ROGER AT THE PLAY.

My friend Sir Roger de Coverley, when we last met together at the club, told me, that he had a great mind to see the new tragedy with me, assuring me at the same time, that he had not been at a play these twenty years. The last I saw, said Sir Roger, was the Committee, which I should not have gone to neither, had not I been told beforehand that it was a good Church of England comedy. He then proceeded to inquire of me who this Distressed Mother was; and upon hearing that she was Hector's widow, he told me, that her husband was a brave man, and that when he was a schoolboy he had read his life at the end of the dictionary. My friend asked me, in the next place, if there would not be some danger in coming home late, in case the Mohocks should be abroad. "I assure you, (says he,) I thought I had fallen into their hands last night; for I observed two or three lusty black men that followed me half way up Fleet Street, and mended their pace behind me, in proportion as I put on to go away from them. You must know, (continued the knight with a smile,) I fancied they had a mind to hunt me : for I remember an honest gentleman in my neighborhood, who was served such a trick in King Charles the Second's time; for which reason he has not ventured himself in town ever since. I might have shown them very good sport, had this been their design; for as I am an old fox-hunter, I should have turned and dodged, and have played them a thousand tricks they had never seen in their lives before." Sir Roger added, that if these gentlemen had any such intention, they did not succeed very well in it; "for I threw them out, (says he,) at the end of Norfolk Street, where I doubled the corner, and got shelter in my lodgings before they could imagine what was become of me. However, (says the knight,) if Captain Sentry will make one with us to-morrow night, and if you will both of you call on me about four o'clock, that we may be at the house before it is full, I will have my own coach in readiness to attend you, for John tells me he has got the fore-wheels mended."

The captain, who did not fail to meet me there at the appointed hour, bid Sir Roger fear nothing, for that he had put on the same sword which he had made use of at the battle of Steenkirk. Sir Roger's servants, and among the rest my old friend the butler, had, I found, provided themselves with good oaken plants, to attend their master upon this occasion. When we had placed him in his coach, with myself at his left hand, the captain before him, and his butler at the head of his footmen in the rear, we convoyed him in safety to the playhouse; where, after having marched up the entry in good order, the captain and I went in with him, and seated him betwixt us in the pit. As soon as the house was full, and the candles lighted, my old friend stood up and looked about him with that pleasure, which a mind seasoned with humanity naturally feels in itself, at the sight of a multitude of people who seemed pleased with one another, and partake of the same common entertainment. I could not but fancy to myself, as the old man stood up in the middle of the pit, that he made a very proper center to a tragic audience. Upon the entering of Pyrrhus, the knight told me, that he did not believe the King of France himself had a better strut. I was, indeed, very attentive to my old friend's remarks, because I looked upon them as a piece of natural criticism, and was well pleased to hear him at the conclusion of almost every scene, telling me that he could not imagine how the play would end. One while he appeared much concerned about Adromache; and a little while after as much for Hermione: and was extremely puzzled to think what would become of Pyrrhus.

When Sir Roger saw Adromache's obstinate refusal to her lover's importunities, he whispered me in the ear, that he was sure she would never have him; to which he added, with a more than ordinary vehemence, you cannot imagine, sir, what it is to have to do with a widow. Upon Pyrrhus his threatening afterwards to leave her, the knight shook his head, and muttered to himself, Ay, do if you can. This part dwelt so much upon my friend's imagination, that at the close of the third act, as I was thinking of something else, he whispered in my ear, " These widows, sir, are the most perverse creatures in the world. But pray, (says he), you that are a critic, is this play according to your dramatic rules, as you call them ? Should your people in tragedy always talk to be understood ? Why, there is not a single sentence in this play that I do not know the meaning of."

The fourth act very luckily begun before I had time to give the old gentleman an answer; " Well, (says the knight, sitting down with great satisfaction,) I suppose we are now to see Hector's ghost." He then re-

newed his attention, and, from time to time fell a
praising the widow. He made, indeed, a little mistake
as to one of her pages, whom, at his first entering, he
took for Astyanax; but he quickly set himself right
in that particular, though, at the same time, he owned
he should have been very glad to have seen the little
boy, "who," says he, "must needs be a very fine child
by the account that is given of him." Upon Hermione's going off with a menace to Pyrrhus, the
audience gave a loud clap; to which Sir Roger added,
"On my word, a notable young baggage!"

As there was a very remarkable silence and stillness
in the audience during the whole action, it was natural
for them to take the opportunity of the intervals between the acts, to express their opinion of the players,
and of their respective parts. Sir Roger hearing a
cluster of them praise Orestes, struck in with them,
and told them, that he thought his friend Pylades was
a very sensible man; as they were afterwards applaud-
ing Pyrrhus, Sir Roger put in a second time, "And
let me tell you, (says he,) though he speaks but little,
I like the old fellow in whiskers as well as any of
them." Captain Sentry, seeing two or three wags who
sat near us, lean with an attentive ear towards Sir
Roger, and fearing lest they should smoke the knight,
plucked him by the elbow, and whispered something
in his ear, that lasted till the opening of the fifth act.
The knight was wonderfully attentive to the account
which Orestes gives of Pyrrhus his death, and at the
conclusion of it, told me it was such a bloody piece of
work, that he was glad it was not done upon the stage.
Seeing afterwards Orestes in his raving fit, he grew
more than ordinary serious, and took occasion to mor-
alize (in his way) upon an evil conscience, adding,

that "Orestes, in his madness, looked as if he saw something."

As we were the first that came into the house, so we were the last that went out of it; being resolved to have a clear passage for our old friend, whom we did not care to venture among the justling of the crowd. Sir Roger went out fully satisfied with his entertainment, and we guarded him to his lodgings in the same manner that we brought him to the play-house; being highly pleased, for my own part, not only with the performance of the excellent piece which had been presented, but with the satisfaction which it had given to the good old man.

SIR ROGER AT VAUXHALL.

As I was sitting in my chamber, and thinking on a subject for my next Spectator, I heard two or three irregular bounces at my landlady's door, and upon the opening of it, a loud cheerful voice inquiring whether the philosopher was at home. The child who went to the door answered very innocently, that he did not lodge there. I immediately recollected that it was my good friend Sir Roger's voice; and that I had promised to go with him on the water to Spring-Garden, in case it proved a good evening. The knight put me in mind of my promise from the staircase, but told me that if I was speculating, he would stay below till I had done. Upon my coming down, I found all the children of the family got about my old friend, and my landlady herself, who is a notable prating gossip, engaged in a conference with him; being mightily pleased with his stroking her little boy upon the head, and bidding him be a good child, and mind his book.

We were no sooner come to the Temple-stairs, but we were surrounded with a crowd of watermen, offering their respective services. Sir Roger, after having looked about him very attentively, spied one with a wooden leg, and immediately gave him orders to get his boat ready. As we were walking towards it, "You must know (says Sir Roger), I never make use of anybody to row me that has not either lost a leg or an arm. I would rather bate him a few strokes of his

42

oar, than not employ an honest man that has been wounded in the Queen's service. If I was a lord or a bishop, and kept a barge, I would not put a fellow in my livery that had not a wooden leg."

My old friend, after having seated himself, and trimmed the boat with his coachman, who, being a very sober man, always serves for ballast on these occasions, we made the best of our way for Fox-hall. Sir Roger obliged the waterman to give us the history of his right leg, and hearing that he had left it at La Hogue, with many particulars which passed in that glorious action, the knight in the triumph of his heart made several reflections on the greatness of the British nation; as, that one Englishman could beat three Frenchmen; that we could never be in danger of Popery so long as we took care of our fleet; that the Thames was the noblest river in Europe; that London bridge was a greater piece of work than any other of the seven wonders of the world; with many other honest prejudices which naturally cleave to the heart of a true Englishman.

After some short pause, the old knight, turning about his head twice or thrice to take a survey of this great metropolis, bid me observe how thick the city was set with churches, and that there was scarce a single steeple on this side Temple-bar. "A most heathenish sight! (says Sir Roger): There is no religion at this end of the town. The fifty new churches will very much mend the prospect; but church-work is slow, church-work is slow!"

I do not remember I have anywhere mentioned in Sir Roger's character, his custom of saluting every-body that passes by him with a good morrow or a good night. This the old man does out of the over-

flowings of humanity, though at the same time it
renders him so popular among all his country neighbors, that it is thought to have gone a good way in
making him once or twice knight of the shire. He
cannot forbear this exercise of benevolence even in
town, when he meets with any one in his morning or
evening walk. It broke from him to several boats
that passed by us upon the water ; but to the knight's
great surprise, as he gave the good night to two or
three young fellows a little before our landing, one of
them, instead of returning the civility, asked us what
queer old put we had in the boat, and whether he was
not ashamed to go a wenching at his years ? with a
great deal of the like Thames ribaldry. Sir Roger
seemed a little shocked at first, but at length assuming
a face of magistracy, told us, " that if he were a Middlesex justice, he would make such vagrants know that
her Majesty's subjects were no more to be abused by
water than by land."

We were now arrived at Spring-Garden, which is
exquisitely pleasant at this time of year. When I
considered the fragrancy of the walks and bowers,
with the choirs of birds that sung upon the trees, and
the loose tribe of people that walked under their
shades, I could not but look upon the place as a kind
of Mahometan paradise. Sir Roger told me it put
him in mind of a little coppice by his house in the
country, which his chaplain used to call an aviary of
nightingales. " You must understand (says the
knight), there is nothing in the world that pleases a
man in love so much as your nightingale. Ah, Mr.
Spectator ! the many moonlight nights that I have
walked by myself, and thought on the widow by the
music of the nightingale ! " He here fetched a deep

sigh, and was falling into a fit of musing, when a mask, who came behind him, gave him a gentle tap upon the shoulder, and asked him if he would drink a bottle of mead with her ? But the knight being startled at so unexpected a familiarity, and displeased to be interrupted in his thoughts of the widow, told her, "She was a wanton baggage," and bid her go about her business.

We concluded our walk with a glass of Burton ale, and a slice of hung-beef. When we had done eating ourselves, the knight called a waiter to him, and bid him carry the remainder to a waterman that had but one leg. I perceived the fellow stared upon him at the oddness of the message, and was going to be saucy ; upon which I ratified the knight's commands with a peremptory look.

As we were going out of the garden my old friend, thinking himself obliged, as a member of the Quorum, to animadvert upon the morals of the place, told the mistress of the house, who sat at the bar, "that he should be a better customer to her garden, if there were more nightingales and fewer strumpets."

DEATH OF SIR ROGER.

WE last night received a piece of ill news at our club, which very sensibly afflicted every one of us. I question not but my readers themselves will be troubled at the hearing of it. To keep them no longer in suspense, Sir Roger de Coverley is dead. He departed this life at his house in the country, after a few weeks' sickness. Sir Andrew Freeport has a letter from one of his correspondents in those parts, that informs him the old man caught a cold at the country sessions, as he was very warmly promoting an address of his own penning, in which he succeeded according to his wishes. But this particular comes from a Whig justice of peace, who was always Sir Roger's enemy and antagonist. I have letters both from the chaplain and Captain Sentry, which mention nothing of it, but are filled with many particulars to the honor of the good old man. I have likewise a letter from the butler, who took so much care of me last summer when I was at the knight's house. As my friend the butler mentions, in the simplicity of his heart, several circumstances the others have passed over in silence, I shall give my reader a copy of his letter, without any alteration or diminution.

" HONORED SIR.

"Knowing that you was my old master's good friend, I could not forbear sending you the melancholy news of his death, which has afflicted the whole country, as well as his poor servants, who loved him, I may say, better than we did our lives. I am afraid he caught his death the last country sessions, where he would go to see justice done to a poor widow woman, and her fatherless children, that had been wronged by a neighboring gentleman; for you know, my good master was always the poor man's friend. Upon his coming home, the first complaint he made was, that he had lost his roast-beef stomach, not being able to touch a sirloin, which was served up according to custom : and you know he used to take great delight in it. From that time forward he grew worse and worse, but still kept a good heart to the last. Indeed we were once in great hopes of his recovery, upon a kind message that was sent him from the widow lady whom he had made love to the forty last years of his life ; but this only proved a lightening before his death. He has bequeathed to this lady, as a token of his love, a great pearl necklace, and a couple of silver bracelets set with jewels, which belonged to my good old lady his mother : he has bequeathed the fine white gelding, that he used to ride a hunting upon, to his chaplain, because he thought he would be kind to him, and has left you all his books. He has, moreover, bequeathed to the chaplain a very pretty tenement with good lands about it. It being a very cold day when he made his will, he left for mourning, to every man in the parish, a great frieze coat, and to every woman a black ridinghood. It was a most moving sight to see him take leave of his poor servants, commending us all for our fidelity, whilst we were not able to speak a word for weeping. As we most of us are grown grayheaded in our dear master's service, he has left us pensions and legacies which we may live very comfortably upon the remaining part of our days. He has bequeathed a great deal more in charity, which is not yet come to my knowledge, and it is peremptorily said in the parish, that he has left money to build a steeple to the church : for he was heard to say some time ago, that if he lived two years longer, Coverley church should have a steeple to it. The chaplain tells everybody that he made a very good end, and never speaks of him without tears. He was buried, according to his own directions, among the family of the Coverlies, on the left hand of his father Sir Arthur. The coffin was carried by six of his tenants, and the pall held up by six of the quorum: the whole parish followed the corpse with heavy hearts, and in their mourning suits; the men in frieze, and the women in riding-hoods. Captain Sentry, my master's nephew, has taken possession of the hall-house, and the whole estate. When my old master saw him, a little before his death, he shook him by the hand, and wished him joy of the estate which was falling to him, desiring him only to make a good use of it, and to pay the several legacies, and the gifts of charity, which he told him he had left as quit-rents upon the estate. The captain truly seems a courteous man, though says but little. He makes much of those whom my master loved, and shows great kindness to the old house-dog, that you know my poor master was so fond of. It would have gone to your heart to have heard the moans the dumb creature made on the day of my master's death. He has never joyed himself since; no more has any of us. It was the melancholiest day for the poor people that ever happened in Worcestershire. This being all from,

" Honored sir, your most sorrowful servant,
"EDWARD BISCUIT.

"P. S. My master desired, some weeks before he died, that a book which comes up to you by the carrier, should be given to Sir Andrew Freeport in his name."

This letter, notwithstanding the poor butler's manner of writing it, gave us such an idea of our good old friend, that, upon the reading of it, there was not a dry eye in the club. Sir Andrew opening the book, found it to be a collection of acts of Parliament. There was, in particular, the act of uniformity, with some passages in it marked by Sir Roger's own hand. Sir Andrew found that they related to two or three points, which he had disputed with Sir Roger the last time he appeared at the club. Sir Andrew, who would have been merry at such an incident on another occasion, at the sight of the old man's handwriting, burst into tears, and put the book into his pocket. Captain Sentry informs me, that the knight has left rings and mourning for every one in the club.

THE TATLER'S COURT.

TRIAL OF THE DEAD IN REASON.

As soon as I had placed myself in the chair of judicature, I ordered my clerk Mr. Lillie to read to the assembly (who were gathered together according to notice) a certain declaration, by way of charge, to open the purpose of my session, which tended only to this explanation, " That as other courts were often called to demand the execution of persons dead in law, so this was held to give the last orders relating to those who are dead in reason." The solicitor of the new company of upholders, near the Hay-market, appeared in behalf of that useful society, and brought in an accusation of a young woman, who herself stood at the bar before me. Mr. Lillie read her indictment, which was in substance, " That whereas Mrs. Rebecca Pindust, of the parish of St. Martin in the Fields, had, by the use of one instrument called a looking-glass, and by the further use of certain attire, made either of cambric, muslin, or other linen wares, upon her head, attained to such an evil heart and magical force in the motion of her eyes and turn of her countenance, that she, the said Rebecca, had put to death several young men of the said parish ; and that the said young men had acknowledged in certain papers, commonly called love-letters, (which were produced in court gilded on the edges, and sealed with a particular wax, with certain amorous and enchanting words wrought upon the said seals,) that they died for the said Rebecca : and whereas the said Rebecca persisted in the said evil practice ; this way of life the said society construed to be, according to former edicts, a state of death, and demanded an order for the interment of the said Rebecca."

I looked upon the maid with great humanity, and desired her to make answer to what was said against her. She said, " it was indeed true, that she had practised all the arts and means she could to dispose of herself happily in marriage, but thought she did not come under the censure expressed in my writings for the same ; and humbly hoped I would not condemn her for the ignorance of her accusers, who, according to their own words, had rather represented her killing, than dead." She further alleged, " That the expressions mentioned in the papers written to her, were become mere words, and that she had been always ready to marry any of those who said they died for her ; but that they made their escape as soon as they found themselves pitied or believed." She ended her discourse, by desiring I would, for the future, settle the meaning of the words, " I die," in letters of love.

Mrs. Pindust behaved herself with such an air of innocence, that she easily gained credit, and was acquitted. Upon which occasion, I gave it as a standing rule, " That any persons, who in any letter, billet, or discourse, should tell a woman he died for her, should, if she pleased, be obliged to live with her, or be immediately interred upon such their own confession, without bail or mainprize."

It happened, that the very next who was brought before me was one of her admirers, who was indicted upon that very head. A letter, which he acknowledged to be his own hand, was read ; in which were the following words ; " Cruel creature, I die for you." It was observable, that he took snuff all the time his accusation was reading. I asked him, "How he came to use these words, if he were not a dead man?" He told me, "He was in love with a lady, and did not know any other way of telling her so; and that all his acquaintance took the same method." Though I was moved with compassion towards him, by reason of the weakness of his parts, yet, for example's sake, I was forced to answer, "Your sentence shall be a warning to all the rest of your companions, not to tell lies for want of wit." Upon this, he began to beat his snuff-box with a very saucy air; and opening it again, "Faith Isaac, (said he,) thou art a very unaccountable old fellow.—Prythee, who gave thee power of life and death? What a pox hast thou to do with ladies and lovers? I suppose thou wouldst have a man be in company with his mistress, and say nothing to her. Dost thou call breaking a jest, telling a lie? Ha! is that thy wisdom, old Stiffrump, ha?" He was going on with this insipid commonplace mirth, sometimes opening his box, sometimes shutting it, then viewing the picture on the lid, and then the workmanship of the hinge, when, in the midst of his eloquence, I ordered his box to be taken from him; upon which he was immediately struck speechless, and carried off stone dead.

The next who appeared, was a hale old fellow of sixty. He was brought in by his relations, who desired leave to bury him. Upon requiring a distinct account of the prisoner, a credible witness deposed, "That he always rose at ten of the clock, played with his cat till twelve, smoked tobacco till one, was at dinner till two, then took another pipe, played at backgammon till six, talked of one Madam Frances, an old mistress of his, till eight, repeated the same account at the tavern till ten, then returned home, took the other pipe, and then to bed." I asked him, what he had to say for himself? "As to what (said he) they mention concerning Madam Frances—" I did not care for hearing a Canterbury tale, and therefore thought myself seasonably interrupted by a young gentleman who appeared in behalf of the old man, and prayed an arrest of judgment; for that he the said young man held certain lands by his the said old man's life. Upon this, the solicitor of the upholders took an occasion to demand him also, and thereupon produced several evidences that witnessed to his life and conversation. It appeared, that each of them divided their hours in matters of equal moment and importance to themselves and to the public. They rose at the same hour: while the old man was playing with his cat, the young one was looking out of his window; while the old man was smoking his pipe, the young man was rubbing his teeth; while one was at dinner, the other was dressing; while one was at backgammon, the other was at dinner; while the old fellow was talking of Madam Frances, the young one was either at play, or toasting women whom he never conversed with. The only difference was, that the young man had never been good for anything; the old man, a man of worth before he knew Madam Frances. Upon the whole, I ordered them to be both interred together, with inscriptions proper to their characters, signifying, "That the old man died in the year 1689, and was buried in the year 1709." And over the young one it was said, "That he departed this world in twenty-fifth year of his death."

The next class of criminals were authors in prose and verse. Those of them who had produced any stillborn work, were immediately dismissed to their burial, and were followed by others, who, notwithstanding some sprightly issue in their life-time, had given proofs of their death, by some posthumous children, that bore no resemblance to their elder brethren. As for those who were the fathers of a mixed progeny, provided always they could prove the last to be a live child, they escaped with life, but not without loss of limbs; for in this case, I was satisfied with amputation of the parts which were mortified.

These were followed by a great crowd of super-annuated benchers of the inns of court, senior fellows of colleges, and defunct statesmen; all whom I ordered to be decimated indifferently, allowing the rest a re-prieve for one year, with a promise of a free pardon in case of resuscitation.

There were still great multitudes to be examined; but finding it very late, I adjourned the court; not without the secret pleasure that I had done my duty, and furnished out an handsome execution.

TRIAL OF THE PETTICOAT.

THE court being prepared for proceeding on the cause of the petticoat, I gave orders to bring in a criminal who was taken up as she went out of the puppet-show about three nights ago, and was now standing in the street with a great concourse of people about her. Word was brought me, that she had en- deavored twice or thrice to come in, but could not do it by reason of her petticoat, which was too large for the entrance of my house, though I had ordered both the folding-doors to be thrown open for its reception. Upon this, I desired the jury of matrons, who stood at my right hand, to inform themselves of her condition, and know whether there were any private reasons why she might not make her appearance separate from her petticoat. This was managed with great discretion, and had such an effect, that upon the return of the verdict from the bench of matrons, I issued out an order forthwith, that the criminal should be stripped of her encumbrances, till she became little enough to enter my house. I had before given directions for an engine of several legs, that could contract or open it- self like the top of an umbrella, in order to place the petticoat upon it, by which means I might take a leisurely survey of it, as it should appear in its proper dimensions. This was all done accordingly; and forth- with, upon the closing of the engine, the petticoat was brought into court. I then directed the machine
58

to be set upon the table, and dilated in such a manner, as to show the garment in its utmost circumference; but my great hall was too narrow for the experiment; for before it was half unfolded, it described so immoderate a circle, that the lower part of it brushed upon my face as I sat in my chair of judicature. I then inquired for the person that belonged to the petticoat; and, to my great surprise, was directed to a very beautiful young damsel, with so pretty a face and shape, that I bid her come out of the crowd, and seated her upon a little crock at my left hand. "My pretty maid, (said I,) do you own yourself to have been the inhabitant of the garment before us?" The girl I found had good sense, and told me with a smile, "That notwithstanding it was her own petticoat, she should be very glad to see an example made of it; and that she wore it for no other reason, but that she had a mind to look as big and burly as other persons of her quality: that she had kept out of it as long as she could, and till she began to appear little in the eyes of all her acquaintance; that if she laid it aside, people would think she was not made like other women." I always give great allowances to the fair sex upon account of the fashion, and therefore was not displeased with the defense of the pretty criminal. I then ordered the vest which stood before us to be drawn up by a pulley to the top of my great hall, and afterwards to be spread open by the engine it was placed upon, in such a manner, that it formed a very splendid and ample canopy over our heads, and covered the whole court of judicature with a kind of silken rotunda, in its form not unlike the cupola of St. Paul's. I entered upon the whole cause with great satisfaction, as I sat under the shadow of it.

The counsel for the petticoat was now called in, and ordered to produce what they had to say against the popular cry which was raised against it. They answered the objections with great strength and solidity of argument, and expatiated in very florid harangues, which they did not fail to set off and furbelow (if I may be allowed the metaphor) with many periodical sentences and turns of oratory. The chief arguments for their client were taken, first, from the great benefit that might arise to our woolen manufactory from this invention, which was calculated as follows : the common petticoat has not above four yards in the circumference ; whereas this over our heads had more in the semi-diameter : so that by allowing it twenty-four yards in the circumference, the five millions of woolen petticoats, which, according to Sir William Petty, (supposing what ought to be supposed in a well-governed state, that all petticoats are made of that stuff,) would amount to thirty millions of those of the ancient mode. A prodigious improvement of the woolen trade ! and what could not fail to sink the power of France in a few years.

To introduce the second argument, they begged leave to read a petition of the rope-makers, wherein it was represented, that the demand for cords, and the price of them, were much risen since this fashion came up. At this, all the company who were present lifted up their eyes into the vault ; and I must confess, we did discover many traces of cordage which were interwoven in the stiffening of the drapery.

A third argument was founded upon a petition of the Greenland trade, which likewise represented the great consumption of whalebone which would be occasioned by the present fashion, and the benefit which would thereby accrue to that branch of the British trade.

To conclude, they gently touched upon the weight and unwieldiness of the garment, which they insinuated might be of great use to preserve the honor of families.

These arguments would have wrought very much upon me, (as I then told the company in a long and elaborate discourse,) had I not considered the great and additional expense which such fashions would bring upon fathers and husbands; and therefore by no means to be thought of till some years after a peace. I further urged, that it would be a prejudice to the ladies themselves, who could never expect to have any money in the pocket, if they laid out so much on the petticoat. To this I added, the great temptation it might give to virgins, of acting in security like married women, and by that means give a check to matrimony, an institution always encouraged by wise societies.

At the same time, in answer to the several petitions produced on that side, I showed one subscribed by the women of several persons of quality, humbly setting forth, that since the introduction of this mode, their respective ladies had (instead of bestowing on them their cast gowns) cut them into shreds, and mixed them with the cordage and buckram, to complete the stiffening of their under-petticoats. For which, and sundry other reasons, I pronounced the petticoat a forfeiture: but to show that I did not make that judgment for the sake of filthy lucre, I ordered it to be folded up, and sent it as a present to a widow gentlewoman, who has five daughters, desiring she would make each of them a petticoat out of it, and send me back the remainder, which I design to cut into stomachers, caps, facings of my waistcoat sleeves, and other garnitures suitable to my age and quality.

I would not be understood, that (while I discard this monstrous invention) I am an enemy to the proper ornaments of the fair sex. On the contrary, as the hand of nature has poured on them such a profusion of charms and graces, and sent them into the world more amiable and finished than the rest of her works; so I would have them bestow upon themselves all the additional beauties that art can supply them with, provided it does not interfere with, disguise, or pervert, those of nature.

I consider woman as a beautiful romantic animal, that may be adorned with furs and feathers, pearls and diamonds, ores and silks. The lynx shall cast its skin at her feet to make her a tippet; the peacock, parrot, and swan shall pay contributions to her muff; the sea shall be searched for shells, and the rocks for gems; and every part of nature furnish out its share towards the embellishment of a creature that is the most consummate work of it. All this I shall indulge them in; but as for the petticoat I have been speaking of, I neither can nor will allow it.

TRIAL OF THE WINE-BREWERS.

THERE is in this city a certain fraternity of chymical operators, who work under ground in holes, caverns, and dark retirements, to conceal their mysteries from the eyes and observation of mankind. These subterraneous philosophers are daily employed in the transmigration of liquors, and, by the power of medical drugs and incantations, raising under the streets of London the choicest products of the hills and valleys of France. They can squeeze Bordeaux out of a sloe, and draw Champagne from an apple. Virgil, in that remarkable prophecy,

Incultisque rubens pendebit sentibus Uva,
"The ripening grape shall hang on every thorn,"

seems to have hinted at this art, which can turn a plantation of northern hedges into a vineyard. These adepts are known among one another by the name of wine-brewers, and I am afraid do great injury, not only to her Majesty's customs, but to the bodies of many of her good subjects.

Having received sundry complaints against these invisible workmen, I ordered the proper officer of my court to ferret them out of their respective caves, and bring them before me, which was yesterday executed accordingly.

The person who appeared against them was a merchant, who had by him a great magazine of wines that

he had laid in before the war: but these gentlemen
(as he said) had so vitiated the nation's palate, that no
man could believe his to be French, because it did not
taste like what they sold for such.   As a man never
pleads better than where his own personal interest is
concerned, he exhibited to the court with great eloquence, That this new corporation of druggists had
inflamed the bills of mortality, and puzzled the college
of physicians with diseases, for which they neither
knew a name or cure.   He accused some of giving all
their customers cholics and megrims; and mentioned
one who had boasted, he had a tun of claret by him,
that in a fortnight's time should give the gout to a
dozen of the healthfullest men in the city, provided
that their constitutions were prepared for it by wealth
and idleness.   He then enlarged, with a great show of
reason, upon the prejudice which these mixtures and
compositions had done to the brains of the English
nation; as is too visible (said he) from many late pam-
phlets, speeches, and sermons, as well as from the
ordinary conversations of the youth of this age.   He
then quoted an ingenious person, who would undertake
to know by a man's writings, the wine he most delighted in; and on that occasion named a certain
satirist, whom he had discovered to be the author of a
lampoon, by a manifest taste of the sloe, which showed
itself in it by much roughness and little spirit.

   In the last place, he ascribed to the unnatural tumults
and fermentations, which these mixtures raise in our
blood, the divisions, heats, and animosities that reign
among us; and in particular, asserted most of the
modern enthusiasms and agitations to be nothing else
but the effects of adulterated port.

   The counsel for the brewers had a face so extremely

inflamed and illuminated with carbuncles, that I did not wonder to see him an advocate for these sophistications. His rhetoric was likewise such as I should have expected from the common draught, which I found he often drank to a great excess. Indeed, I was so surprised at his figure and parts, that I ordered him to give me a taste of his usual liquor ; which I had no sooner drank, but I found a pimple rising in my forehead ; and felt such a sensible decay in my understanding, that I would not proceed in the trial till the fume of it was entirely dissipated.

This notable advocate had little to say in the defense of his clients, but that they were under a necessity of making claret if they would keep open their doors, it being the nature of mankind to love everything that is prohibited. He further pretended to reason, that it might be as profitable to the nation to make French wine as French hats, and concluded with the great advantage that this had already brought to part of the kingdom. Upon which he informed the court, " That the lands in Herefordshire were raised two years' purchase since the beginning of the war."

When I had sent out my summons to these people, I gave at the same time orders to each of them to bring the several ingredients he made use of in distinct phials, which they had done accordingly, and ranged them into two rows on each side of the court. The workmen were drawn up in ranks behind them. The merchant informed me, that in one row of phials were the several colors they dealt in, and in the other the tastes. He then showed me on the right hand one who went by the name of Tom Tintoret, who (as he told me) was the greatest master in his coloring of any vintner in London. To give me a proof of his art, he took a glass

5

of fair water; and by the infusion of three drops out
of one of his phials, converted it into a most beautiful
pale Burgundy. Two more of the same kind heightened
it into a perfect Languedoc: from thence it passed into
a florid Hermitage: and after having gone through two
or three other changes, by the addition of a single drop,
ended in a very deep Pontac. This ingenious virtuoso,
seeing me very much surprised at his art, told me, that
he had not an opportunity of showing it in perfection,
having only made use of water for the ground-work
of his coloring; but that if I were to see an operation
upon liquors of stronger bodies, the art would appear
to much greater advantage. He added, " That he
doubted not but it would please my curiosity to see the
cider of one apple take only a vermilion, when another,
with a less quantity of the same infusion, would rise
into a dark purple, according to the different texture of
parts in the liquor." He informed me also, " That he
could hit the different shades and degrees of red, as they
appear in the pink and the rose, the clove and the carna-
tion, as he had Rhenish or Moselle, Perry or White
Port, to work in."

I was so satisfied with the ingenuity of this virtuoso,
that, after having advised him to quit so dishonest a
profession, I promised him, in consideration of his great
genius, to recommend him as a partner to a friend of
mine, who has heaped up great riches, and is a scarlet
dyer.

The artists on my other hand were ordered in the
second place to make some experiments of their skill
before me: upon which the famous Harry Sippet stept
out, and asked me, " What I would be pleased to
drink ? " At the same time he filled out three or four
white liquors in a glass, and told me, " That it should

be what I pleased to call for ; " adding very learnedly,
" That the liquor before him was as the naked substance or first matter of his compound, to which he
and his friend, who stood over against him, could give
what accidents or form they pleased." Finding him
so great a philosopher, I desired he would convey into
it the qualities and essence of right Bourdeaux.
" Coming, coming, sir," (said he,) with the air of a
drawer ; and after having cast his eye on the several
tastes and flavors that stood before him, he took up a
little cruet that was filled with a kind of inky juice,
and pouring some of it out into the glass of white
wine, presented it to me, and told me, " This was the
wine over which most of the business of the last term
had been despatched." I must confess, I looked upon
that sooty drug which he held up in his cruet, as the
quintessence of English Bourdeaux, and therefore desired him to give me a glass of it by itself, which he
did with great unwillingness. My cat at that time
sat by me, upon the elbow of my chair ; and as I did
not care for making the experiment upon myself, I
reached it to her to sip of it, which had like to have
cost her her life ; for notwithstanding it flung her at
first into freakish tricks, quite contrary to her usual
gravity, in less than a quarter of an hour she fell into
convulsions ; and had it not been a creature more
tenacious of life than any other, would certainly have
died under the operation.

I was so incensed by the tortures of my innocent
domestic, and the unworthy dealings of these men,
that I told them, if each of them had as many lives as
the injured creature before them, they deserved to forfeit them for the pernicious arts which they used for
their profit. I therefore bid them look upon them-

selves as no better than a kind of assassins and murderers within the law. However, since they had dealt so clearly with me, and laid before me their whole practise, I dismissed them for that time; with a particular request, That they would not poison any of my friends and acquaintance, and take to some honest livelihood without loss of time.

For my own part, I have resolved hereafter to be very careful in my liquors, and have agreed with a friend of mine in the army, upon their next march, to secure me two hogsheads of the best stomach-wine in the cellars of Versailles, for the good of my lucubrations, and the comfort of my old age.

STATESWOMEN.

PARTY PATCHES.

ABOUT the middle of last winter I went to see an opera at the theater in the Haymarket, where I could not but take notice of two parties of very fine women, that had placed themselves in the opposite side boxes, and seemed drawn up in a kind of battle-array one against another. After a short survey of them, I found they were patched differently; the faces, on one hand, being spotted on the right side of the forehead, and those upon the other on the left: I quickly perceived that they cast hostile glances upon one another; and that their patches were placed in those different situations, as party-signals to distinguish friends from foes. In the middle boxes, between these two opposite bodies, were several ladies who patched indifferently on both sides of their faces, and seemed to sit there with no other intention but to see the opera. Upon inquiry I found, that the body of Amazons on my right hand were Whigs, and those on my left, Tories; and that those who had placed themselves in the middle boxes were a neutral party, whose faces had not yet declared themselves. These last, however, as I afterwards found, diminished daily, and took their party with one side or the other; insomuch that I observed in several of them, the patches, which were before dispersed equally, are now all gone over to the Whig or the Tory side of the face. The censorious say, that the men whose hearts are aimed at, are very

often the occasions that one part of the face is thus
dishonored, and lies under a kind of disgrace, while
the other is so much set off and adorned by the owner;
and that the patches turn to the right or to the left,
according to the principles of the man who is most in
favor. But whatever may be the motives of a few
fantastical coquettes, who do not patch for the public
good so much as for their own private advantage, it is
certain, that there are several women of honor who
patch out of principle, and with an eye to the interest
of their country. Nay, I am informed that some of
them adhere so stedfastly to their party, and are so far
from sacrificing their zeal for the public to their passions for any particular person, that in a late draught
of marriage-articles a lady has stipulated with her
husband, that whatever his opinions are, she shall be
at liberty to patch on which side she pleases.

I must here take notice, that Rosalinda, a famous
Whig partisan, has most unfortunately a very beautiful mole on the Tory part of her forehead; which
being very conspicuous, has occasioned many mistakes,
and given an handle to her enemies to misrepresent
her face, as though it had revolted from the Whig interest. But, whatever this natural patch may seem to
insinuate, it is well known that her notions of government are still the same. This unlucky mole, however,
has misled several coxcombs; and like the hanging out
of false colors, made some of them converse with
Rosalinda in what they thought the spirit of her party,
when on a sudden she has given them an unexpected
fire, that has sunk them all at once. If Rosalinda is
unfortunate in her mole, Nigranilla is as unhappy in a
pimple, which forces her, against her inclinations, to
patch on the Whig side.

I am told that many virtuous matrons, who formerly have been taught to believe that this artificial spotting of the face was unlawful, are now reconciled by a zeal for their cause, to what they could not be prompted by a concern for their beauty. This way of declaring war upon one another, puts me in mind of what is reported of the tigress, that several spots rise in her skin when she is angry; or, as Mr. Cowley has imitated the verses that stand as the motto of this paper,

—She swells with angry pride,
And calls forth all her spots on every side.

When I was in the theater the time above mentioned, I had the curiosity to count the patches on both sides, and found the Tory patches to be about twenty stronger than the Whig; but to make amends for this small inequality, I the next morning found the whole puppet-show filled with faces spotted after the Whiggish manner. Whether or no the ladies had retreated hither in order to rally their forces, I cannot tell; but the next night they came in so great a body to the opera, that they outnumbered the enemy.

This account of party-patches will, I am afraid, appear improbable to those who live at a distance from the fashionable world; but as it is a distinction of a very singular nature, and what perhaps may never meet with a parallel, I think I should not have discharged the office of a faithful Spectator, had I not recorded it.

I have endeavored to expose this party-rage in women, as it only serves to aggravate the hatred and animosities that reign among men, and in a great measure deprives the fair sex of those peculiar charms with which nature has endowed them.

When the Romans and Sabines were at war, and just upon the point of giving battle, the women who were allied to both of them, interposed with so many tears and entreaties, that they prevented the mutual slaughter which threatened both parties, and united them together in a firm and lasting peace.

I would recommend this noble example to our British ladies, at a time when their country is torn with so many unnatural divisions, that if they continue, it will be a misfortune to be born in it. The Greeks thought it so improper for women to interest themselves in competitions and contentions, that for this reason, among others, they forbade them, under pain of death, to be present at the Olympic games, notwithstanding these were the public diversions of all Greece.

As our English women excel those of all nations in beauty, they should endeavor to outshine them in all other accomplishments proper to the sex, and to distinguish themselves as tender mothers and faithful wives, rather than as furious partisans. Female virtues are of a domestic turn. The family is the proper province for private women to shine in. If they must be showing their zeal for the public, let it not be against those who are perhaps of the same family, or at least of the same religion or nation, but against those who are the open, professed, undoubted enemies of their faith, liberty, and country. When the Romans were pressed with a foreign enemy, the ladies voluntarily contributed all their rings and jewels to assist the government under the public exigence, which appeared so laudable an action in the eyes of their countrymen, that from thenceforth it was permitted by a law to pronounce public orations at the funeral

of a woman in praise of the deceased person, which
till that time was peculiar to men.

Would our English ladies, instead of sticking on a
patch against those of their own country, show themselves so truly public-spirited as to sacrifice every one
her necklace against the common enemy, what decrees ought not to be made in favor of them!

Since I am recollecting upon this subject such passages as occur to my memory out of ancient authors,
I cannot omit a sentence in the celebrated funeral ora-
tion of Pericles, which he made in honor of those brave
Athenians that were slain in a fight with the Lacedæ-
monians. After having addressed himself to the
several ranks and orders of his countrymen, and shown
them how they should behave themselves in the public
cause, he turns to the female part of his audience ;
" And as for you, (says he,) I shall advise you in very
few words : aspire only to those virtues that are peculiar to your sex ; follow your natural modesty, and
think it your greatest commendation not to be talked
of one way or other."

WOMEN AND LIBERTY.

IT is with great satisfaction I observe, that the women of our island, who are the most eminent for virtue and good sense, are in the interest of the present government. As the fair sex very much recommend the cause they are engaged in, it would be no small misfortune to a sovereign, though he had all the male part of the nation on his side, if he did not find himself king of the most beautiful half of his subjects. Ladies are always of great use to the party they espouse, and never fail to win over numbers to it. Lovers, according to Sir William Petty's computation, make at least the third part of the sensible men of the British nation; and it has been an uncontroverted maxim in all ages, that, though a husband is sometimes a stubborn sort of a creature, a lover is always at the devotion of his mistress. By this means, it lies in the power of every fine woman, to secure at least half a dozen able-bodied men to his Majesty's service. The female world are, likewise, indispensably necessary in the best causes, to manage the controversial part of them, in which no man of tolerable breeding is ever able to refute them. Arguments out of a pretty mouth are unanswerable.

There are many reasons why the women of Great Britain should be on the side of the Freeholder, and enemies to the person who would bring in arbitrary government and Popery. As there are several of our ladies who amuse themselves in the reading of travels, they cannot but take notice, what uncomfortable lives those of their own sex lead, where passive obedience is professed and practised in its utmost perfection. In those countries, the men have no property but in their wives, who are the slaves to slaves : every married woman being subject to a domestic tyrant, that requires from her the same vassalage which he pays to his sultan. If the ladies would seriously consider the evil consequences of arbitrary power, they would find, that it spoils the shape of the foot in China, where the barbarous politics of the men so diminish the basis of the female figure, as to unqualify a woman for an evening walk or country-dance. In the East Indies, a widow, who has any regard to her character, throws herself into the flames of her husband's funeral pile, to show, forsooth, that she is faithful and loyal to the memory of her deceased lord. In Persia, the daughters of Eve, as they call them, are reckoned in the inventory of their goods and chattels : and it is a usual thing, when a man sells a bale of silk or a drove of camels, to toss half a dozen women into the bargain. Through all the dominions of the Great Turk, a woman thinks herself happy, if she can get but the twelfth share of a husband, and is thought of no manner of use in the creation but to keep up a proper number of slaves for the commander of the faithful. I need not set forth the ill usage which the fair ones meet with, in those despotic governments that lie nearer us. Every one hath heard of the several ways of locking up women in Spain and Italy ; where, if there is any power lodged in any of the sex, it is not among the young and the beautiful, whom nature seems to have formed for it, but among the old and withered matrons, known by the frightful name of *gouvernantes* and

duennas. If any should allege the freedoms indulged
to the French ladies, he must own that these are
owing to the natural gallantry of the people, not to
their form of government, which excludes, by its very
constitution, every female from power, as naturally
unfit to hold the scepter of that kingdom.

Women ought, in reason, to be no less averse to
Popery than to arbitrary power. Some merry authors
have pretended to demonstrate, that the Roman Catholic religion could never spread in a' nation where
women would have more modesty than to expose their
innocent liberties to a confessor. Others of the same
turn have assured us, that the fine British complexion,
which is so peculiar to our ladies, would suffer very
much from a fish-diet : and that a whole Lent would
give such a sallowness to the celebrated beauties of
this island, as would scarce make them distinguishable
from those of France. I shall only leave to the serious consideration of the countrywomen, the danger
any of them might have been in, (had Popery been our
natural religion,) of being forced by their relations to
a state of perpetual virginity. The most blooming
toast in the island might have been a nun ; and many
a lady, who is now a mother of fine children, condemned to a condition of life, disagreeable to herself
and unprofitable to the world. To this I might add,
the melancholy objects they would be daily entertained
with, of several sightly men delivered over to an invio-
lable celibacy. Let a young lady imagine to herself, the
brisk embroidered officer, who now makes love to her
with so agreeable an air, converted into a monk ; or
the beau, who now addresses himself to her in a full-
bottomed wig, distinguished by a little bald pate
covered with a black leather skull-cap. I forbear to

mention many other objections, which the ladies, who are no strangers to the doctrines of Popery, will easily recollect : though I do not in the least doubt but those I have already suggested, will be sufficient to persuade my fair readers to be zealous in the Protestant cause.

The freedom and happiness of our British ladies is so singular, that it is a common saying in foreign countries, " If a bridge were built across the seas, all the women in Europe would flock into England." It has been observed, that the laws relating to them are so favorable, that one would think they themselves had given votes in enacting them. All the honors and indulgences of society are due to them by our customs ; and, by our constitution, they have all the privileges of English-born subjects, without the burdens. I need not acquaint my fair fellow-freeholders, that every man who is anxious for our sacred and civil rights, is a champion in their cause ; since we enjoy in common a religion agreeable to that reasonable nature, of which we equally partake ; and since, in point of property, our law makes no distinction of sexes.

We may, therefore, justly expect from them, that they will act in concert with us for the preservation of our laws and religion, which cannot subsist, but under the government of his present Majesty ; and would necessarily be subverted, under that of a person bred up in the most violent principles of Popery and arbitrary power. Thus may the fair sex contribute to fix the peace of a brave and generous people who, for many ages, have disdained to bear any tyranny but theirs ; and be as famous in history, as those illustrious matrons, who, in the infancy of Rome, reconciled the Romans and the Sabines, and united the two contending parties under their new king.

THE LADIES' ASSOCIATION.

I have heard that several ladies of distinction, upon the reading of my former paper, are studying methods how to make themselves useful to the public. One has a design of keeping an open tea-table, where every man shall be welcome that is a friend to King George. Another is for setting up an assembly for basset, where none shall be admitted to punt that have not taken the oaths. A third is upon an invention of a dress, which will put every Tory lady out of countenance: I am not informed of the particulars, but am told in general, that she has contrived to show her principles by the setting of her commode; so that it will be impossible for any woman, that is disaffected, to be in the fashion. Some of them are of opinion that the fan may be made use of, with good success, against Popery, by exhibiting the corruptions of the Church of Rome in various figures; and that their abhorrence of the superstitious use of beads, may be very aptly expressed in the make of a pearl necklace. As for the civil part of our constitution, it is unanimously agreed, among the leaders of the sex, that there is no glory in making a man their slave, who has not naturally a passion for liberty; and to disallow of all professions of passive obedience, but from a lover to his mistress.

It happens very luckily for the interests of the Whigs, that their very enemies acknowledge the finest women of Great Britain to be of that party. The
80

Tories are forced to borrow their toasts from their antagonists; and can scarce find beauties enough of their own side, to supply a single round of October. One may, indeed, sometimes discover among the malignants of the sex a face that seems to have been naturally designed for a Whig lady ; but then it is so often flushed with rage, or soured with disappointments, that one cannot but be troubled to see it thrown away upon the owner. Would the pretty malecontent be persuaded to love her king and country, it would diffuse a cheerfulness through all her features, and give her quite another air. I would, therefore, advise these my gentle readers, as they consult the good of their faces, to forbear frowning upon loyalists, and pouting at the government. In the mean time, what may we not hope, from a cause which is recommended by all the allurement of beauty and the force of truth ! It is, therefore, to be hoped, that every fine woman will make this laudable use of her charms ; and that she may not want to be frequently reminded of this great duty, I will only desire her to think of her country every time she looks in her glass.

But because it is impossible to prescribe such rules as shall be suitable to the sex in general, I shall consider them under their several divisions of maids, wives, and widows.

As for virgins, who are unexperienced in the wiles of men, they would do well to consider, how little they are to rely on the faith of lovers who, in less than a year, have broken their allegiance to their lawful sovereign ; and what credit is to be given to the vows and protestations of such as show themselves so little afraid of perjury. Besides, what would an innocent young lady think, should she marry a man without

6

examining his principles, and afterwards find herself got with child by a rebel?

In the next place, every wife ought to answer for her man. If the husband be engaged in a seditious club, or drinks mysterious healths, or be frugal of his candles on a rejoicing night, let her look to him, and keep him out of harm's way; or the world will be apt to say, she has a mind to be a widow before her time. She ought, in such cases, to exert the authority of the curtain lecture; and if she finds him of a rebellious disposition, to tame him, as they do birds of prey, by dinning him in the ears all night long.

Widows may be supposed women of too good sense not to discountenance all practises that have a tendency to the destruction of mankind. Besides, they have a greater interest in property than either maids or wives, and do not hold their jointures by the precarious tenure of portions or pin-money. So that it is as unnatural for a dowager, as a freeholder, to be an enemy to our constitution.

As nothing is more instructive than examples, I would recommend to the perusal of our British virgins, the story of Clelia, a Roman spinster, whose behavior is represented by all their historians, as one of the chief motives that discouraged the Tarquins from prosecuting their attempt to regain the throne, from whence they had been expelled. Let the married women reflect upon the glory acquired by the wife of Coriolanus, who, when her husband, after long exile, was returning into his country with fire and sword, diverted him from so cruel and unnatural an enterprise. And let those who have outlived their husbands, never forget their countrywoman Boadicea, who headed her troops in person against the invasion of a

Roman army, and encouraged them with this memorable saying, "I, who am a woman, am resolved upon victory or death : but as for you, who are men, you may, if you please, choose life and slavery."

But I do not propose to our British ladies, that they should turn Amazons in the service of their sovereign, nor so much as let their nails grow for the defense of their country. The men will take the work of the field off their hands, and show the world, that English valor cannot be matched when it is animated by English beauty. I do not, however, disapprove the project which is now on foot for a "Female Association;" and since I hear the fair confederates cannot agree among themselves upon a form, shall presume to lay before them the following rough draft, to be corrected or improved, as they in their wisdom shall think fit.

"We, the consorts, relicts, and spinsters, of the isle of Great Britain, whose names are under-written, being most passionately offended at the falsehood and perfidiousness of certain faithless men, and at the lukewarmth and indifference of others, have entered into a voluntary association for the good and safety of our constitution. And we do hereby engage ourselves to raise and arm our vassels for the service of his Majesty King George, and him to defend, with our tongues and hearts, our eyes, eye-lashes, favorites, lips, dimples, and every other feature, whether natural or acquired. We promise publicly and openly to avow the loyalty of our principles in every word we shall utter, and every patch we shall stick on. We do further promise, to annoy the enemy with all the flames, darts, and arrows, with which nature has armed us; never to correspond with them by sigh, ogle, or billet-doux;

not to have any intercourse with them, either in snuff or tea; nor to accept the civility of any man's hand, who is not ready to use it in the defense of his country. We are determined, in so good a cause, to endure the greatest hardships and severities, if there should be occasion; and even to wear the manufacture of our country, rather than appear the friends of a foreign interest in the richest French brocade. And forgetting all private feuds, jealousies, and animosities, we do unanimously oblige ourselves, by this our association, to stand and fall by one another, as loyal and faithful sisters and fellow-subjects."

N.B. This association will be lodged at Mr. Motteux's, where attendance will be given to the subscribers, who are to be ranged in their respective columns, as maids, wives, and widows.

MEETING OF THE ASSOCIATION.

By our latest advices, both from town and country, it appears that the ladies of Great Britain, who are able to bear arms, that is, to smile or frown to any purpose, have already begun to commit hostilities upon the men of each opposite party. To this end we are assured, that many of them on both sides exercise before their glasses every morning; that they have already cashiered several of their followers as mutineers, who have contradicted them in some political conversations; and that the Whig ladies in particular design very soon to have a general review of their forces at a play bespoken by one of their leaders. This set of ladies, indeed, as they daily do duty at court, are much more expert in the use of their airs and graces than their female antagonists, who are most of them bred in the country; so that the sister-hood of loyalists, in respect of the fair malecontents, are like an army of regular forces, compared with a raw, undisciplined militia.

It is to this misfortune in their education that we may ascribe the rude and opprobrious language with which the disaffected part of the sex treat the present royal family. A little lively rustic, who hath been trained up in ignorance and prejudice, will prattle treason a whole winter's evening, and string together a parcel of silly seditious stories, that are equally void of decency and truth. Nay, you sometimes meet with a zealous matron, who sets up for the pattern of a parish, uttering such invectives as are highly misbecoming her, both as a woman and a subject. In answer, therefore, to such disloyal termagants, I shall repeat to them a speech of the honest and blunt Duke du Sully, to an assembly of Popish ladies, who were railing very bitterly against Henry the Fourth, at his accession to the French throne; "Ladies," said he, "you have a very good king, if you know when you are well. However, set your hearts at rest, for he is not a man to be scolded or scratched out of his kingdom."

But as I never care to speak of the fair sex, unless I have an occasion to praise them, I shall take my leave of these ungentle damsels ; and only beg of them not to make themselves less amiable than nature designed them, by being rebels to the best of their abilities, and endeavoring to bring their country into bloodshed and confusion. Let me, therefore, recommend to them the example of those beautiful associates, whom I mentioned in my former paper, as I have received the particulars of their behavior from the person with whom I lodged their association.

This association being written at length in a large roll of the finest vellum, with three distinct columns for the maids, wives, and widows, was opened for the subscribers near a fortnight ago. Never was a subscription for a raffling or an opera more crowded. There is scarce a celebrated beauty about town that you may not find in one of the three lists ; insomuch, that if a man, who did not know the design, should read only the names of the subscribers, he would fancy every column to be a catalogue of toasts. Mr. Motteux has been heard to say more than once, that if he had the portraits of all the associates, they would make a finer auction of pictures than he or anybody else had exhibited.

Several of these ladies, indeed, criticised upon the form of the association. One of them, after the perusal of it, wondered that among the features to be used in defense of their country, there was no mention made of *teeth ;* upon which she smiled very charmingly, and discovered as fine a set as ever eye beheld. Another, who was a tall lovely prude, holding up her head in a most majestic manner, said, with some disdain, she thought a *good neck* might have done his Majesty as much service as smiles or dimples. A third looked upon the association as defective, because so necessary a word as *hands* was omitted; and by her manner of taking up the pen, it was easy to guess the reason of her objection.

Most of the persons who associated have done much more than by the letter of the association they were obliged to ; having not only set their names to it, but subscribed their several aids and subsidies for the carrying on so good a cause. In the virgin column is one who subscribes fifteen lovers, all of them good men and true. There is another who subscribes five admirers, with one tall handsome black man, fit to be a colonel. In short, there is scarce one in this list who does not engage herself to supply a quota of brisk young fellows, many of them already equipt with hats and feathers. Among the rest, was a pretty sprightly coquette, with sparkling eyes, who subscribed two quivers of arrows.

In the column of wives, the first that took pen in hand, writ her own name and one vassal, meaning her husband. Another subscribes her husband and three sons. Another, her husband and six coach-horses. Most in this catalogue paired themselves with their respective mates, answering for them as men of honest principles, and fit for the service.

N. B. There were two in this column that wore association ribbons; the first of them subscribed her husband, and her husband's friend; the second a husband and five lovers; but upon inquiry into their characters, they are both of them found to be Tories, who hung out false colors to be spies upon the association, or to insinuate to the world by their subscriptions, as if a lady of Whig principles could love any man besides her husband.

The widow's column is headed by a fine woman who calls herself Boadicea, and subscribes six hundred tenants. It was, indeed, observed that the strength of the association lay most in this column; every widow, in proportion to her jointure, having a great number of admirers, and most of them distinguished as able men. Those who have examined this list, compute that there may be three regiments raised out of it, in which there shall not be one man under six foot high.

I must not conclude this account without taking notice of the association-ribbon, by which these beautiful confederates have agreed to distinguish themselves. It is, indeed, so very pretty an ornament, that I wonder any Englishwoman will be without it. A lady of the association who bears this badge of allegiance upon her breast, naturally produces a desire in every male beholder, of gaining a place in a heart which carries on it such a visible mark of its fidelity. When the beauties of our island are thus industrious to show their principles as well as their charms, they raise the sentiments of their countrymen, and inspire them at the same time both with loyalty and love. What numbers of proselytes may we not expect, when the most amiable of the Britons thus exhibit to their admirers the only terms upon which they are to hope for any correspondence or alliance with them! It is well known that the greatest blow the French nation ever received, was the dropping of a fine lady's garter, in the reign of King Edward the Third. The most remarkable battles which have been since gained over that nation, were fought under the auspices of a blue ribbon. As our British ladies have still the 'same faces, and our men the same hearts, why may we not hope for the same glorious achievements from the influence of this beautiful breast-knot?

POLITICS AND THE FAN.

It is with great pleasure that I see a race of female patriots springing up in this island. The fairest among the daughters of Great Britain no longer confine their cares to a domestic life, but are grown anxious for the welfare of their country, and show themselves good stateswomen as well as good housewives.

Our she-confederates keep pace with us in quashing that rebellion which had begun to spread itself among part of the fair sex. If the men who are true to their king and country have taken Preston and Perth, the ladies have possessed themselves of the opera and the play-house with as little opposition or bloodshed. The non-resisting women, like their brothers in the Highlands, think no post tenable against an army that makes so fine an appearance; and dare not look them in the face, when they are drawn up in battle-array.

As an instance of this cheerfulness in our fair fellow-subjects to oppose the designs of the Pretender, I did but suggest in one of my former papers, "That the fan might be made use of with good success against Popery, by exhibiting the corruptions of the church of Rome in various figures;" when immediately they took the hint, and have since had frequent consultations upon several ways and methods "to make the fan useful." They have unanimously agreed upon the following resolutions, which are indeed very suitable to ladies who are at the same time the most beautiful

90

and the most loyal of their sex. To hide their faces
behind the fan, when they observe a Tory gazing upon
them. Never to peep through it, but in order to pick
out men, whose principles make them worth the con-
quest. To return no other answer to a Tory's addresses, than by counting the sticks of it all the while
he is talking to them. To avoid dropping it in the
neighborhood of a malecontent, that he may not have
an opportunity of taking it up. To show their dis-
belief of any Jacobite story by a flirt of it. To fall
a fanning themselves when a Tory comes into one of
their assemblies, as being disordered at the sight of
him.

These are the uses by which every fan may in the
hands of a fine woman become serviceable to the public. But they have at present under consideration,
certain fans of a Protestant make, that they may have
a more extensive influence, and raise an abhorrence of
Popery in a whole crowd of beholders : for they intend
to let the world see what party they are of, by figures
and designs upon these fans; as the knights-errant
used to distinguish themselves by devices on their
shields.

There are several sketches of pictures which have
been already presented to the ladies for their approbation, and out of which several have made their choice.
A pretty young lady will very soon appear with a fan,
which has on it a nunnery of lively black-eyed vestals,
who are endeavoring to creep out at the grates. Another has a fan mounted with a fine paper, on which
is represented a group of people upon their knees very
devoutly worshiping an old ten-penny nail. A certain lady of great learning has chosen for her device
the council of Trent; and another, who has a good

satirical turn, has filled her fan with the figure of a
huge tawdry woman, representing the whore of Babylon; which she is resolved to spread full in the face of
any sister-disputant, whose arguments have a tendency
to Popery. The following designs are already executed on several mountings. The ceremony of the
holy pontiff opening the mouth of a cardinal in a full
consistory. An old gentleman with a triple crown
upon his head, and big with child, being the portrait
of Pope Joan. Bishop Bonner purchasing great quantities of fagots and brushwood, for the conversion of
heretics. A figure reaching at a scepter with one
hand, and holding a chaplet of beads in the other;
with a distant view of Smithfield.

When our ladies make their zeal thus visible upon
their fans, and every time they open them, display an
error of the church of Rome, it cannot but have a good
effect, by showing the enemies of our present establishment the folly of what they are contending for.
At least, every one must allow that fans are much
more innocent engines for propagating the Protestant
religion, than racks, wheels, gibbets, and the like ma-
chines, which are made use of for the advancement of
the Roman Catholic. Besides, as every lady will of
course study her fan, she will be a perfect mistress of
the controversy, at least in one point of Popery; and
as her curiosity will put her upon the perusal of every
other fan that is fashionable, I doubt not but in a
very little time there will be scarce a woman of quality in Great Britain, who would not be an overmatch
for an Irish priest.

The beautiful part of this island, whom I am proud
to number amongst the most candid of my readers,
will likewise do well to reflect, that our dispute at

present concerns our civil as well as religious rights. I shall therefore only offer it to their thoughts as a point that highly deserves their consideration, whether the fan may not also be made use of with regard to our political constitution. As a Freeholder, I would not have them confine their cares for us as we are Protestants, but at the same time have an eye to our happiness as we are Britons. In this case they would give a new turn to the minds of their countrymen, if they would exhibit on their fans the several grievances of a tyrannical government. Why might not an audience of Muley Ishmael, or a Turk dropping his handkerchief in his seraglio, be proper subjects to express their abhorrence both of despotic power, and of male tyranny ? or if they have a fancy for burlesque, what would they think of a French cobbler cutting shoes for several of his fellow-subjects out of an old apple-tree ? On the contrary, a fine woman, who would maintain the dignity of her sex, might bear a string of galley slaves, dragging their chains the whole breadth of her fan; and at the same time, to celebrate her own triumphs, might order every slave to be drawn with the face of one of her admirers.

I only propose these as hints to my gentle readers, which they may alter or improve as they shall think fit : but cannot conclude without congratulating our country upon this disposition among the most amiable of its inhabitants, to consider in their ornaments the advantage of the public as well as of their persons. It was with the same spirit, though not with the same politeness, that the ancient British women had the figures of monsters painted on their naked bodies, in order (as our historians tells us) to make themselves beautiful in the eyes of their countrymen, and terrible to their enemies. If this project goes on, we may boast, that our sister Whigs have the finest fans, as well as the most beautiful faces, of any ladies in the world. At least, we may venture to foretell, that the figures in their fans will lessen the Tory interest, much more than those in the Oxford Almanacs will advance it.

PRETTY DISAFFECTION.

WHEN the Athenians had long contended against the power of Philip, he demanded of them to give up their orators, as well knowing their opposition would be soon at an end if it were not irritated from time to time by these tongue-warriors. I have endeavored, for the same reason, to gain our female adversaries, and by that means to disarm the party of its principal strength. Let them give us up their women, and we know by experience how inconsiderable a resistance we are to expect from their men.

This sharp political humor has but lately prevailed in so great a measure as it now does among the beautiful part of our species. They used to employ themselves wholly in the scenes of a domestic life, and provided a woman could keep her house in order, she never troubled herself about regulating the commonwealth. The eye of the mistress was wont to make her pewter shine, and to inspect every part of her household furniture as much as her looking-glass. But at present our discontented matrons are so conversant in matters of state, that they wholly neglect their private affairs; for we may always observe that a gossip in politics is a slattern in her family.

It is indeed a melancholy thing to see the disorders of a household that is under the conduct of an angry stateswoman, who lays out all her thoughts upon the public, and is only attentive to find out miscarriages in the ministry. Several women of this turn are so earnest in contending for hereditary right, that they wholly neglect the education of their sons and heirs; and are so taken up with their zeal for the church, that they cannot find time to teach their children their catechism. A lady who thus intrudes into the province of the men, was so astonishing a character among the old Romans, that when Amaesia presented herself to speak before the senate, they looked upon it as a prodigy, and sent messengers to inquire of the oracle, what it might portend to the commonwealth?

It would be manifestly to the disadvantage of the British cause, should our pretty loyalists profess an indifference in state affairs, while their disaffected sisters are thus industrious to the prejudice of their country; and accordingly we have the satisfaction to find our she-associates are not idle upon this occasion. It is owing to the good principles of these his Majesty's fair and faithful subjects, that our country-women appear no less amiable in the eyes of the male world, than they have done in former ages. For where a great number of flowers grow, the ground at a distance seems entirely covered with them, and we must walk into it, before we can distinguish the several weeds that spring up in such a beautiful mass of colors. Our great concern is, to find deformity can arise among so many charms, and that the most lovely parts of the creation can make themselves the most disagreeable. But it is an observation of the philosophers, that the best things may be corrupted into the worst; and the ancients did not scruple to affirm, that the Furies and the Graces were of the same sex.

As I should do the nation and themselves good
service, if I could draw the ladies, who still hold out
against his Majesty, into the interest of our present
establishment, I shall propose to their serious consideration, the several inconveniences which those
among them undergo, who have not yet surrendered
to the government.

They should first reflect on the great sufferings and
persecutions to which they expose themselves by the
obstinacy of their behavior. They lose their elec-
tions in every club where they are set up for toasts.
They are obliged by their principles to stick a patch
on the most unbecoming side of their foreheads. They
forego the advantage of birth-day suits. They are
insulted by the loyalty of claps and hisses every time
they appear at a play. They receive no benefit from
the army, and are never the better for all the young
fellows that wear hats and feathers. They are forced
to live in the country and feed their chickens; at the
same time that they might show themselves at court,
and appear in brocade, if they behaved themselves
well. In short, what must go to the heart of every
fine woman, they throw themselves quite out of the
fashion.

The above-mentioned motive must have an influence
upon the gay part of the sex; and as for those who
are acted by more sublime and moral principles, they
should consider, that they cannot signalize themselves
as malecontents, without breaking through all the
amiable instincts and softer virtues, which are peculiarly ornamental to womankind. Their timorous,
gentle, modest behavior; their affability, meekness,
good-breeding, and many other beautiful dispositions
of mind, must be sacrificed to a blind and furious

7

zeal for they do not know what. A man is startled when he sees a pretty bosom heaving with such party-rage, as is disagreeable even in that sex, which is of a more coarse and rugged make. And yet such is our misfortune, that we sometimes see a pair of stays ready to burst with sedition; and hear the most masculine passions exprest in the sweetest voices. I have lately been told of a country-gentlewoman, pretty much famed for this virility of behavior in party-disputes, who, upon venting her notions very freely in a strange place, was carried before an honest justice of the peace. This prudent magistrate observing her to be a large black woman, and finding by her discourse that she was no better than a rebel in a riding-hood, began to suspect her for my Lord Nithisdale; till a stranger came to her rescue, who assured him, with tears in his eyes, that he was her husband.

In the next place, our British ladies may consider, that by interesting themselves so zealously in the affairs of the public, they are engaged, without any necessity, in the crimes which are often committed even by the best of parties, and which they are naturally exempted from by the privilege of their sex. The worst character a female could formerly arrive at, was of being an ill woman; but by their present conduct, she may likewise deserve the character of an ill subject. They come in for their share of political guilt, and have found a way to make themselves much greater criminals than their mothers before them.

I have great hopes that these motives, when they are assisted by their own reflections, will incline the fair ones of the adverse party to come over to the national interest, in which their own is so highly concerned; especially if they consider, that by these su-

perfluous employments, which they take upon them
as partisans, they do not only dip themselves in an
unnecessary guilt, but are obnoxious to a grief and
anguish of mind, which doth not properly fall within
their lot.   And here I would advise every one of these
exasperated ladies, who indulge that opprobrious eloquence which is so much in fashion, to reflect on
Æsop's fable of the viper.   " This little animal, (says
the old moralist,) chancing to meet with a file, began
to lick it with her tongue till the blood came ; which
gave her a very silly satisfaction, as imagining the
blood came from the file, notwithstanding all the
smart was in her own tongue."

HUMORS OF THE TOWN.

THE ROYAL EXCHANGE.

THERE is no place in the town which I so much love to frequent as the Royal Exchange. It gives me a secret satisfaction, and, in some measure, gratifies my vanity, as I am an Englishman, to see so rich an assembly of countrymen and foreigners consulting together upon the private business of mankind, and making this metropolis a kind of emporium for the whole earth. I must confess I look upon high-change to be a great council, in which all considerable nations have their representatives. Factors in the trading world are what ambassadors are in the politic world; they negotiate affairs, conclude treaties, and maintain a good correspondence between those wealthy societies of men that are divided from one another by seas and oceans, or live on the different extremities of a continent. I have often been pleased to hear disputes adjusted between an inhabitant of Japan and an alderman of London, or to see a subject of the Great Mogul entering into a league with one of the Czar of Muscovy. I am infinitely delighted in mixing with these several ministers of commerce, as they are distinguished by their different walks and different languages: sometimes I am jostled among a body of Armenians; sometimes I am lost in a crowd of Jews; and sometimes make one in a group of Dutchmen. I am a Dane, Swede, or Frenchman at different times; or rather fancy myself like the old philosopher, who upon being asked what countryman he was, replied, that he was a citizen of the world.

Though I very frequently visit this busy multitude of people, I am known to nobody there but my friend Sir Andrew, who often smiles upon me as he sees me bustling in the crowd, but at the same time connives at my presence without taking any further notice of me. There is indeed a merchant of Egypt, who just knows me by sight, having formerly remitted me some money to Grand Cairo ; but as I am not versed in the modern Coptic, our conferences go no further than a bow and a grimace.

This grand scene of business gives me an infinite variety of solid and substantial entertainments. As I am a great lover of mankind, my heart naturally overflows with pleasure at the sight of a prosperous and happy multitude, insomuch, that at many public solemnities I cannot forbear expressing my joy with tears that have stolen down my cheeks. For this reason I am wonderfully delighted to see such a body of men thriving in their own private fortunes, and at the same time promoting the public stock; or, in other words, raising estates for their own families, by bringing into their country whatever is wanting, and carrying out of it whatever is superfluous.

Nature seems to have taken a peculiar care to disseminate the blessings among the different regions of the world, with an eye to this mutual intercourse and traffic among mankind, that the natives of the several parts of the globe might have a kind of dependence upon one another, and be united together by this common interest. Almost every degree produces something peculiar to it. The food often grows in one country, and the sauce in another. The fruits of

Portugal are corrected by the products of Barbadoes ; the infusion of a China plant sweetened with the pith of an Indian cane. The Philippine Islands give a flavor to our European bowls. The single dress of a woman of quality is often the product of a hundred climates. The muff and the fan come together from the different ends of the earth. The scarf is sent from the torrid zone, and the tippet from beneath the pole. The brocade petticoat rises out of the mines of Peru, and the diamond necklace out of the bowels of Indostan.

If we consider our own country in its natural prospect, without any of the benefits and advantages of commerce, what a barren, uncomfortable spot of earth falls to our share! Natural historians tell us, that no fruit grows originally among us besides hips and haws, acorns and pig-nuts, with other delicacies of the like nature ; that our climate of itself, and without the as_ sistance of art, can make no further advances towards a plum than to a sloe, and carries an apple to no greater a perfection than a crab : that our melons, our peaches, our figs, our apricots, and cherries, are strangers among us, imported in different ages, and naturalized in our English gardens ; and that they would all degenerate and fall away into the trash of our own country, if they were wholly neglected by the planter, and left to the mercy of our sun and soil. Nor has traffic more enriched our vegetable world, than it has improved the whole face of nature among us. Our ships are laden with the harvest of every climate : our tables are stored with spices, and oils, and wines; our rooms are filled with pyramids of China, and adorned with the workmanship of Japan : our morning's draught comes to us from the remotest corners of the earth; we repair our bodies by the drugs of America, and repose ourselves under Indian canopies. My friend Sir Andrew calls the vineyards of France our gardens; the spice-islands our hot-beds; the Persians our silk-weavers, and the Chinese our potters. Nature indeed furnishes us with the bare necessaries of life, but traffic gives us a great variety of what is useful, and at the same time supplies us with everything that is convenient and ornamental. Nor is it the least part of this our happiness, that while we enjoy the remotest products of the north and south, we are free from those extremities of weather which give them birth; that our eyes are refreshed with the green fields of Britain, at the same time that our palates are feasted with fruits that rise between the tropics.

For these reasons there are not more useful members in a commonwealth than merchants. They knit mankind together in a mutual intercourse of good offices, distribute the gifts of nature, find work for the poor, and wealth to the rich, and magnificence to the great. Our English merchant converts the tin of his own country into gold, and exchanges his wool for rubies. The Mahometans are clothed in our British manufacture, and the inhabitants of the frozen zone warmed with the fleeces of our sheep.

When I have been upon the Change, I have often fancied one of our old kings standing in person, where he is represented in effigy, and looking down upon the wealthy concourse of people with which that place is every day filled. In this case, how would he be surprised to hear all the languages of Europe spoken in this little spot of his former dominions, and to see so many private men, who in his time would have been the vassals of some powerful baron, negotiating like princes for greater sums of money than were formerly to be met with in the royal treasury! Trade, without enlarging the British territories, has given us a kind of additional empire: it has multiplied the number of the rich, made our landed estates infinitely more valuable than they were formerly, and added to them an accession of other estates as valuable as the lands themselves.

STAGE LIONS.

THERE is nothing that of late years has afforded matter of greater amusement to the town than Signior Nicolini's combat with a lion in the Haymarket, which has been very often exhibited to the general satisfaction of most of the nobility and gentry in the kingdom of Great Britain. Upon the first rumor of this intended combat, it was confidently affirmed, and is still believed by many in both galleries, that there would be a tame lion sent from the Tower every opera night, in order to be killed by Hydaspes; this report, though altogether groundless, so universally prevailed in the upper regions of the playhouse, that some of the most refined politicians in those parts of the audience gave it out in whisper, that the lion was a cousin-german of the tiger who made his appearance in King William's days, and that the stage would be supplied with lions at the public expense, during the whole session. Many likewise were the conjectures of the treatment which this lion was to meet with from the hands of Signior Nicolini: some supposed that he was to subdue him in recitativo, as Orpheus used to serve the wild beasts in his time, and afterwards to knock him on the head; some fancied that the lion would not pretend to lay his paws upon the hero, by reason of the received opinion, that a lion will not hurt a virgin: several, who pretended to have seen the opera in Italy, had informed their friends, that the lion was to act a part in High-Dutch, and roar twice or thrice to a thorough-bass, before he fell at the feet of Hydaspes. To clear up a matter that was so variously reported, I have made it my business to examine whether this pretended lion is really the savage he appears to be, or only a counterfeit.

But before I communicate my discoveries, I must acquaint the reader, that upon my walking behind the scenes last winter, as I was thinking on something else, I accidentally justled against a monstrous animal that extremely startled me, and upon my nearer survey of it, appeared to be a lion rampant. The lion seeing me very much surprised, told me, in a gentle voice, that I might come by him if I pleased: "For," says he, "I do not intend to hurt anybody." I thanked him very kindly, and passed by him. And in a little time after saw him leap upon the stage, and act his part with very great applause. It has been observed by several, that the lion has changed his manner of acting twice or thrice since his first appearance; which will not seem strange, when I acquaint my reader that the lion has been changed upon the audience three several times. The first lion was a candle-snuffer, who being a fellow of a testy, choleric temper, over-did his part, and would not suffer himself to be killed so easily as he ought to have done; besides, it was observed of him, that he grew more surly every time he came out of the lion, and having dropt some words in ordinary conversation, as if he had not fought his best, and that he suffered himself to be thrown upon his back in the scuffle, and that he would wrestle with Mr. Nicolini for what he pleased, out of his lion's skin, it was thought proper to discard him; and it is verily believed, to this day, that had he been brought upon the stage another time, he would certainly have done mischief. Besides, it was objected against the first lion, that he reared himself so high upon his hinder paws, and walked in so erect a posture, that he looked more like an old man than a lion.

The second lion was a tailor by trade, who belonged to the playhouse, and had the character of a mild and peaceable man in his profession. If the former was too furious, this was too sheepish for his part; insomuch, that after a short modest walk upon the stage, he would fall at the first touch of Hydaspes, without grappling with him, and giving him an opportunity of showing his variety of Italian trips. It is said, indeed, that he once gave him a rip in his flesh-colored doublet; but this was only to make work for himself, in his private character of a tailor. I must not omit that it was this second lion who treated me with so much humanity behind the scenes.

The acting lion at present is, as I am informed, a country gentleman, who does it for his diversion, but desires his name may be concealed. He says, very handsomely, in his own excuse, that he does not act for gain; that he indulges an innocent pleasure in it; and that it is better to pass away an evening in this manner than in gaming and drinking: but at the same time says, with a very agreeable raillery upon himself, that if his name should be known, the ill-natured world might call him, " the ass in the lion's skin." This gentleman's temper is made out of such a happy mixture of the mild and the choleric, that he outdoes both his predecessors, and has drawn together greater audiences than have been known in the memory of man.

I must not conclude my narrative, without taking notice of a groundless report that has been raised to a gentleman's disadvantage, of whom I must declare myself an admirer; namely, that Signior Nicolini and the lion have been seen sitting peaceably by one another, and smoking a pipe together behind the scenes; by which their common enemies would insinuate, that it is but a sham combat which they represent upon the stage: but upon inquiry I find, that if any such correspondence has passed between them, it was not till the combat was over, when the lion was to be looked upon as dead, according to the received rules of the drama. Besides, this is what is practised every day in Westminster Hall, where nothing is more usual than to see a couple of lawyers, who have been tearing each other to pieces in the court, embracing one another as soon as they are out of it.

I would not be thought, in any part of this relation, to reflect upon Signior Nicolini, who in acting this part only complies with the wretched taste of his audience ; he knows very well, that the lion has many more admirers than himself; as they say of the famous equestrian statue on the Pont Neuf at Paris, that more people go to see the horse than the king who sits upon it. On the contrary, it gives me a just indignation to see a person whose action gives new majesty to kings, resolution to heroes, and softness to lovers, thus sinking from the greatness of his behavior, and degraded into the character of the London Prentice. I have often wished, that our tragedians would copy after this great master in action. Could they make the same use of their arms and legs, and inform their faces with as significant looks and passions, how glorious would an English tragedy appear with that action which is capable of giving a dignity to the forced thoughts, cold conceits, and unnatural expressions of an Italian opera ! In the mean time, I have related this combat of the lion, to show what are at present the reigning entertainments of the politer part of Great Britain.

THE POLITICAL UPHOLSTERER.

THERE lived some years since within my neighborhood a very grave person, an upholsterer, who seemed a man of more than ordinary application to business. He was a very early riser, and was often abroad two or three hours before any of his neighbors. He had a particular carefulness in the knitting of his brows, and a kind of impatience in all his motions, that plainly discovered he was always intent on matters of importance. Upon my inquiry into his life and conversation, I found him to be the greatest newsmonger in our quarter; that he rose before day to read the Postman; and that he would take two or three turns to the other end of the town before his neighbors were up, to see if there were any Dutch mails come in. He had a wife and several children; but was much more inquisitive to know what passed in Poland than in his own family, and was in greater pain and anxiety of mind for King Augustus's welfare than that of his nearest relations. He looked extremely thin in a dearth of news, and never enjoyed himself in a westerly wind. This indefatigable kind of life was the ruin of his shop: for about the time that his favorite prince left the crown of Poland, he broke and disappeared.

This man and his affairs had been long out of mind, till about three days ago, as I was walking in St. James's Park, I heard somebody at a distance hemming after me: and who should it be but my old neighbor the upholsterer. I saw he was reduced to extreme poverty, by certain shabby superfluities in his dress: for, notwithstanding that it was a very sultry day for the time of year, he wore a loose great coat and a muff, with a long campaign-wig out of curl; to which he had added the ornament of a pair of black garters buckled under the knee. Upon his coming up to me, I was going to inquire into his present circumstances; but was prevented by his asking me, with a whisper, "Whether the last letters brought any accounts that one might rely upon from Bender?" I told him, "None that I heard of;" and asked him, "Whether he had yet married his eldest daughter?" He told me "No. But pray," says he, "tell me sincerely, what are your thoughts of the king of Sweden?" (for though his wife and children were starving, I found his chief concern at present was for this great monarch). I told him, "that I looked upon him as one of the first heroes of the age." "But pray," says he, "do you think there is anything in the story of his wound?" and finding me surprised at the question, "Nay," says he, "I only propose it to you." I answered, "that I thought there was no reason to doubt it." "But why in the heel," says he, "more than in any other part of the body?" "Because," says I, "the bullet chanced to light there."

This extraordinary dialogue was no sooner ended, but he began to launch out into a long dissertation upon the affairs of the North; and after having spent some time on them, he told me, he was in a great perplexity how to reconcile the Supplement with the English Post, and had been just now examining what the other papers say upon the same subject. "The Daily Courant" (says he) has these words, "We have advices from very good hands, that a certain prince has some matters of great importance under consideration." This is very mysterious; but the Postboy leaves us more in the dark, for he tells us, " That there are private intimations of measures taken by a certain prince, which time will bring to light." Now the Postman, (says he,) who used to be very clear, refers to the same news in these words ; " The late conduct of a certain prince affords great matter of speculation." This certain prince, (says the upholsterer,) whom they are all so cautious of naming, I take to be ——," upon which, though there was nobody near us, he whispered something in my ear, which I did not hear, or think worth my while to make him repeat.

We were now got to the upper end of the Mall, where were three or four very odd fellows sitting together upon the bench. These I found were all of them politicians, who used to sun themselves in that place every day about dinner-time. Observing them to be curiosities in their kind, and my friend's acquaintance, I sat down among them.

The chief politician of the bench was a great assertor of paradoxes. He told us, with a seeming concern, that by some news he had lately read from Muscovy, it appeared to him that there was a storm gathering in the Black Sea, which might in time do hurt to the naval forces of this nation. To this he added, that for his part, he could not wish to see the Turk driven out of Europe, which he believed could not but be prejudicial to our woolen manufacture. He then told us, that he looked upon those extraordinary revolutions which had lately happened in these parts of the world, to have risen chiefly from two persons who were not much talked of ; and those, says he, are Prince Menzikoff,

and the Duchess of Mirandola. He backed his asser-
tions with so many broken hints, and such a show of
depth and wisdom, that we gave ourselves up to his
opinions.

The discourse at length fell upon a point which
seldom escapes a knot of true-born Englishmen, whether
in case of a religious war, the Protestants would not be
too strong for the Papists? This we unanimously determined on the Protestant side. One who sat on my
right hand, and, as I found by his discourse, had been
in the West Indies, assured us, that it would be a very
easy matter for the Protestants to beat the pope at sea ;
and added, that whenever such a war does break out,
it must turn to the good of the Leeward Islands. Upon
this, one who sat at the end of the bench, and, as I afterwards found, was the geographer of the company, said,
that in case the Papists should drive the Protestants
from these parts of Europe, when the worst came to
the worst, it would be impossible to beat them out of
Norway and Greenland, provided the northern crowns
hold together, and the Czar of Muscovy stand neuter.

He further told us for our comfort, that there were
vast tracts of lands about the pole, inhabited neither
by Protestants nor Papists, and of greater extent than
all the Roman Catholic dominions in Europe.

When we had fully discussed this point, my friend
the upholsterer began to exert himself upon the present negotiations of peace, in which he deposed princes,
settled the bounds of kingdoms, and balanced the power
of Europe, with great justice and impartiality.

I at length took my leave of the company, and was
going away ; but had not been gone thirty yards,
before the upholsterer hemmed again after me. Upon
his advancing towards me, with a whisper, I expected

to hear some secret piece of news, which he had not thought fit to communicate to the bench; but instead of that, he desired me in my ear to lend him half-a-crown. In compassion to so needy a statesman, and to dissipate the confusion I found he was in, I told him, if he pleased, I would give him five shillings, to receive five pounds of him when the Great Turk was driven out of Constantinople; which he very readily accepted, but not before he had laid down to me the impossibility of such an event, as the affairs of Europe now stand.

This paper I design for the particular benefit of those worthy citizens who live more in a coffee-house than in their shops, and whose thoughts are so taken up with the affairs of the allies, that they forget their customers.

A VISIT FROM THE UPHOLSTERER.

A COMMON civility to an impertinent fellow, often draws upon one a great many unforeseen troubles; and if one doth not take particular care, will be interpreted by him as an overture of friendship and intimacy. This I was very sensible of this morning. About two hours before day, I heard a great rapping at my door, which continued some time, till my maid could get herself ready to go down and see what was the occasion of it. She then brought me up word, that there was a gentleman who seemed very much in haste, and said he must needs speak with me. By the description she gave me of him, and by his voice, which I could hear as I lay in my bed, I fancied him to be my old acquaintance the upholsterer, whom I met the other day in St. James's Park. For which reason I bid her tell the gentleman, whoever he was, that I was indisposed, that I could see nobody, and that, if he had anything to say to me, I desired he would leave it in writing. My maid, after having delivered her message, told me, that the gentleman said he would stay at the next coffee-house till I was stirring, and bid her be sure to tell me, that the French were driven from the Scarp, and that the Douay was invested. He gave her the name of another town, which I found she had dropped by the way. As much as I love to be informed of the success of my brave countrymen, I do not care for hearing of a victory before day, and was therefore very much out of humor at this unseasonable visit. I had no sooner recovered my temper, and was falling asleep, but I was immediately startled by a second rap; and upon my maid's opening the door, heard the same voice ask her, if her master was yet up? and at the same time bid her tell me, that he was come on purpose to talk with me about a piece of home-news that everybody in town will be full of two hours hence. I ordered my maid, as soon as she came into the room, without hearing her message, to tell the gentleman, that whatever his news was, I would rather hear it two hours hence than now ; and that I persisted in my resolution not to speak with anybody that morning. The wench delivered my answer presently, and shut the door. It was impossible for me to compose myself to sleep after two such unexpected alarms ; for which reason I put on my clothes in a very peevish humor. I took several turns about my chamber, reflecting with a great deal of anger and contempt on these volunteers in politics, that undergo all the pain, watchfulness, and disquiet of a first minister, without turning it to the advantage either of themselves or their country ; and yet it is surprising to consider how numerous this species of men is. There is nothing more frequent than to find a tailor breaking his rest on the affairs of Europe, and to see a cluster of porters sitting upon the ministry. Our streets swarm with politicians, and there is scarce a shop which is not held by a statesman. As I was musing after this manner, I heard the upholsterer at the door delivering a letter to my maid, and begging her, in very great hurry, to give it to her master as soon as ever he was awake, which I opened and found as follows :

" Mr. Bickerstaffe,

" I was to wait upon you about a week ago, to let
you know, that the honest gentlemen whom you conversed
with upon the bench at the end of the Mall, having heard
that I had received five shillings of you, to give you a
hundred pounds upon the Great Turk's being driven out
of Europe, desired me to acquaint you, that every one of
that company would be willing to receive five shillings, to
pay a hundred pounds on the same conditions. Our last
advices from Muscovy making this a fairer bet than it
was a week ago, I do not question but you will accept the
wager.

But this is not my present business. If you remember,
I whispered a word in your ear as we were walking up the
Mall, and you see what has happened since. If I had
seen you this morning, I would have told you in your ear
another secret. I hope you will be recovered of your in-
disposition by to-morrow morning, when I will wait on
you at the same hour as I did this ; my private circumstances being such, that I cannot well appear in this
quarter of the town after it is day.

I have been so taken up with the late good news from
Holland, and the expectation of further particulars, as well
as with other transactions, of which I will tell you more
to-morrow morning, that I have not slept a wink these
three nights.

I have reason to believe, that Picardy will soon follow
the example of Artois, in case the enemy continue in their
present resolution of flying away from us. I think I told
you last time we were together my opinion about the
Deulle.

The honest gentlemen upon the bench bid me tell you,
they would be glad to see you often among them. We
shall be there all the warm hours of the day during the
present posture of affairs.

This happy opening of the campaign, will, I hope, give us a very joyful summer; and I propose to take many a pleasant walk with you, if you will sometimes come into the Park; for that is the only place in which I can be free from the malice of my enemies. Farewell till three-o'clock to-morrow morning.

I am

Your most humble servant, &c.

" P. S. The king of Sweden is still at Bender."

I should have fretted myself to death at this promise of a second visit, if I had not found in his letter an intimation of the good news which I have since heard at large. I have, however, ordered my maid to tie up the knocker of my door, in such a manner as she would do if I were really indisposed. By which means I hope to escape breaking my morning's rest.

THE FORTUNE HUNTER.

"MR. SPECTATOR,

"I am amazed that, among all the variety of characters with which you have enriched your speculations, you have never given us a picture of those audacious young fellows among us, who commonly go by the name of fortune-stealers. You must know, sir, I am one who live in a continual apprehension of this sort of people, that lie in wait, day and night, for our children, and may be considered as a kind of kidnappers within the law. I am the father of a young heiress, whom I begin to look upon as marriageable, and who has looked upon herself as such for above these six years. She is now in the eighteenth year of her age. The fortune-hunters have already cast their eyes upon her, and take care to plant themselves in her view whenever she appears in any public assembly. I have myself caught a young jackanapes, with a pair of silver fringed gloves, in the very fact. You must know, sir, I have kept her as a prisoner of state ever since she was in her teens. Her chamber windows are cross-barred, she is not permitted to go out of the house but with her keeper, who is a stayed relation of my own ; I have likewise forbid her the use of pen and ink for this twelve months last past, and do not suffer a band-box to be carried into her room before it has been searched. Notwithstanding these precautions, I am at my wits' end for fear of any sudden surprise. There were, two or three nights ago, some fiddles heard in the street, which I am afraid portend me no good ; not to mention a tall Irishman, that has been walking before my house more than once this winter. My kinswoman likewise informs me, that the girl has talked to her twice or thrice of a gentleman in a fair wig, and that she loves to go to church more than ever she did in her life. She gave me the slip about a week ago, upon which my whole house was in alarm. I immediately despatched a hue and cry after her to the 'Change, to her mantuamaker, and to the young ladies that visit her ; but after above an hour's search she returned of herself, having been taking a walk, as she told me, by Rosamond's pond. I have hereupon turned off her woman, doubled her guards, and given new instructions to my relation, who, to give her her due, keeps a watchful eye over all her motions. This, sir, keeps me in a perpetual anxiety, and makes me very often watch when my daughter sleeps, as I am afraid she is even with me in her turn. Now, sir, what I would desire of you is, to represent to this fluttering tribe of young fellows, who are for making their fortunes by these indirect means, that stealing a man's daughter for the sake of her portion, is but a kind of tolerated robbery ; and that they make but a poor amends to the father, whom they plunder after this manner, by going to bed with his child. Dear sir, be speedy in your thoughts on this subject, that, if possible, they may appear before the disbanding of the army.

I am, sir,

Your most humble servant,

TIM. WATCHWELL."

Themistocles, the great Athenian general, being asked whether he would choose to marry his daughter to an indigent man of merit, or to a worthless man of an estate, replied, that he would prefer a man without an estate, to an estate without a man. The worst of it is our modern fortune-hunters are those who turn their heads that way, because they are good for nothing else. If a young fellow finds he can make nothing of Cook and Littleton, he provides himself with a ladder of ropes, and by that means very often enters upon the premises.

The same art of scaling has likewise been practised with good success by many military engineers. Stratagems of this nature make parts and industry superfluous, and cut short the way to riches.

Nor is vanity a less motive than idleness to this kind of mercenary pursuit. A fop who admires his person in a glass, soon enters into a resolution of making his fortune by it, not questioning but every woman that falls in his way will do him as much justice as he does himself. When an heiress sees a man throwing particular graces into his ogle, or talking loud within her hearing, she ought to look to herself; but if withal she observes a pair of red-heels, a patch, or any other particularity in his dress, she cannot take too much care of her person. These are baits not to trifled with, charms that have done a world of execution, and made their way into hearts which have been thought impregnable. The force of a man with these qualifications is so well known, that I am credibly informed there are several female undertakers about the 'Change, who upon the arrival of a likely man out of a neighboring kingdom, will furnish him with proper dress from head to foot, to be paid for at double price on the day of marriage.

We must, however, distinguish between fortune-hunters and fortune-stealers. The first are those assiduous gentlemen who employ their whole lives in the chase, without ever coming at the quarry. Suffenus has combed and powdered at the ladies for thirty years together, and taken his stand in a side box, till he is grown wrinkled under their eyes. He is now laying the same snares for the present generation of beauties, which he practised on their mothers. Cottilus, after having made his applications to more than you meet with in Mr. Cowley's ballad of mistresses, was at last smitten with a city lady of £20,000 sterling; but died of old age before he could bring matters to bear. Nor must I here omit my worthy friend Mr. Honeycomb, who has often told us in the club, that for twenty years successively, upon the death of a childless rich man, he immediately drew on his boots, called for his horse, and made up to the widow. When he is rallied upon his ill success, Will. with his usual gaiety tells us, that he always found her pre-engaged.

Widows are indeed the great game of your fortune-hunters. There is scarce a young fellow in the town of six foot high, that has not passed in review before one or other of these wealthy relics. Hudibras's Cupid, who

—took his stand
Upon a widow's jointure land,

is daily employed in throwing darts and kindling flames. But as for widows, they are such a subtle generation of people, that they may be left to their own conduct; or if they make a false step in it, they are answerable for it to nobody but themselves. The young innocent creatures who have no knowledge and experience of the world, are those whose safety I would principally consult in this speculation. The stealing of such an one should, in my opinion, be as punishable as a rape. Where there is no judgment, there is no choice; and why the inveigling a woman before she is come to years of discretion, should not be as criminal as the seducing of her before she is ten years old, I am at a loss to comprehend.

TOM FOLIO.

Tom Folio is a broker in learning, employed to get together good editions, and stock the libraries of great men. There is not a sale of books begins till Tom Folio is seen at the door. There is not an auction where his name is not heard, and that too in the very nick of time, in the critical moment, before the last decisive stroke of the hammer. There is not a subscription goes forward, in which Tom is not privy to the first rough draught of the proposals; nor a catalogue printed, that doth not come to him wet from the press. He is an universal scholar, so far as the titlepage of all authors, knows the manuscripts in which they were discovered, the editions through which they have passed, with the praises or censures which they have received from the several members of the learned world. He has a greater esteem for Aldus and Elzevir, than for Virgil and Horace. If you talk of Herodotus, he breaks out into a panegyric upon Harry Stephens. He thinks he gives you an account of an author, when he tells the subject he treats of, the name of the editor, and the year in which it was printed. Or if you draw him into further particulars, he cries up the goodness of the paper, extols the diligence of the corrector, and is transported with the beauty of the letter. This he looks upon to be sound learning and substantial criticism. As for those who talk of the fineness of style, and the justness of thought, or describe the brightness of any particular passages; nay, though they write themselves in the genius and spirit of the author they admire, Tom looks upon them as men of superficial learning and flashy parts.

I had yesterday morning a visit from this learned idiot, (for that is the light in which I consider every pedant,) when I discovered in him some little touches of the coxcomb, which I had not before observed. Being very full of the figure which he makes in the republic of letters, and wonderfully satisfied with his great stock of knowledge, he gave me broad intimations, that he did not "believe" in all points as his forefathers had done. He then communicated to me a thought of a certain author upon a passage of Virgil's account of the dead, which I made the subject of a late paper. This thought hath taken very much among men of Tom's pitch and understanding, though universally exploded by all that know how to construe Virgil, or have any relish of antiquity. Not to trouble my reader with it, I found upon the whole, that Tom did not believe a future state of rewards and punishments, because Æneas, at his leaving the empire of the dead, passed through the gate of ivory, and not through that of horn. Knowing that Tom had not sense enough to give up an opinion which he had once received, that he might avoid wrangling, I told him, that Virgil possibly had his oversights as well as another author. "Ah! Mr. Bickerstaffe," says he, "you would have another opinion of him, if you would read him in Daniel Heinsius's edition. I have perused him myself several times in that edition," continued he; "and after the strictest and most malicious examination, could find but two faults in him: one of them is in the Æneid, where there are two commas instead of

a parenthesis; and another in the third Georgic, where
you may find a semicolon turned upside down."
" Perhaps," (said I,) " these were not Virgil's thoughts,
but those of the transcriber." "I do not design it,"
says Tom, " as a reflection on Virgil : on the contrary,
I know that all the manuscripts ' reclaim' against
such a punctuation. Oh! Mr. Bickerstaffe," says he,
" what would a man give to see one simile of Virgil
writ in his own hand?" I asked him which was the
simile he meant; but was answered, "Any simile in
Virgil." He then told me all the secret history in the
commonwealth of learning; of modern pieces that had
the names of ancient authors annexed to them; of all
the books that were now writing or printing in the
several parts of Europe; of many amendments which
are made, and not yet published; and a thousand other
particulars, which I would not have my memory
burthened with for a Vatican.

At length, being fully persuaded that I thoroughly
admired him, and looked upon him as a prodigy of
learning, he took his leave. I know several of Tom's
class who are professed admirers of Tasso without
understanding a word of Italian; and one in particular, that carries a *Pastor Fido* in his pocket, in which
I am sure he is acquainted with no other beauty but
the clearness of the character.

There is another kind of pedant, who, with all Tom
Folio's impertinencies, hath greater superstructures
and embellishments of Greek and Latin, and is still
more insupportable than the other, in the same degree as he is more learned. Of this kind very often
are editors, commentators, interpreters, scholiasts, and
critics; and in short, all men of deep learning without
common sense. These persons set a greater value on

themselves for having found out the meaning of a passage in Greek, than upon the author for having written it; nay, will allow the passage itself not to have any beauty in it, at the same time that they would be considered as the greatest men in the age for having interpreted it. They will look with contempt upon the most beautiful poems that have been composed by any of their contemporaries; but will lock themselves up in their studies for a twelve-month together, to correct, publish, and expound, such trifles of antiquity as a modern author would be contemned for. Men of the strictest morals, severest lives, and the gravest professions, will write volumes upon an idle sonnet that is originally in Greek or Latin; give editions of the most immoral authors, and spin out whole pages upon the various readings of a lewd expression. All that can be said in excuse for them is, that their works sufficiently show they have no taste of their authors; and that what they do in this kind, is out of their great learning, and not out of any levity or lasciviousness of temper.

A pedant of this nature is wonderfully well described in six lines of Boileau, with which I shall conclude his character:

Un Pédant enyvré de sa vaine science,
Tout herissé de Grec, tout bouffi d'arrogance,
Et qui de mille Auteurs retenus mot pour mot,
Dans sa tête entassez n'a souvent fait qu'un Sot,
Croit qu'un Livre fait tout, et que sans Aristote
La Raison ne voit goute, et le bon Sens radote.

THE MAN OF THE TOWN.

My friend Will. Honeycomb values himself very much upon what he calls the knowledge of mankind, which has cost him many disasters in his youth; for Will. reckons every misfortune that he has met with among the women, and every rencounter among the men, as parts of his education, and fancies he should never have been the man he is, had not he broke windows, knocked down constables, disturbed honest people with his midnight serenades, and beat time up a lewd woman's quarters, when he was a young fellow. The engaging in adventures of this nature Will. calls the studying of mankind; and terms this knowledge of the town, the knowledge of the world. Will. ingenuously confesses, that for half his life his head ached every morning with reading of men overnight; and at present comforts himself under certain pains which he endures from time to time, that without them he could not have been acquainted with the gallantries of the age. This Will. looks upon as the learning of a gentleman, and regards all other kinds of science as the accomplishments of one whom he calls a scholar, a bookish man, or a philosopher.

For these reasons Will. shines in mixed company, where he has the discretion not to go out of his depth, and has often a certain way of making his real ignorance appear a seeming one. Our club, however, has frequently caught him tripping, at which times

130

they never spare him. For as Will. often insults us with the knowledge of the town, we sometimes take our revenge upon him by our knowledge of books.

He was last week producing two or three letters which he writ in his youth to a coquette lady. The raillery of them was natural, and well enough for a mere man of the town ; but, very unluckily, several of the words were wrong spelt. Will. laught this off at first as well as he could, but finding himself pushed on all sides, and especially by the templar, he told us, with a little passion, that he never liked pedantry in spelling, and that he spelt like a gentleman, and not like a scholar : upon this Will. had recourse to his old topic of showing the narrow-spiritedness, the pride, and ignorance of pedants; which he carried so far, that upon my retiring to my lodgings, I could not forbear throwing together such reflections as occurred to me upon that subject.

A man who has been brought up among books, and is able to talk of nothing else, is a very indifferent companion, and what we call a pedant. But, methinks, we should enlarge the title, and give it every one that does not know how to think out of his profession, and particular way of life.

What is a greater pedant than a mere man of the town ? Bar him the play-houses, a catalogue of the reigning beauties, and an account of a few fashionable distempers that have befallen him, and you strike him dumb. How many a pretty gentleman's knowledge lies all within the verge of the court ? He will tell you the names of the principal favorites, repeat the shrewd sayings of a man of quality, whisper an intrigue that is not yet blown upon by common fame; or, if the sphere of his observations is a little larger than ordinary, will perhaps enter into all the incidents, turns, and revolutions in a game of ombre. When he has gone thus far, he has shown you the whole circle of his accomplishments, his parts are drained, and he is disabled from any further conversation. What are these but rank pedants? and yet these are the men who value themselves most on their exemption from the pedantry of colleges.

I might here mention the military pedant, who always talks in a camp, and is storming towns, making lodgments and fighting battles from one end of the year to the other. Everything he speaks smells of gunpowder; if you take away his artillery from him, he has not a word to say for himself. I might likewise mention the law pedant, that is perpetually putting cases, repeating the transactions of Westminster Hall, wrangling with you upon the most indifferent circumstances of life, and not to be convinced of the distance of a place, or of the most trivial point in conversation, but by dint of argument. The state pedant is wrapped up in news, and lost in politics. If you mention either of the kings of Spain or Poland, he talks very notably; but if you go out of the gazette you drop him. In short, a mere courtier, a mere soldier, a mere scholar, a mere anything, is an insipid pedantic character, and equally ridiculous.

Of all the species of pedants, which I have mentioned, the book pedant is much the most supportable; he has at least an exercised understanding, and a head which is full though confused, so that a man who converses with him may often receive from him hints of things that are worth knowing, and what he may possibly turn to his own advantage, though they are of little use to the owner. The worst kind of pedants among learned men, are such as are naturally endowed with a very small share of common sense, and have read a great number of books without taste or distinction.

The truth of it is, learning, like traveling, and all other methods of improvement, as it finishes good sense, so it makes a silly man ten thousand times more insufferable, by supplying variety of matter to his impertinence, and giving him an opportunity of abounding in absurdities.

THE TRUNK-MAKER AT THE PLAY.

THERE is nothing which lies more within the province of a Spectator than public shows and diversions; and as among these there are none which can pretend to vie with those elegant entertainments that are exhibited in our theaters, I think it particularly incumbent on me to take notice of everything that is remarkable in such numerous and refined assemblies.

It is observed, that of late years there has been a certain person in the upper gallery of the play-house, who, when he is pleased with anything that is acted upon the stage, expresses his approbation by a loud knock upon the benches or the wainscot, which may be heard over the whole theater. This person is commonly known by the name of the "Trunk-maker in the upper gallery." Whether it be, that the blow he gives on these occasions resembles that which is often heard in the shops of such artisans, or that he was supposed to have been a real trunk-maker, who, after the finishing of his day's work, used to unbend his mind at these public diversions with his hammer in his hand, I cannot certainly tell. There are some, I know, who have been foolish enough to imagine it is a spirit which haunts the upper gallery, and from time to time makes those strange noises; and the rather, because he is observed to be louder than ordinary every time the ghost of Hamlet appears. Others have reported that it is a dumb man, who has chosen this

way of uttering himself, when he is transported with
anything he sees or hears.   Others will have it to be
the play-house thunderer, that exerts himself after
this manner in the upper gallery, when he has nothing
to do upon the roof.

But having made it my business to get the best in-
formation I could in a matter of this moment, I find
that the Trunk-maker, as he is commonly called, is a
large black man, whom nobody knows.   He generally
leans forward on a huge oaken plant, with great attention to everything that passes upon the stage.   He
is never seen to smile; but upon hearing anything
that pleases him, he takes up his staff with both hands,
and lays it upon the next piece of timber that stands
in his way with exceeding vehemence : after which he
composes himself in his former posture, till such time
as something new sets him again at work.

It has been observed, his blow is so well timed, that
the most judicious critic could never except against it.
As soon as any shining thought is expressed in the
poet, or any uncommon grace appears in the actor, he
smites the bench or wainscot.   If the audience does
not concur with him, he smites a second time ; and if
the audience is not yet awaked, looks round him with
great wrath, and repeats the blow a third time, which
never fails to produce the clap.   He sometimes lets
the audience begin the clap of themselves, and at the
conclusion of their applause ratifies it with a single
thwack.

He is of so great use to the play-house, that it is
said a former director of it, upon his not being able
to pay his attendance by reason of sickness, kept one
in pay to officiate for him till such time as he recovered; but the person so employed, though he laid

about him with incredible violence, did it in such wrong places, that the audience soon found out that it was not their old friend the Trunk-maker.

It has been remarked, that he has not yet exerted himself with vigor this season. He sometimes plies at the opera; and upon Nicolini's first appearance, was said to have demolished three benches in the fury of his applause. He has broken half a dozen oaken plants upon Dogget; and seldom goes away from a tragedy of Shakespeare, without leaving the wainscot extremely shattered.

The players do not only connive at this his obstreperous approbation, but very cheerfully repair at their own cost whatever damage he makes. They had once a thought of erecting a kind of wooden anvil for his use, that should be made of a very sounding plank, in order to render his strokes more deep and mellow; but as this might not have been distinguished from the music of a kettle-drum, the project was laid aside.

In the mean while I cannot but take notice of the great use it is to an audience, that a person should thus preside over their heads, like the director of a concert, in order to awaken their attention, and beat time to their applauses; or, to raise my simile, I have sometimes fancied the Trunk-maker in the upper gallery to be like Virgil's ruler of the wind, seated upon the top of a mountain, who, when he struck his scepter upon the side of it, roused an hurricane, and set the whole cavern in an uproar.

It is certain the Trunk-maker has saved many a good play, and brought many a graceful actor into reputation, who would not otherwise have been taken notice of. It is very visible, as the audience is not a little abashed if they find themselves betrayed into a

clap, when their friend in the upper gallery does not
come into it; so the actors do not value themselves
upon the clap, but regard it as a mere *brutum fulmen*,
or empty noise, when it has not the sound of the
oaken plant in it. I know it has been given out by
those who are enemies to the Trunk-maker, that he
has sometimes been bribed to be in the interest of a
bad poet, or a vicious player; but this is a surmise
which has no foundation; his strokes are always just,
and his admonitions seasonable; he does not deal
about his blows at random, but always hits the right
nail upon the head. That inexpressible force where-
with he lays them on, sufficiently shows the evidence
and strength of his conviction. His zeal for a good
author is indeed outrageous, and breaks down every
fence and partition, every board and plank, that stands
within the expression of his applause.

As I do not care for terminating my thoughts in
barren speculations, or in reports of pure matter of
fact, without drawing something from them for the
advantage of my countrymen, I shall take the liberty
to make an humble proposal, that whenever the
Trunk-maker shall depart this life, or whenever he
shall have lost the spring of his arm by sickness, old
age, infirmity, or the like, some able-bodied critic
should be advanced to this post, and have a competent
salary settled on him for life, to be furnished with
bamboos for operas, crab-tree cudgels for comedies,
and oaken plants for tragedy, at the public expense.
And to the end that this place should be always disposed of according to merit, I would have none preferred to it, who has not given convincing proofs both
of a sound judgment and a strong arm, and who could
not, upon occasion, either knock down an ox, or write

a comment upon Horace's Art of Poetry. In short, I would have him a due composition of Hercules and Apollo, and so rightly qualified for this important office, that the Trunk-maker may not be missed by our posterity.

COFFEE-HOUSE POLITICIANS.

WHEN I consider this great city in its several quarters and divisions, I look upon it as an aggregate of various nations distinguished from each other by their respective customs, manners, and interests. The courts of two countries do not so much differ from one another, as the court and city in their peculiar ways of life and conversation. In short, the inhabitants of St. James's, notwithstanding they live under the same laws, and speak the same language, are a distinct people from those of Cheapside, who are likewise removed from those of the Temple on the one side, and those of Smithfield on the other, by several climates and degrees in their way of thinking and conversing together.

For this reason, when any public affair is upon the anvil, I love to hear the reflections that arise upon it in the several districts and parishes of London and Westminster, and to ramble up and down a whole day together, in order to make myself acquainted with the opinions of my ingenious countrymen. By this means I know the faces of all the principal politicians within the bills of mortality; and as every coffee-house has some particular statesman belonging to it, who is the mouth of the street where he lives, I always take care to place myself near him, in order to know his judgment on the present posture of affairs. The last progress that I made with this intention was about three months ago, when we had a current report of the king of France's death. As I foresaw this would produce a new face of things in Europe, and many curious speculations in our British coffee-houses, I was very desirous to learn the thoughts of our most eminent politicians on that occasion.

That I might begin as near the fountain-head as possible, I first of all called in at St. James's, where I found the whole outward room in a buzz of politics. The speculations were but very indifferent towards the door, but grew finer as you advanced to the upper end of the room, and were so very much improved by a knot of theorists who sat in the inner room, within the steams of the coffee-pot, that I there heard the whole Spanish monarchy disposed of, and all the line of Bourbon provided for, in less than a quarter of an hour.

I afterwards called in at Giles's, where I saw a board of French gentlemen sitting upon the life and death of their *Grand Monarque.* Those among them who had espoused the Whig interest, very positively affirmed, that he departed this life about a week since, and therefore proceeded without any further delay to the release of their friends on the galleys, and to their own re-establishment; but finding they could not agree among themselves, I proceeded on my intended progress.

Upon my arrival at Jenny Man's, I saw an alert young fellow that cocked his hat upon a friend of his who entered just at the same time with myself, and accosted him after the following manner: " Well, Jack, the old prig is dead at last. Sharp 's the word. Now or never, boy. Up to the walls of Paris directly." With several other deep reflections of the same nature.

I met with very little variation in the politics between Charing Cross and Covent Garden. And upon my going into Will's, I found their discourse was gone off from the death of the French king to that of Monsieur Boileau, Racine, Corneille, and several other poets, whom they regretted on this occasion, as persons who would have obliged the world with very noble elegies on the death of so great a prince, and so eminent a patron of learning.

At a coffee-house near the Temple, I found a couple of young gentlemen engaged very smartly in a dispute on the succession to the Spanish monarchy. One of them seemed to have been retained as advocate for the Duke of Anjou, the other for his Imperial Majesty. They were both for regulating the title to that kingdom by the statute laws of England; but finding them going out of my depth, I passed forward to Paul's Churchyard, where I listened with great attention to a learned man, who gave the company an account of the deplorable state of France during the minority of the deceased king.

I then turned on my right hand into Fish Street, where the chief politician of that quarter, upon hearing the news, (after having taken a pipe of tobacco, and ruminating for some time,) "If," says he, "the king of France is certainly dead, we shall have plenty of mackerel this season; our fishery will not be disturbed by privateers, as it has been for these ten years past." He afterwards considered how the death of this great man would affect our pilchards, and by several other remarks infused a general joy into his whole audience.

I afterwards entered a by coffee-house that stood at the upper end of a narrow lane, where I met with a Nonjuror, engaged very warmly with a Laceman who

was the great support of a neighboring conventicle.
The matter in debate was, whether the late French
king was most like Augustus Cæsar or Nero. The
controversy was carried on with great heat on both
sides, and as each of them looked upon me very frequently during the course of their debate, I was under
some apprehension that they would appeal to me, and
therefore laid down my penny at the bar, and made
the best of my way to Cheapside.

I here gazed upon the signs for some time before I
found one to my purpose. The first object I met in
the coffee-room was a person who expressed a great
grief for the death of the French king; but upon his
explaining himself, I found his sorrow did not arise
from the loss of the monarch, but for his having sold
out of the bank about three days before he heard the
news of it; upon which a haberdasher, who was the
oracle of the coffee-house, and had his circle of admirers
about him, called several to witness that he had declared his opinion above a week before, that the French
king was certainly dead; to which he added, that considering the late advices we had received from France,
it was impossible that it could be otherwise. As he
was laying these together, and dictating to his hearers
with great authority, there came in a gentleman from
Garraway's, who told us that there were several letters
from France just come in, with advice that the king
was in good health, and was gone out a hunting the
very morning the post came away: upon which the
haberdasher stole off his hat that hung upon a wooden
peg by him, and retired to his shop with great confusion. This intelligence put a stop to my travels,
which I had prosecuted with much satisfaction; not
being a little pleased to hear so many different opin-

ions upon so great an event, and to observe how naturally upon such a piece of news every one is apt to consider it with a regard to his own particular interest
and advantage.

LONDON CRIES.

THERE is nothing which more astonishes a foreigner and frights a country squire, than the Cries of London. My good friend Sir Roger often declares, that he cannot get them out of his head, or go to sleep for them, the first week that he is in town. On the contrary, Will. Honeycomb calls them the *Ramage de la Ville* and prefers them to the sounds of larks and nightingales, with all the music of the fields and woods. I have lately received a letter from some very odd fellow upon this subject, which I shall leave with my reader, without saying anything further of it.

"SIR,

I am a man out of all business, and would willingly turn my head to anything for an honest livelihood. I have invented several projects for raising many millions of money without burthening the subject, but I cannot get the parliament to listen to me, who look upon me, forsooth, as a crack and a projector ; so that despairing to enrich either myself or my country by this public-spiritedness, I would make some proposals to you relating to a design which I have very much at heart, and which may procure me an handsome subsistence, if you will be pleased to recommend it to the cities of London and Westminster.

"The post I would aim at is to be Comptroller-general of the London Cries, which are at present under no manner of rules or discipline. I think I am pretty well qualified for this place, as being a man of very strong lungs, of

great insight into all the branches of our British trades
and manufactures, and of a competent skill in music.

"The cries of London may be divided into vocal and in-
strumental. As for the latter, they are at present under a
very great disorder. A freeman of London has the privilege of disturbing a whole street, for an hour together,
with the twanking of a brass-kettle or a frying-pan. The
watchman's thump at midnight startles us in our beds as
much as the breaking in of a thief. The sow-gelder's
horn has indeed something musical in it, but this is seldom
heard within the liberties. I would therefore propose,
that no instrument of this nature should be made use of,
which I have not tuned and licensed, after having care-
fully examined in what manner it may affect the ears of
her Majesty's liege subjects.

"Vocal cries are of a much larger extent, and, indeed,
so full of incongruities and barbarisms, that we appear a
distracted city to foreigners, who do not comprehend the
meaning of such enormous outcries. Milk is generally
sold in a note above *ela*, and it sounds so exceeding shrill,
that it often sets our teeth on edge. The chimney-sweeper
is confined to no certain pitch ; he sometimes utters himself in the deepest bass, and sometimes in the sharpest
treble ; sometimes in the highest, and sometimes in the
lowest note of the gamut. The same observation might
be made on the retailers of small coal, not to mention
broken glasses or brick-dust. In these, therefore, and the
like cases, it should be my care to sweeten and mellow the
voices of these itinerant tradesmen, before they make their
appearance in our streets, as also to accommodate their
cries to their respective wares ; and to take care in particular that those may not make the most noise who have
the least to sell, which is very observable in the venders
of card-matches, to whom I cannot but apply that old
proverb of "Much cry, but little wool."

"Some of these last-mentioned musicians are so very

10

loud in the sale of these trifling manufactures, that an
honest splenetic gentleman of my acquaintance bargained
with one of them never to come into the street where he
lived : but what was the effect of this contract ? why, the
whole tribe of card-match-makers which frequent the
quarter, passed by his door the very next day, in hopes of
being bought off after the same manner.

"It is another great imperfection in our London cries,
that there is no just time nor measure observed in them.
Our news should, indeed, be published in a very quick
time, because it is a commodity that will not keep cold.
It should not, however, be cried with the same precipita-
tion as ' fire : ' yet this is generally the case. A bloody
battle alarms the town from one end to another in an instant. Every motion of the French is published in so
great a hurry, that one would think the enemy were at
our gates. This likewise I would take upon me to regulate
in such a manner, that there should be some distinction
made between the spreading of a victory, a march, or an
encampment, a Dutch, a Portugal, or a Spanish mail.
Nor must I omit under this head, those excessive alarms
with which several boisterous rustics infest our streets
in turnip season ; and which are more inexcusable, because these are wares which are in no danger of cooling
upon their hands.

" There are others who affect a very slow time, and are,
in my opinion, much more tunable than the former ; the
cooper, in particular, swells his last note in an hollow
voice, that is not without its harmony : nor can I forbear
being inspired with a most agreeable melancholy, when I
hear that sad and solemn air with which the public is very
often asked, if they have any chairs to mend ? Your own
memory may suggest to you many other lamentable ditties
of the same nature, in which the music is wonderfully
languishing and melodious.

" I am always pleased with that particular time of the

year which is proper for the pickling of dill and cucumbers ; but, alas, this cry, like the song of the nightingale, is not heard above two months. It would, therefore, be worth while to consider whether the same air might not in some cases be adapted to other words.

" It might likewise deserve our most serious consideration, how far, in a well-regulated city, those humorists are to be tolerated, who, not contented with the traditional cries of their forefathers, have invented particular songs and tunes of their own : such as was, not many years since, the pastry-man, commonly known by the name of the colly-molly-puff ; and such as is at this day the vender of powder and wash-balls, who, if I am rightly informed, goes under the name of Powder Watt.

" I must not here omit one particular absurdity which runs through this whole vociferous generation, and which renders their cries very often not only incommodious, but altogether useless to the public ; I mean that idle accomplishment which they all of them aim at, of crying so as not to be understood. Whether or no they have learned this from several of our affected singers, I will not take upon me to say ; but most certain it is, that people know the wares they deal in rather by their tunes than by their words ; insomuch, that I have sometimes seen a country boy run out to buy apples of a bellows-mender, and gingerbread from a grinder of knives and scissors. Nay, so strangely infatuated are some very eminent artists of this particular grace in a cry, that none but their acquaintance are able to guess at their profession ; for who else can know that, " Work if I had it," should be the signification of a corn-cutter.

" Forasmuch, therefore, as persons of this rank are seldom men of genius or capacity, I think it would be very proper, that some man of good sense, and sound judgment, should preside over these public cries, who should permit none to lift up their voices in our streets, that have not tunable throats, and are not only able to overcome the noise of the crowd, and the rattling of coaches, but also to vend their respective merchandises in apt phrases, and in the most distinct and agreeable sounds. I do therefore humbly recommend myself as a person rightly qualified for this post : and if I meet with fitting encouragement, shall communicate some other projects which I have by me, that may no less conduce to the emolument of the public.

> " I am, sir, &c.,
> " RALPH CROTCHET."

THE CAT-CALL.

I HAVE lately received the following letter from a country gentleman.

" MR. SPECTATOR,

The night before I left London I went to see a play, called, The Humorous Lieutenant. Upon the rising of the curtain I was very much surprised with the great consort of cat-calls which was exhibited that evening, and began to think with myself that I had made a mistake, and gone to a music-meeting instead of the play-house. It appeared, indeed, a little odd to me, to see so many persons of quality of both sexes assembled together at a kind of caterwauling ; for I cannot look upon that performance to have been anything better, whatever the musicians themselves might think of it. As I had no acquaintance in the house to ask questions of, and was forced to go out of town early the next morning, I could not learn the secret of this matter. What I would therefore desire of you, is, to give some account of this strange instrument, which I found the company called a cat-call ; and particularly to let me know whether it be a piece of music lately come from Italy. For my own part, to be free with you, I would rather hear an English fiddle ; though I durst not show my dislike whilst I was in the play-house, it being my chance to sit the very next man to one of the performers.

"I am, sir,

" Your most affectionate friend and servant,

" JOHN SHALLOW, Esq."

In compliance with 'Squire Shallow's request, I de-sign this paper as a dissertation upon the cat-call. In order to make myself a master of the subject, I pur-chased one the beginning of last week, though not without great difficulty, being informed at two or three toy-shops that the players had lately bought them all up. I have since consulted many learned antiquaries in relation to its original, and find them very much divided among themselves upon that particular. A Fellow of the Royal Society, who is my good friend, and a great proficient in the mathematical part of music, concludes from the simplicity of its make, and the uniformity of its sound, that the cat-call is older than any of the inventions of Jubal. He observes very well, that musical instruments took their first rise from the notes of birds, and other melodious animals; and what, says he, was more natural than for the first ages of mankind to imitate the voice of a cat that lived under the same roof with them? he added, that the cat had contributed more to harmony than any other animal; as we are not only beholden to her for this wind-instrument, but for our string music in general.

Another virtuoso of my acquaintance will not allow the cat-call to be older than Thespis, and is apt to think it appeared in the world soon after the ancient comedy; for which reason it has still a place in our dramatic entertainments: nor must I here omit what a curious gentleman, who is lately returned from his travels, has more than once assured me, namely, that there was lately dug up at Rome the statue of a Momus, who holds an instrument in his right hand very much resem-bling our modern cat-call.

There are others who ascribe this invention to

Orpheus, and look upon the cat-call to be one of those instruments which that famous musician made use of to draw the beasts about him. It is certain, that the roasting of a cat does not call together a greater audience of that species, than this instrument, if dexterously played upon in proper time and place.

But notwithstanding these various and learned conjectures, I cannot forbear thinking that the cat-call is originally a piece of English music. Its resemblance to the voice of some of our British songsters, as well as the use of it, which is peculiar to our nation, confirms me in this opinion. It has at least received great improvements among us, whether we consider the instrument itself, or those several quavers and graces which are thrown into the playing of it. Every one might be sensible of this, who heard that remarkable overgrown cat-call which was placed in the center of the pit, and presided over all the rest at the celebrated performance lately exhibited in Drury Lane.

Having said thus much concerning the original of the cat-call, we are in the next place to consider the use of it. The cat-call exerts itself to most advantage in the British theater: it very much improves the sound of nonsense, and often goes along with the voice of the actor who pronounces it, as the violin or harpsichord accompanies the Italian recitativo.

It has often supplied the place of the ancient chorus, in the words of Mr. * * * In short, a bad poet has as great an antipathy to a cat-call, as many people have to a real cat.

Mr. Collier, in his ingenious essay upon music, has the following passage:

" I believe it is possible to invent an instrument that shall have a quite contrary effect to those martial ones now in use: an instrument that shall sink the spirits, and shake the nerves, and curdle the blood, and inspire despair, and cowardice, and consternation, at a surprising rate. It is probable the roaring of a lion, the warbling of cats and screech-owls, together with a mixture of the howling of dogs, judiciously imitated and compounded, might go a great way in this invention. Whether such anti-music as this might not be of service in a camp, I shall leave to the military men to consider."

What this learned gentleman supposes in speculation, I have known actually verified in practise. The cat-call has struck a damp into generals, and frighted heroes off the stage. At the first sound of it I have seen a crowned head tremble, and a princess fall into fits. The humorous lieutenant himself could not stand it; nay, I am told that even Almanzor looked like a mouse, and trembled at the voice of this terrifying instrument.

As it is of a dramatic nature, and peculiarly appropriated to the stage, I can by no means approve the thought of that angry lover, who, after an unsuccessful pursuit of some years, took leave of his mistress in a serenade of cat-calls.

I must conclude this paper with the account I have lately received of an ingenious artist, who has long studied this instrument, and is very well versed in all the rules of the drama. He teaches to play on it by book, and to express by it the whole art of criticism. He has his base and his treble cat-call; the former for tragedy, the latter for comedy; only in tragi-comedies they may both play together in consort. He has a particular squeak to denote the violation of each of the unities, and has different sounds to show whether he aims at the poet or the player. In short, he teaches the smut-note, the fustian-note, the stupid-note, and has composed a kind of air that may serve as an act-tune to an incorrigible play, and which takes in the whole compass of the cat-call.

THE NEWSPAPER.

THERE is no humor in my countrymen, which I am more inclined to wonder at, than their general thirst after news. There are about half a dozen ingenious men, who live very plentifully upon this curiosity of their fellow-subjects. They all of them receive the same advices from abroad, and very often in the same words; but their way of cooking it is so different, that there is no citizen, who has an eye to the public good, that can leave the coffee-house with peace of mind, before he has given every one of them a reading. These several dishes of news are so very agreeable to the palate of my countrymen, that they are not only pleased with them when they are served up hot, but when they are again set cold before them by those penetrating politicians, who oblige the public with their reflections and observations upon every piece of intelligence that is sent us from abroad. The text is given us by one set of writers, and the comment by another.

But notwithstanding we have the same tale told us in so many different papers, and if occasion requires, in so many articles of the same paper; notwithstanding a scarcity of foreign posts we hear the same story repeated, by different advices from Paris, Brussels, the Hague, and from every great town in Europe; notwithstanding the multitude of annotations, explanation, reflections, and various readings which it passes through, our time lies heavy on our hands till the

154

arrival of a fresh mail: we long to receive further particulars, to hear what will be the next step, or what
will be the consequence of that which has been lately
taken. A westerly wind keeps the whole town in suspense, and puts a stop to conversation.

This general curiosity has been raised and inflamed
by our late wars, and, if rightly directed, might be of
good use to a person who has such a thirst awakened
in him. Why should not a man who takes delight in
reading everything that is new, apply himself to history, travels, and other writings of the same kind,
where he will find perpetual fuel for his curiosity, and
meet with much more pleasure and improvement, than
in these papers of the week? An honest tradesman,
who languishes a whole summer in expectation of a
battle, and perhaps is balked at last, may here meet
with half a dozen in a day. He may read the news of
a whole campaign in less time than he now bestows
upon the products of any single post. Fights, con-
quests, and revolutions lie thick together. The reader's
curiosity is raised and satisfied every moment, and his
passions disappointed or gratified, without being detained in a state of uncertainty from day to day, or
lying at the mercy of sea and wind. In short, the mind
is not here kept in a perpetual gape after knowledge,
nor punished with that eternal thirst which is the
portion of all our modern newsmongers and coffee-
house politicians.

All matters of fact, which a man did not know before, are news to him; and I do no see how any haberdasher in Cheapside is more concerned in the present
quarrel of the Cantons, than he was in that of the
League. At least, I believe every one will allow me,
it is of more importance to an Englishman to know the

history of his ancestors, than that of his contemporaries who live upon the banks of the Danube or the Borysthenes. As for those who are of another mind, I shall recommend to them the following letter, from a projector, who is willing to turn a penny by this remarkable curiosity of his countrymen.

" MR. SPECTATOR,

You must have observed, that men who frequent coffee-houses, and delight in news, are pleased with everything that is matter of fact, so it be what they have not heard before. A victory, or a defeat, are equally agreeable to them. The shutting of a cardinal's mouth pleases them one post, and the opening of it another. They are glad to hear the French court is removed to Marli, and are afterwards as much delighted with its return to Versailles. They read the advertisements with the same curiosity as the articles of public news ; and are as pleased to hear of a piebald horse that is strayed out of a field near Islington, as of a whole troop that has been engaged in any foreign adventure. In short, they have a relish for everything that is news, let the matter of it be what it will ; or to speak more properly, they are men of a voracious appetite, but no taste. Now, sir, since the great fountain of news, I mean the war, is very near being dried up ; and since these gentlemen have contracted such an inextinguishable thirst after it ; I have taken their case and my own into consideration, and have thought of a project which may turn to the advantage of us both. I have thoughts of publishing a daily paper, which shall comprehend in it all the most remarkable occurrences in every little town, village, and hamlet, that lie within ten miles of London, or in other words, within the verge of the penny-post. I have pitched upon this scene of intelligence for two reasons ; first, because the carriage of letters will be very cheap ; and secondly, because I may receive them every day.

By this means my readers will have their news fresh and fresh, and many worthy citizens, who cannot sleep with any satisfaction at present, for want of being informed how the world goes, may go to bed contentedly, it being my design to put out my paper every night at nine-a-clock precisely. I have already established correspondences in these several places, and received very good intelligence.

" By my last advices from Knightsbridge I hear that a horse was clapped into the pound on the third instant, and that he was not released when the letters came away.

" We are informed from Pankridge, that a dozen weddings were lately celebrated in the mother-church of that place, but are referred to their next letters for the names of the parties concerned.

" Letters from Brompton advise, that the widow Blight had received several visits from John Mildew, which affords great matter of speculation in those parts.

" By a fisherman which lately touched at Hammersmith, there is advice from Putney, that a certain person well known in that place, is like to lose his election for churchwarden ; but this being boat-news, we cannot give entire credit to it.

" Letters from Paddington bring little more than that William Squeak, the sow-gelder, passed through that place the fifth instant.

" They advise from Fulham, that things remained there in the same state they were. They had intelligence, just as the letters came away, of a tub of excellent ale just set a-broach at Parsons Green ; but this wanted confirmation.

" I have here, sir, given you a specimen of the news with which I intend to entertain the town, and which when drawn up regularly in the form of a newspaper, will, I doubt not, be very acceptable to many of those public-spirited readers, who take more delight in acquainting themselves with other people's business than their own. I hope a paper of this kind, which lets us know what is done near home, may be more useful to us than those which are filled with advices from Zug and Bender, and make some amends for that dearth of intelligence, which we justly apprehend from times of peace. If I find that you receive this project favorably, I will shortly trouble you with one or two more ; and in the mean time am, most worthy sir, with all due respect,

" Your most obedient and most humble servant."

COFFEE-HOUSE DEBATES.

It is sometimes pleasant enough to consider the different notions which different persons have of the same thing. If men of low condition very often set a value on things which are not prized by those who are in a higher station of life, there are many things these esteem which are in no value among persons of an inferior rank. Common people are, in particular, very much astonished, when they hear of those solemn contests and debates, which are made among the great upon the punctilios of a public ceremony; and wonder to hear that any business of consequence should be retarded by those little circumstances, which they represent to themselves as trifling and insignificant. I am mightily pleased with a porter's decision in one of Mr. Southern's plays, which is founded upon that fine distress of a virtuous woman's marrying a second husband, while her first was yet living. The first husband, who was supposed to have been dead, returning to his house after a long absence, raises a noble perplexity for the tragic part of the play. In the mean while, the nurse and the porter conferring upon the difficulties that would ensue in such a case, honest Samson thinks the matter may be easily decided, and solves it very judiciously, by the old proverb, that if his first master be still living, " The man must have his mare again." There is nothing in my time which has so much surprised and confounded the greatest part of my honest
159

countrymen, as the present controversy between Count Rechteren and Monsieur Mesnager, which employs the wise heads of so many nations, and holds all the affairs of Europe in suspense.

Upon my going into a coffee-house yesterday, and lending an ear to the next table, which was encompassed with a circle of inferior politicians, one of them, after having read over the news very attentively, broke out into the following remarks. "I am afraid (says he) this unhappy rupture between the footmen at Utrecht will retard the peace of Christendom. I wish the pope may not be at the bottom of it. His Holiness has a very good hand at fomenting a division, as the poor Swiss Cantons have lately experienced to their cost. If Monsieur What-d'ye-call-him's domestics will not come to an accommodation, I do not know how the quarrel can be ended, but by a religious war."

"Why truly," says a wiseacre that sat by him, "were I as the king of France, I would scorn to take part with the footmen of either side: here's all the business of Europe stands still, because Monsieur Mesnager's man has had his head broke. If Count Rectrum had given them a pot of ale after it, all would have been well, without any of this bustle; but they say he is a warm man, and does not care to be made mouths at."

Upon this, one, who had held his tongue hitherto, began to exert himself; declaring that he was very well pleased the plenipotentiaries of our Christian princes took this matter into their serious consideration; for that lacqueys were never so saucy and pragmatical as they are now-a-days, and that he should be glad to see them taken down in the treaty of peace, if it might be done without prejudice to the public affairs.

One, who sat at the other end of the table, and seemed to be in the interests of the French king, told them, that they did not take the matter right, for that his most Christian Majesty did not resent this matter because it was an injury done to Monsieur Mesnager's footmen; " for (says he) what are Monsieur Mesnager's footmen to him ? but because it was done to his subjects. Now, (says he,) let me tell you, it would look very odd for a subject of France to have a bloody nose, and his sovereign not to take notice of it. He is obliged in honor to defend his people against hostilities; and if the Dutch will be so insolent to a crowned head, as, in anywise, to cuff or kick those who are under his protection, I think he is in the right to call them to an account for it."

This distinction set the controversy upon a new foot, and seemed to be very well approved by most that heard it, till a little warm fellow, who declared himself a friend to the house of Austria, fell most unmercifully upon his Gallic Majesty, as encouraging his subjects to make mouths at their betters, and afterwards screening them from the punishment that was due to their insolence. To which he added, that the French nation was so addicted to grimace, that if there was not a stop put to it at the general congress, there would be no walking the streets for them in a time of peace, especially if they continued masters of the West Indies. The little man proceeded with a great deal of warmth, declaring, that if the allies were of his mind, he would oblige the French king to burn his galleys, and tolerate the Protestant religion in his dominions, before he would sheath his sword. He concluded with calling Monsieur Mesnager an insignificant prig.

11

The dispute was now growing very warm, and one does not know where it would have ended, had not a young man of about one and twenty, who seems to have been brought up with an eye to the law, taken the debate into his hand, and given it as his opinion, that neither Count Rechteren nor Monsieur Mesnager had behaved themselves right in this affair. " Count Rechteren (says he) should have made affidavit that his servants had been affronted, and then Monsieur Mesnager would have done him justice, by taking away their liveries from them, or some other way that he might have thought the most proper ; for let me tell you, if a man makes a mouth at me, I am not to knock the teeth out of it for his pains. Then again, as for Monsieur Mesnager, upon his servant's being beaten, why ! he might have had his action of assault and battery. But as the case now stands, if you will have my opinion, I think they ought to bring it to referees."

I heard a great deal more of this conference, but I must confess with little edification ; for all I could learn at last from these honest gentlemen was, that the matter in debate was of too high a nature for such heads as theirs, or mine, to comprehend.

THE VISION OF PUBLIC CREDIT.

In one of my late rambles, or rather speculations, I looked into the great hall where the Bank is kept, and was not a little pleased to see the directors, secretaries, and clerks, with all the other members of that wealthy corporation, ranged in their several stations, according to the parts they act in that just and regular œconomy. This revived in my memory the many discourses which I had both read and heard concerning the decay of public credit, with the methods of restoring it, and which, in my opinion, have always been defective, because they have always been made with an eye to separate interests and party principles.

The thoughts of the day gave my mind employment for the whole night, so that I fell insensibly into a kind of methodical dream, which disposed all my contemplations into a vision or allegory, or what else the reader shall please to call it.

Methoughts I returned to the great hall, where I had been the morning before, but, to my surprise, instead of the company that I left there, I saw towards the upper end of the hall a beautiful virgin, seated on a throne of gold. Her name (as they told me) was Public Credit. The walls, instead of being adorned with pictures and maps, were hung with many Acts of Parliament written in golden letters. At the upper end of the hall was the Magna Charta, with the Act of Uniformity on the right hand, and the Act of Toleration on the left. At the lower end of the hall was the Act of Settlement, which was placed full in the eye of the virgin that sat upon the throne. Both the sides of the hall were covered with such Acts of Parliament as had been made for the establishment of public funds. The lady seemed to set an unspeakable value upon these several pieces of furniture, insomuch that she often refreshed her eye with them, and often smiled with a secret pleasure as she looked upon them ; but, at the same time, showed a very particular uneasiness, if she saw anything approaching that might hurt them. She appeared, indeed, infinitely timorous in all her behavior; and, whether it was from the delicacy of her constitution, or that she was troubled with vapors, as I was afterwards told by one who I found was none of her well-wishers, she changed color and startled at everything she heard. She was likewise (as I afterwards found) a greater valetudinarian than any I had ever met with, even in her own sex, and subject to such momentary consumptions, that, in the twinkling of an eye, she would fall away from the most florid complexion, and the most healthful state of body, and wither into a skeleton. Her recoveries were often as sudden as her decays, insomuch that she would revive in a moment out of a wasting distemper, into a habit of the highest health and vigor.

I had very soon an opportunity of observing these quick turns and changes in her constitution. There sat at her feet a couple of secretaries, who received every hour letters from all parts of the world, which the one or the other of them was perpetually reading to her ; and, according to the news she heard, to which she was exceedingly attentive, she changed color, and discovered many symptoms of health or sickness.

Behind the throne was a prodigious heap of bags of money, which were piled upon one another so high, that they touched the ceiling. The floor, on her right hand and on her left, was covered with vast sums of gold that rose up in pyramids on either side of her: but this I did not so much wonder at, when I heard, upon inquiry, that she had the same virtue in her touch, which the poets tell us a Lydian king was formerly possessed of; and that she could convert whatever she pleased into that precious metal.

After a little dizziness, and confused hurry of thought, which a man often meets with in a dream, methoughts the hall was alarmed, the doors flew open, and there entered half a dozen of the most hideous phantoms that I had ever seen (even in a dream) before that time. They came in two by two, though matched in the most dissociable manner, and mingled together in a kind of dance. It would be tedious to describe their habits and persons, for which reason I shall only inform my reader, that the first couple were Tyranny and Anarchy ; the second were Bigotry and Atheism ; the third, the genius of a commonwealth and a young man of about twenty-two years of age, whose name I could not learn. He had a sword in his right hand, which in the dance he often brandished at the Act of Settlement; and a citizen, who stood by me, whispered in my ear, that he saw a spunge in his left hand. The dance of so many jarring natures put me in mind of the sun, moon, and earth, in the Rehearsal, that danced together for no other end but to eclipse one another.

The reader will easily suppose, by what has been before said, that the lady on the throne would have been almost frighted to distraction, had she seen but any one of these specters; what then must have been her condition when she saw them all in a body? She fainted and died away at the sight.

Et neque jam color est misto candore rubori;
Nec vigor, et vires, et quæ modo visa placebant;
Nec corpus remanet—   Ov. MET. lib. iii.

There was a great change in the hill of money bags and the heaps of money; the former shrinking, and falling into so many empty bags, that I now found not above a tenth part of them had been filled with money. The rest that took up the same space, and made the same figure as the bags that were really filled with money, had been blown up with air, and called into my memory the bags full of wind, which Homer tells us his hero received as a present from Æolus. The great heaps of gold, on either side the throne, now appeared to be only heaps of paper, or little piles of notched sticks, bound up together in bundles, like Bath fagots.

Whilst I was lamenting this sudden desolation that had been made before me, the whole scene vanished: in the room of the frightful specters, there now entered a second dance of apparitions very agreeably matched together, and made up of very amiable phantoms. The first pair was Liberty with Monarchy at her right hand; the second was Moderation leading in Religion; and the third, a person whom I had never seen, with the genius of Great Britain. At the first entrance the lady revived; the bags swelled to their former bulk; the pile of fagots, and heaps of paper, changed into pyramids of guineas: and, for my own part, I was so transported with joy, that I awaked; though, I must confess, I would fain have fallen asleep again to have closed my vision, if I could have done it.

TALES AND ALLEGORIES.

THE VISIONS OF MIRZAH.

WHEN I was at Grand Cairo I picked up several oriental manuscripts, which I have still by me. Among others I met with one entitled, The Visions of Mirzah, which I have read over with great pleasure. I intend to give it to the public when I have no other entertainment for them; and shall begin with the first vision, which I have translated word for word as follows:

" ON the fifth day of the moon, which according to the custom of my forefathers I always kept holy, after having washed myself, and offered up my morning devotions, I ascended the high hills of Bagdat, in order to pass the rest of the day in meditation and prayer. As I was here airing myself on the tops of the mountains, I fell into a profound contemplation on the vanity of human life; and passing from one thought to another, surely, said I, man is but a shadow and life a dream. Whilst I was thus musing, I cast my eyes towards the summit of a rock that was not far from me, where I discovered one in the habit of a shepherd, with a musical instrument in his hand. As I looked upon him he applied it to his lips, and began to play upon it. The sound of it was exceeding sweet, and wrought into a variety of tunes that were inexpressibly melodious, and altogether different from anything I had ever heard. They put me in mind of those heavenly airs that are played to the departed souls of good men upon their first arrival in paradise, to wear out the impressions of their last agonies, and qualify them for the pleasures of that happy place. My heart melted away in secret raptures.

I had been often told that the rock before me was the haunt of a genius; and that several had been entertained with music who had passed by it, but never heard that the musician had before made himself visible. When he had raised my thoughts, by those transporting airs which he played, to taste the pleasures of his conversation, as I looked upon him like one astonished, he beckoned to me, and by the waving of his hand directed me to approach the place where he sat. I drew near with that reverence which is due to a superior nature; and as my heart was entirely subdued by the captivating strains I had heard, I fell down at his feet and wept. The genius smiled upon me with a look of compassion and affability that familiarized him to my imagination, and at once dispelled all the fears and apprehensions with which I approached him. He lifted me from the ground, and taking me by the hand, Mirzah, said he, I have heard thee in thy soliloquies, follow me.

He then led me to the highest pinnacle of the rock, and placed me on the top of it. Cast thy eyes eastward, said he, and tell me what thou seest. I see, said I, a huge valley and a prodigious tide of water rolling through it. The valley that thou seest, said he, is the vale of misery, and the tide of water that thou seest is part of the great tide of eternity. What is the reason, said I, that the tide I see rises out of a thick mist at one end, and again loses itself in a thick mist at the other? What thou seest, says he, is that portion of eternity which is called time, measured out by the sun, and reaching from the beginning of the world to its consummation. Examine now, said he, this sea that is thus bounded with darkness at both ends, and tell me what thou discoverest in it. I see a bridge, said I, standing in the midst of the tide. The bridge thou seest, said he, is human life; consider it attentively. Upon a more leisurely survey of it, I found that it consisted of threescore and ten entire arches, with several broken arches, which added to those that were entire, made up the number about an hundred. As I was counting the arches the genius told me that this bridge consisted at first of a thousand arches; but that a great flood swept away the rest, and left the bridge in the ruinous condition I now beheld it. But tell me, further, said he, what thou discoverest on it. I see multitudes of people passing over it, said I, and a black cloud hanging on each end of it. As I looked more attentively, I saw several of the passengers dropping through the bridge, into the great tide that flowed underneath it; and upon further examination, perceived there were innumerable trap-doors that lay concealed in the bridge, which the passengers no sooner trod upon, but they fell through them into the tide and immediately disappeared. These hidden pit-falls were set very thick at the entrance of the bridge, so that throngs of people no sooner broke through the cloud, but many of them fell into them. They grew thinner towards the middle, but multiplied and lay closer together towards the end of the arches that were entire.

There were indeed some persons, but their number was very small, that continued a kind of hobbling march on the broken arches, but fell through one after another, being quite tired and spent with so long a walk.

I passed some time in the contemplation of this

wonderful structure, and the great variety of objects which it presented. My heart was filled with a deep melancholy to see several dropping unexpectedly in the midst of mirth and jollity, and catching at everything that stood by them to save themselves. Some were looking up towards the heavens in a thoughtful posture, and in the midst of a speculation stumbled and fell out of sight. Multitudes were very busy in the pursuit of baubles that glittered in their eyes and danced before them, but often when they thought themselves within the reach of them, their footing failed and down they sunk. In this confusion of objects, I observed some with scimetars in their hands, and others with urinals, who ran to and fro upon the bridge, thrusting several persons upon trap-doors which did not seem to lie in their way, and which they might have escaped, had they not been thus forced upon them.

The genius seeing me indulge myself in this melancholy prospect, told me I had dwelt long enough upon it : take thine eyes off the bridge, said he, and tell me if thou seest anything thou dost not comprehend. Upon looking up, what mean, said I, those great flights of birds that are perpetually hovering about the bridge, and settling upon it from time to time ? I see vultures, harpies, ravens, cormorants, and among many other feathered creatures, several little winged boys, that perch in great numbers upon the middle arches. These, said the genius, are envy, avarice, superstition, despair, love, with the like cares and passions, that infest human life.

I here fetched a deep sigh ; alas, said I, man was made in vain ! How is he given away to misery and mortality ! tortured in life, and swallowed up in death !

The genius, being moved with compassion towards me,
bid me quit so uncomfortable a prospect. Look no
more, said he, on man in the first stage of his existence, in his setting out for eternity; but cast thine eye
on that thick mist into which the tide bears the
several generations of mortals that fall into it. I
directed my sight as I was ordered, and (whether or
no the good genius strengthened it with any super-
natural force, or dissipated part of the mist that was
before too thick for the eye to penetrate) I saw the
valley opening at the farther end, and spreading forth
into an immense ocean, that had a huge rock of adamant running through the midst of it, and dividing it
into two equal parts. The clouds still rested on one
half of it, insomuch that I could discover nothing in it:
but the other appeared to me a vast ocean planted
with innumerable islands, that were covered with fruits
and flowers, and interwoven with a thousand little
shining seas that ran among them. I could see persons dressed in glorious habits with garlands upon
their heads, passing among the trees, lying down by
the sides of the fountains, or resting on beds of flowers;
and could hear a confused harmony of singing birds,
falling waters, human voices, and musical instruments. Gladness grew in me upon the discovery of
so delightful a scene. I wished for the wings of an
eagle, that I might fly away to those happy seats; but
the genius told me there was no passage to them, except through the gates of death that I saw opening
every moment upon the bridge. The islands, said he,
that lie so fresh and green before thee, and with which
the whole face of the ocean appears spotted as far as
thou canst see, are more in number than the sands on
the sea-shore; there are myriads of islands behind

those which thou here discoverest, reaching farther than thine eye, or even thine imagination, can extend itself. These are the mansions of good men after death, who, according to the degree and kinds of virtue in which they excelled, are distributed among these several islands, which abound with pleasures of different kinds and degrees, suitable to the relishes and perfections of those who are settled in them: every island is a paradise, accommodated to its respective inhabitants. Are not these, O Mirzah, habitations worth contending for? Does life appear miserable, that gives thee opportunities of earning such a reward? Is death to be feared, that will convey thee to so happy an existence? Think not man was made in vain, who has such an eternity reserved for him. I gazed with inexpressible pleasure on these happy islands. At length, said I, show me now, I beseech thee, the secrets that lie hid under those dark clouds which cover the ocean on the other side of the rock of adamant. The genius making me no answer, I turned about to address myself to him a second time, but I found that he had left me. I then turned again to the vision which I had been so long contemplating, but, instead of the rolling tide, the arched bridge, and the happy islands, I saw nothing but the long hollow valley of Bagdat, with oxen, sheep, and camels grazing upon the sides of it."

THE TALE OF MARRATON.

The Americans believe that all creatures have souls, not only men and women, but brutes, vegetables, nay, even the most inanimate things, as stocks and stones. They believe the same of all the works of art, as of knives, boats, looking-glasses : and that as any of these things perish, their souls go into another world, which is habited by the ghosts of men and women. For this reason they always place by the corpse of their dead friend a bow and arrows, that he may make use of the souls of them in the other world, as he did of their wooden bodies in this. How absurd soever such an opinion as this may appear, our European philosophers have maintained several notions altogether as improbable. Some of Plato's followers in particular, when they talk of the world of ideas, entertain us with substances and beings no less extravagant and chimerical. Many Aristotelians have likewise spoken as unintelligibly of their substantial forms. I shall only instance Albertus Magnus, who in his dissertation upon the loadstone, observing that fire will destroy its magnetic virtues, tells us that he took particular notice of one as it lay glowing amidst an heap of burning coals, and that he perceived a certain blue vapor to arise from it, which he believed might be the substantial form, that is, in our West Indian phrase, the soul of the loadstone.

There is a tradition among the Americans, that one of their countrymen descended in a vision to the great repository of souls, or, as we call it here, to the other world; and that upon his return he gave his friends a distinct account of everything he saw among those regions of the dead. A friend of mine, whom I have formerly mentioned, prevailed upon one of the interpreters of the Indian kings, to inquire of them, if possible, what tradition they have among them of this matter; which, as well as he could learn by those many questions which he asked them at several times, was in substance as follows.

The visionary, whose name was Marraton, after having traveled for a long space under an hollow mountain, arrived at length on the confines of this world of spirits; but could not enter it by reason of a thick forest made up of bushes, brambles, and pointed thorns, so perplexed and interwoven with one another, that it was impossible to find a passage through it. Whilst he was looking about for some track or pathway that might be worn in any part of it, he saw an huge lion couched under the side of it, who kept his eye upon him in the same posture as when he watches for his prey. The Indian immediately started back, whilst the lion rose with a spring, and leaped towards him. Being wholly destitute of all other weapons, he stooped down to take up an huge stone in his hand: but to his infinite surprise grasped nothing, and found the supposed stone to be only the apparition of one. If he was disappointed on this side, he was as much pleased on the other, when he found the lion, which had seized on his left shoulder, had no power to hurt him, and was only the ghost of that ravenous creature which it appeared to be. He no sooner got rid of his impotent enemy, but he marched up to the wood, and after having surveyed it for some time, endeavored

to press into one part of it that was a little thinner
than the rest; when again, to his great surprise, he
found the bushes made no resistance, but that he
walked through briers and brambles with the same
ease as through the open air; and, in short, that the
whole wood was nothing else but a wood of shades.
He immediately concluded, that this huge thicket of
thorns and brakes was designed as a kind of fence or
quick-set hedge to the ghosts it enclosed; and that
probably their soft substances might be torn by these
subtle points and prickles, which were too weak to
make any impressions in flesh and blood. With this
thought he resolved to travel through this intricate
wood; when by degrees he felt a gale of perfumes
breathing upon him, that grew stronger and sweeter
in proportion as he advanced. He had not proceeded
much farther when he observed the thorns and briers
to end, and give place to a thousand beautiful green
trees covered with blossoms of the finest scents and
colors, that formed a wilderness of sweets, and were
a kind of lining to those ragged scenes which he had
before passed through. As he was coming out of this
delightful part of the wood, and entering upon the
plains it enclosed, he saw several horsemen rushing by
him, and a little while after heard the cry of a pack
of dogs. He had not listened long before he saw the
apparition of a milk-white steed, with a young man on
the back of it, advancing upon full stretch after the
souls of about an hundred beagles that were hunting
down the ghost of an hare, which ran away before
them with an unspeakable swiftness. As the man on
the milk-white steed came by him, he looked upon him
very attentively, and found him to be the young prince
Nicharagua, who died about half a year before, and by

12

reason of his great virtues was at that time lamented over all the western parts of America.

He had no sooner got out of the wood, but he was entertained with such a landskip of flowery plains, green meadows, running streams, sunny hills, and shady vales, as were not to be represented by his own expressions, nor, as he said, by the conceptions of others. This happy region was peopled with innumerable swarms of spirits, who applied themselves to exercises and diversions according as their fancies led them. Some of them were tossing the figure of a coit; others were pitching the shadow of a bar; others were breaking the apparition of a horse; and multitudes employing themselves upon ingenious handicrafts with the souls of departed utensils; for that is the name which in the Indian language they give their tools when they are burnt or broken. As he traveled through this delightful scene, he was very often tempted to pluck the flowers that rose everywhere about him in the greatest variety and profusion, having never seen several of them in his own country; but he quickly found, that though they were objects of his sight, they were not liable to his touch. He at length came to the side of a great river, and being a good fisherman himself, stood upon the banks of it some time to look upon an angler that had taken a great many shapes of fishes, which lay flouncing up and down by him.

I should have told my reader, that this Indian had been formerly married to one of the greatest beauties of his country, by whom he had several children. This couple were so famous for their love and constancy to one another, that the Indians to this day, when they give a married man joy of his wife, wish

that they may live together like Marraton and Yaratilda. Marraton had not stood long by the fisherman
when he saw the shadow of his beloved Yaratilda,
who had for some time fixed her eye upon him, before
he discovered her. Her arms were stretched out
towards him, floods of tears ran down her eyes; her
looks, her hands, her voice called him over to her;
and at the same time seemed to tell him that the river
was unpassable. Who can describe the passion made
up of joy, sorrow, love, desire, astonishment, that rose
in the Indian upon the sight of his dear Yaratilda?
he could express it by nothing but his tears, which ran
like a river down his cheeks as he looked upon her.
He had not stood in this posture long, before he
plunged into the stream that lay before him; and
finding it to be nothing but the phantom of a river,
stalked on the bottom of it till he arose on the other
side. At his approach Yaratilda flew into his arms,
whilst Marraton wished himself disencumbered of
that body which kept her from his embraces. After
many questions and endearments on both sides, she
conducted him to a bower which she had dressed with
her own hands with all the ornaments that could be
met with in those blooming regions. She had made it
gay beyond imagination, and was every day adding
something new to it. As Marraton stood astonished
at the unspeakable beauty of her habitation, and ravished with the fragrancy that came from every part of
it, Yaratilda told him that she was preparing this
bower for his reception, as well knowing that his piety
to his God, and his faithful dealing towards men, would
certainly bring him to that happy place, whenever his
life should be at an end. She then brought two of her
children to him, who died some years before, and re-

sided with her in the same delightful bower; advising him to breed up those others which were still with him in such a manner, that they might hereafter all of them meet together in this happy place.

This tradition tells us further, that he had afterwards a sight of those dismal habitations which are the portion of ill men after death; and mentions several molten seas of gold, in which were plunged the souls of barbarous Europeans, who put to the swords so many thousands of poor Indians for the sake of that precious metal: but having already touched upon the chief points of this tradition, and exceeded the measure of my paper, I shall not give any further account of it.

THE GOLDEN SCALES.

I was lately entertaining myself with comparing Homer's balance, in which Jupiter is represented as weighing the fates of Hector and Achilles, with a passage of Virgil, wherein that deity is introduced as weighing the fates of Turnus and Æneas. I then considered how the same way of thinking prevailed in the eastern parts of the world, as in those noble passages of Scripture, where we are told, that the great king of Babylon, the day before his death, had been weighed in the balance, and been found wanting. In other places of the holy writings, the Almighty is described as weighing the mountains in scales, making the weight for the winds, knowing the balancings of the clouds ; and, in others, as weighing the actions of men, and laying their calamities together in a balance. Milton, as I have observed in a former paper, had an eye to several of these foregoing instances, in that beautiful description wherein he represents the archangel and the evil spirit as addressing themselves for the combat, but parted by the balance which appeared in the heavens, and weighed the consequences of such a battle.

These several amusing thoughts having taken possession of my mind some time before I went to sleep, and mingling themselves with my ordinary ideas, raised in my imagination a very odd kind of vision. I was, methought, replaced in my study, and seated in my elbow-chair, where I had indulged the foregoing speculations, with my lamp burning by me, as usual. Whilst I was here meditating on several subjects of morality, and considering the nature of many virtues and vices, as materials for those discourses with which I daily entertain the public; I saw, methought, a pair of golden scales hanging by a chain in the same metal over the table that stood before me; when, on a sudden, there were great heaps of weights thrown down on each side of them. I found upon examining these weights, they showed the value of everything that is in esteem among men. I made an essay of them, by putting the weight of wisdom in one scale, and that of riches in another, upon which the latter, to show its comparative lightness, immediately " flew up and kick'd the beam."

But, before I proceed, I must inform my reader, that these weights did not exert their natural gravity, till they were laid in the golden balance, insomuch that I could not guess which was light or heavy, whilst I held them in my hand. This I found by several instances, for upon my laying a weight in one of the scales, which was inscribed by the word Eternity; though I threw in that of time, prosperity, affliction, wealth, poverty, interest, success, with many other weights, which in my hand seemed very ponderous, they were not able to stir the opposite balance, nor could they have prevailed, though assisted with the weight of the sun, the stars, and the earth.

Upon emptying the scales, I laid several titles and honors, with pomps, triumphs, and many weights of the like nature, in one of them, and seeing a little glittering weight lie by me, I threw it accidentally into the other scale, when, to my great surprise, it proved so exact a counterpoise, that it kept the balance in an equilibrium. This little glittering weight was inscribed upon the edges of it with the word Vanity. I found there were several other weights which were equally heavy, and exact counterpoises to one another; a few of them I tried, as avarice and poverty, riches and content, with some others.

There were likewise several weights that were of the same figure, and seemed to correspond with each other, but were entirely different when thrown into the scales, as religion and hypocrisy, pedantry and learning, wit and vivacity, superstition and devotion, gravity and wisdom, with many others.

I observed one particular weight lettered on both sides, and upon applying myself to the reading of it, I found on one side written, " In the dialect of men," and underneath it, " CALAMITIES ;" on the other side was written, " In the language of the gods," and underneath, " BLESSINGS." I found the intrinsic value of this weight to be much greater than I imagined, for it overpowered health, wealth, good-fortune, and many other weights, which were much more ponderous in my hand than the other.

There is a saying among the Scotch, that " an ounce of mother is worth a pound of clergy ;" I was sensible of the truth of this saying, when I saw the difference between the weight of natural parts and that of learning. The observation which I made upon these two weights opened to me a new field of discoveries, for notwithstanding the weight of natural parts was much heavier than that of learning, I observed that it weighed an hundred times heavier than it did before, when I put learning into the same scale with it. I made the same observation upon faith and morality ; for not-

withstanding the latter outweighed the former sepa-
rately, it received a thousand times more additional
weight from its conjunction with the former, than what
it had by itself. This odd phenomenon showed itself
in other particulars, as in wit and judgment, philosophy
and religion, justice and humanity, zeal and charity,
depth of sense and perspicuity of style, with innumerable other particulars, too long to be mentioned in this
paper.

As a dream seldom fails of dashing seriousness with
impertinence, mirth with gravity, methought I made
several other experiments of a more ludicrous nature,
by one of which I found that an English octavo was
very often heavier than a French folio ; and by another,
that an old Greek or Latin author weighed down a
whole library of moderns. Seeing one of my Spectators
lying by me, I laid it into one of the scales, and flung
a twopenny piece in the other. The reader will not
inquire into the event, if he remembers the first trial
which I have recorded in this paper. I afterwards
threw both the sexes into the balance ; but as it is not
for my interest to disoblige either of them, I shall desire to be excused from telling the result of this experiment. Having an opportunity of this nature in my
hands, I could not forbear throwing into one scale the
principles of a Tory, and in the other those of a Whig ;
but as I have all along declared this to be a neutral
paper, I shall likewise desire to be silent under this
head also, though upon examining one of the weights,
I saw the word TEKEL engraven on it in capital
letters.

I made many other experiments, and though I have
not room for them all in this day's speculation, I may
perhaps reserve them for another. I shall only add,

that upon my awaking I was sorry to find my golden
scales vanished, but resolved for the future to learn
this lesson from them, not to despise or value any
things for their appearances, but to regulate my esteem
and passions towards them according to their real and
intrinsic value.

HILPA AND SHALUM.

HILPA was one of the 150 daughters of Zilpah, of the race of Cohu, by whom some of the learned think is meant Cain. She was exceedingly beautiful, and when she was but a girl of threescore and ten years of age, received the addresses of several who made love to her. Among these were two brothers, Harpath and Shalum. Harpath, being the first-born, was master of that fruitful region which lies at the foot of Mount Tirzah, in the southern parts of China. Shalum (which is to say the planter, in the Chinese language) possessed all the neighboring hills, and that great range of mountains which goes under the name of Tirzah. Harpath was of a haughty, contemptuous spirit; Shalum was of a gentle disposition, beloved both by God and man.

It is said that, among the antediluvian women, the daughters of Cohu had their minds wholly set upon riches; for which reason, the beautiful Hilpa preferred Harpath to Shalum, because of his numerous flocks and herds, that covered all the low country which runs along the foot of Mount Tirzah, and is watered by several fountains and streams breaking out of the sides of that mountain.

Harpath made so quick a despatch of his courtship, that he married Hilpa in the hundredth year of her age, and being of an insolent temper, laughed to scorn his brother Shalum for having pretended to the beautiful Hilpa, when he was master of nothing but a long

186

chain of rocks and mountains. This so much provoked
Shalum, that he is said to have cursed his brother in
the bitterness of his heart, and to have prayed that
one of his mountains might fall upon his head, if ever
he came within the shadow of it.

From this time forward Harpath would never venture out of the valleys, but came to an untimely end in
the 250th year of his age, being drowned in a river as
he attempted to cross it. This river is called, to this
day, from his name who perished in it, the river Harpath, and what is very remarkable, issues out of one
of those mountains which Shalum wished might fall
upon his brother, when he cursed him in the bitterness
of his heart.

Hilpa was in the 160th year of her age at the death
of her husband, having brought him but fifty children,
before he was snatched away, as has been already related. Many of the antediluvians made love to the
young widow, though no one was thought so likely to
succeed in her affections as her first lover Shalum, who
renewed his court to her about ten years after the
death of Harpath; for it was not thought decent in
those days that a widow should be seen by a man
within ten years after the decease of her husband.

Shalum, falling into a deep melancholy, and resolv-
ing to take away that objection which had been raised
against him when he made his first addresses to Hilpa,
began, immediately after her marriage with Harpath,
to plant all that mountainous region which fell to his
lot in the division of this country. He knew how to
adapt every plant to its proper soil, and is thought to
have inherited many traditional secrets of that art
from the first man. This employment turned at length
to his profit as well as to his amusement: his moun-

tains were in a few years shaded with young trees, that gradually shot up into groves, woods, and forests, intermixed with walks, and lawns, and gardens; insomuch that the whole region, from a naked and desolate prospect, began now to look like a second Paradise. The pleasantness of the place, and the agreeable disposition of Shalum, who was reckoned one of the mildest and wisest of all who lived before the flood, drew into it multitudes of people who were perpetually employed in the sinking of wells, the digging of trenches, and the hollowing of trees, for the better distribution of water through every part of this spacious plantation.

The habitations of Shalum looked every year more beautiful in the eyes of Hilpa, who, after the space of 70 autumns, was wonderfully pleased with the distant prospect of Shalum's hills; which were then covered with innumerable tufts of trees and gloomy scenes, that gave a magnificence to the place, and converted it into one of the finest landscapes the eye of man could behold.

The Chinese record a letter which Shalum is said to have written to Hilpa, in the eleventh year of her widowhood. I shall here translate it, without departing from that noble simplicity of sentiments, and plainness of manners, which appears in the original.

Shalum was at this time 180 years old, and Hilpa 170.

Shalum, master of Mount Tirzah, to Hilpa, mistress of the Valleys.

In the 788th year of the Creation.

"What have I not suffered, O thou daughter of Zilpah, since thou gavest thyself away in marriage to my rival!

I grew weary of the light of the sun, and have been ever since covering myself with woods and forests. These threescore and ten years have I bewailed the loss of thee on the tops of Mount Tirzah, and soothed my melancholy among a thousand gloomy shades of my own raising. My dwellings are at present as the garden of God ; every part of them is filled with fruits, and flowers, and fountains. The whole mountain is perfumed for thy reception. Come up into it, O my beloved, and let us people this spot of the new world with a beautiful race of mortals ; let us multiply exceedingly among these delightful shades, and fill every quarter of them with sons and daughters. Remember, O thou daughter of Zilpah, that the age of men is but a thousand years ; that beauty is the admiration but of a few centuries. It flourishes as a mountain oak, or as a cedar on the top of Tirzah, which in three or four hundred years will fade away, and never be thought of by posterity, unless a young wood springs from its roots. Think well on this, and remember thy neighbor in the mountains."

The letter had so good an effect upon Hilpa, that she answered it in less than a twelve-month after the following manner.

Hilpa, mistress of the Valleys, to Shalum, master of Mount Tirzah.

In the 789th year of the Creation.

" What have I to do with thee, O Shalum ? Thou praisest Hilpa's beauty, but art thou not secretly enamored with the verdure of her meadows ? Art thou not more affected with the prospect of her green valley, than thou wouldest be with the sight of her person ? The lowings of my herds, and the bleatings of my flocks, make a pleasant echo in thy mountains, and sound sweetly in thy ears. What though I am delighted with the wavings of thy forests, and those breezes of perfumes which flow from the top of Tirzah : are these like the riches of the valley ?

"I know thee, O Shalum ; thou art more wise and happy than any of the sons of men. Thy dwellings are among the cedars ; thou searchest out the diversity of soils, thou understandest the influence of the stars, and markest the change of seasons. Can a woman appear lovely in the eyes of such a one ? Disquiet me not, O Shalum ; let me alone, that I may enjoy those goodly possessions which are fallen to my lot. Win me not by thy enticing words. May thy trees increase and multiply ; mayest thou add wood to wood, and shade to shade ; but tempt not Hilpa to destroy thy solitude, and make thy retirement populous."

The Chinese say, that a little time afterwards she accepted of a treat, in one of the neighboring hills, to which Shalum had invited her. This treat lasted for two years, and is said to have cost Shalum five hundred antelopes, two thousand ostriches, and a thousand tun of milk ; but what most of all recommended it, was that variety of delicious fruits and pot-herbs, in which no person then living could any way equal Shalum.

He treated her in the bower which he had planted amidst the wood of nightingales. The wood was made up of such fruit trees and plants as are most agreeable to the several kinds of singing birds ; so that it had drawn into it all the music of the country, and was filled, from one end of the year to the other, with the most agreeable concert in season.

He showed her every day some beautiful and surprising scene in this new region of wood-lands ; and as, by this means, he had all the opportunities he could

wish for of opening his mind to her, he succeeded so
well, that upon her departure, she made him a kind of
promise, and gave him her word to return him a positive answer in less than fifty years.

She had not been long among her own people in
the valleys, when she received new overtures, and at
the same time a most splendid visit, from Mishpach,
who was a mighty man of old, and had built a great
city, which he called after his own name. Every
house was made for at least a thousand years, nay,
there were some that were leased out for three lives;
so that the quantity of stone and timber consumed in
this building is scarce to be imagined by those who
live in the present age of the world. This great man
entertained her with the voice of musical instruments,
which had been lately invented, and danced before
her to the sound of the timbrel. He also presented
her with several domestic utensils wrought in brass
and iron, which had been newly found out for the convenience of life. In the mean time, Shalum grew very
uneasy with himself, and was sorely displeased at
Hilpa, for the reception which she had given to Mishpach, insomuch that he never wrote to her, or spoke
of her, during a whole revolution of Saturn ; but,
finding that this intercourse went no further than a
visit, he again renewed his addresses to her, who,
during his long silence, is said very often to have cast
a wishing eye upon Mount Tirzah.

Her mind continued wavering about twenty years
longer, between Shalum and Mishpach ; for though
her inclinations favored the former, her interest
pleaded very powerfully for the other. While her
heart was in this unsettled condition, the following
accident happened, which determined her choice. A

high tower of wood, that stood in the city of Mishpach, having caught fire by a flash of lightning, in a few days reduced the whole town to ashes. Mishpach resolved to rebuild the place, whatever it should cost him; and, having already destroyed all the timber of the country, he was forced to have recourse to Shalum, whose forests were now two hundred years old. He purchased these woods, with so many herds of cattle and flocks of sheep, and with such a vast extent of fields and pastures, that Shalum was now grown more wealthy than Mishpach; and, therefore, appeared so charming in the eyes of Zilpah's daughter, that she no longer refused him in marriage. On the day in which he brought her up into the mountains, he raised a most prodigious pile of cedar, and of every sweet-smelling wood, which reached above 300 cubits in height: he also cast into the pile bundles of myrrh, and sheaves of spikenard, enriching it with every spicy shrub, and making it fat with the gums of his plantations. This was the burnt-offering which Shalum offered in the day of his espousals: the smoke of it ascended up to heaven, and filled the whole country with incense and perfume.

THE VISION OF JUSTICE.

I was last week taking a solitary walk in the garden of Lincoln's Inn, (a favor that is indulged me by several of the benchers who are my intimate friends, and grown old with me in this neighborhood,) when, according to the nature of men in years, who have made but little progress in the advancement of their fortune or their fame, I was repining at the sudden rise of many persons who are my juniors, and indeed at the unequal distribution of wealth, honor, and all other blessings of life. I was lost in this thought, when the night air came upon me, and drew my mind into a far more agreeable contemplation. The heaven above me appeared in all its glories, and presented me with such an hemisphere of stars, as made the most agreeable prospect imaginable to one who delights in the study of nature. It happened to be a freezing night, which had purified the whole body of air into such a bright, transparent æther, as made every constellation visible; and at the same time gave such a particular glowing to the stars, that I thought it the richest sky I had ever seen. I could not behold a scene so wonderfully adorned and lighted up, (if I may be allowed that expression,) without suitable meditations on the Author of such illustrious and amazing objects. For on these occasions, philosophy suggests motives to religion, and religion adds pleasures to philosophy.

As soon as I had recovered my usual temper and

13   193

serenity of soul, I retired to my lodgings with the satisfaction of having passed away a few hours in the proper employments of a reasonable creature, and promising myself that my slumbers would be sweet. I no sooner fell into them, but I dreamed a dream, or saw a vision, (for I knew not which to call it,) that seemed to rise out of my evening meditation, and had something in it so solemn and serious, that I cannot forbear communicating it; though I must confess, the wildness of imagination (which in a dream is always loose and irregular) discovers itself too much in several parts of it.

Methought I saw the azure sky diversified with the same glorious luminaries which had entertained me a little before I fell asleep. I was looking very attentively on that sign in the heavens which is called by the name of the Balance, when on a sudden there appeared in it an extraordinary light, as if the sun should rise at midnight. By its increasing in breadth and luster, I soon found that it approached towards the earth; and at length could discern something like a shadow hovering in the midst of a great glory, which in a little time after I distinctly perceived to be the figure of a woman. I fancied at first it might have been the Angel or Intelligence that guided the constellation from which it descended; but upon a nearer view, I saw about her all the emblems with which the Goddess of Justice is usually described. Her countenance was unspeakably awful and majestic, but exquisitely beautiful to those whose eyes were strong enough to behold it; her smiles transported with rapture, her frowns terrified to despair. She held in her hand a mirror endowed with the same qualities as that which the painters put into the hand of Truth.

There streamed from it a light, which distinguished itself from all the splendors that surrounded her, more than a flash of lightning shines in the midst of daylight. As she moved it in her hand, it brightened the heavens, the air, or the earth. When she had descended so low as to be seen and heard by mortals, to make the pomp of her appearance more supportable, she threw darkness and clouds about her, that tempered the light into a thousand beautiful shades and colors, and multiplied that luster, which was before too strong and dazzling, into a variety of milder glories.

In the mean time the world was in an alarm, and all the inhabitants of it gathered together upon a spacious plain ; so that I seemed to have all the species before my eyes. A voice was heard from the clouds, declaring the intention of this visit, which was to restore and appropriate to every one living what was his due. The fear and hope, joy and sorrow, which appeared in that great assembly after this solemn declaration, are not to be expressed. The first edict was then pronounced, "That all titles and claims to riches and estates, or to any parts of them, should be immediately vested in the rightful owner." Upon this, the inhabitants of the earth held up the instruments of their tenure, whether in parchment, paper, wax, or any other form of conveyance ; and as the goddess moved the mirror of truth which she held in her hand, so that the light which flowed from it fell upon the multitude, they examined the several instruments by the beams of it. The rays of this mirror had a particular quality of setting fire to all forgery and falsehood. The blaze of papers, the melting of seals, and crackling of parchments, made a very odd scene. The fire very often ran through two or three lines only, and then stopped ;

though I could not but observe, that the flame chiefly broke out among the interlineations and codicils. The light of the mirror as it was turned up and down, pierced into all the dark corners and recesses of the universe, and by that means detected many writings and records which had been hidden or buried by time, chance, or design. This occasioned a wonderful revolution among the people. At the same time, the spoils of extortion, fraud, and robbery, with all the fruits of bribery and corruption, were thrown together into a prodigious pile, that almost reached to the clouds, and was called the Mount of Restitution; to which all injured persons were invited, to receive what belonged to them.

One might see crowds of people in tattered garments come up, and change clothes with others that were dressed with lace and embroidery. Several who were plums, or very near it, became men of moderate fortunes; and many others, who were overgrown in wealth and possessions, had no more left than what they usually spent. What moved my concern most was, to see a certain street of the greatest credit in Europe from one end to the other become bankrupt.

The next command was, for the whole body of mankind to separate themselves into their proper families: which was no sooner done, but an edict was issued out, requiring all children "to repair to their true and natural fathers." This put a great part of the assembly in motion; for as the mirror was moved over them, it inspired every one with such a natural instinct, as directed them to their real parents. It was a very melancholy spectacle to see the fathers of very large families become vacant, and bachelors undone by a charge of sons and daughters. You might see a presumptive heir of a great estate ask blessing of his coachman, and a celebrated toast paying her duty to a valet de chambre. Many under vows of celibacy appeared surrounded with a numerous issue. This change of parentage would have caused great lamentation, but that the calamity was pretty common; and that generally those who lost their children, had the satisfaction of seeing them put into the hands of their dearest friends.

Men were no sooner settled in their right to their possessions and their progeny, but there was a third order proclaimed, " That all posts of dignity and honor in the universe should be conferred on persons of the greatest merit, abilities, and perfection." The handsome, the strong, and the wealthy, immediately pressed forward; but not being able to bear the splendor of the mirror which played upon their faces, they immediately fell back among the crowd: but as the goddess tried the multitude by her glass, as the eagle does its young ones by the luster of the sun, it was remarkable, that every one turned away his face from it, who had not distinguished himself either by virtue, knowledge, or capacity in business, either military or civil. This select assembly was drawn up in the center of a prodigious multitude, which was diffused on all sides, and stood observing them, as idle people use to gather about a regiment that are exercising their arms. They were drawn up in three bodies: in the first, were men of virtue; in the second, men of knowledge; and in the third, the men of business. It was impossible to look at the first column without a secret veneration, their aspects were so sweetened with humanity, raised with contemplation, emboldened with resolution, and adorned with the most agreeable

airs, which are those that proceed from secret habits
of virtue. I could not but take notice, that there were
many faces among them which were unknown, not only
to the multitude, but even to several of their own body.

In the second column, consisting of the men of
knowledge, there had been great disputes before they
fell into the ranks, which they did not do at last without positive command of the goddess who presided
over the assembly. She had so ordered it, that men
of the greatest genius and strongest sense were placed
at the head of the column : behind these were such as
had formed their minds very much on the thoughts
and writings of others. In the rear of the column,
were men who had more wit than sense, or more learning than understanding. All living authors of any
value were ranged in one of these classes; but I must
confess, I was very much surprised to see a great body
of editors, critics, commentators, and grammarians,
meet with so very ill a reception. They had formed
themselves into a body, and with a great deal of arrogance demanded the first station in the column of
knowledge; but the goddess, instead of complying
with their request, clapped them all into liveries, and
bid them know themselves for no other but lacqueys
of the learned.

The third column were men of business, and consisting of persons in military and civil capacities. The
former marched out from the rest, and placed themselves in the front, at which the other shook their
heads at them, but did not think fit to dispute the
post with them. I could not but make several observations upon this last column of people; but I have
certain private reasons why I do not think fit to communicate them to the public. In order to fill up all

the posts of honor, dignity, and profit, there was a draught made out of each column, of men who were masters of all three qualifications in some degree, and were preferred to stations of the first rank. The second draught was made out of such as were possessed of any two of the qualifications, who were disposed of in stations of a second dignity. Those who were left, and were endowed only with one of them, had their suitable posts. When this was over, there remained many places of trust and profit unfilled, for which there were fresh draughts made out of the surrounding multitude, who had any appearance of these excellencies, or were recommended by those who possessed them in reality.

All were surprised to see so many new faces in the most eminent dignities; and for my own part, I was very well pleased to see that all my friends either kept their present posts, or were advanced to higher.

The male world were dismissed by the Goddess of Justice, and disappeared, when on a sudden the whole plain was covered with women. So charming a multitude filled my heart with unspeakable pleasure; and as the celestial light of the mirror shone upon their faces, several of them seemed rather persons that descended in the train of the goddess, than such who were brought before her to their trial. The clack of tongues, and confusion of voices, in this new assembly, was so very great, that the goddess was forced to command silence several times, and with some severity, before she could make them attentive to her edicts. They were all sensible, that the most important affair among womankind was then to be settled, which every one knows to be the point of place. This had raised innumerable disputes among them, and put the whole sex into a tumult. Every one produced her claim, and pleaded her pretensions. Birth, beauty, wit, or wealth, were words that rung in my ears from all parts of the plain. Some boasted of the merit of their husbands; others, of their own power in governing them. Some pleaded their unspotted virginity; others, their numerous issue. Some valued themselves as they were the mothers, and others as they were the daughters, of considerable persons. There was not a single accomplishment unmentioned, or unpractised. The whole congregation was full of singing, dancing, tossing, ogling, squeaking, smiling, sighing, fanning, frowning, and all those irresistible arts which women put in practise to captivate the hearts of reasonable creatures. The goddess, to end this dispute, caused it to be proclaimed, " That every one should take place according as she was more or less beautiful." This declaration gave great satisfaction to the whole assembly, which immediately bridled up, and appeared in all its beauties. Such as believed themselves graceful in their motion, found an occasion of falling back, advancing forward, or making a false step, that they might show their persons in the most becoming air. Such as had fine necks and bosoms, were wonderfully curious to look over the heads of the multitude, and observe the most distant parts of the assembly. Several clapped their hands on their foreheads, as helping their sight to look upon the glories that surrounded the goddess, but in reality to show fine hands and arms. The ladies were yet better pleased when they heard, that in the decision of this great controversy, each of them should be her own judge, and take her place according to her own opinion of herself, when she consulted her looking-glass.

The goddess then let down the mirror of truth in a golden chain, which appeared larger in proportion as it descended and approached nearer to the eyes of the beholders. It was the particular property of this looking-glass to banish all false appearances, and show people what they are. The whole woman was represented, without regard to the usual external features, which were made entirely conformable to their real characters. In short, the most accomplished (taking in the whole circle of female perfections) were the most beautiful; and the most defective, the most deformed. The goddess so varied the motion of the glass, and placed it in so many different lights, that each had an opportunity of seeing herself in it.

It is impossible to describe the rage, the pleasure, or astonishment, that appeared in each face upon its representation in the mirror: multitudes started at their own form, and would have broke the glass if they could have reached it. Many saw their blooming features wither as they looked upon them, and their self-admiration turned into a loathing and abhorrence. The lady who was thought so agreeable in her anger, and was so often celebrated for a woman of fire and spirit, was frighted at her own image, and fancied she saw a fury in the glass. The interested mistress beheld a harpy, and the subtle jilt a sphinx. I was very much troubled in my own heart, to see such a destruction of fine faces; but at the same time had the pleasure of seeing several improved, which I had before looked upon as the greatest master-pieces of nature. I observed, that some few were so humble, as to be surprised at their own charms; and that many a one, who had lived in the retirement and severity of a vestal, shined forth in all the graces and attractions of a siren. I was ravished at the sight of a particular image in the mirror, which I think the most beautiful object that my eyes ever beheld.   There was something more than human in her countenance: her eyes was so full of light, that they seemed to beautify everything they looked upon.   Her face was enlivened with such a florid bloom, as did not so properly seem the mark of health, as of immortality. Her shape, her nature, and her mien, were such as distinguished her even there where the whole fair sex was assembled.

I was impatient to see the lady represented by so divine an image, whom I found to be the person that stood at my right hand, and in the same point of view with myself.   This was a little old woman, who in her prime had been about five foot high, though at present shrunk to about three quarters of that measure.   Her natural aspect was puckered up with wrinkles, and her head covered with gray hairs.   I had observed all along an innocent cheerfulness in her face, which was now heightened into rapture as she beheld herself in the glass.   It was an odd circumstance in my dream, (but I cannot forbear relating it,) I conceived so great an inclination towards her, that I had thoughts of discoursing her upon the point of marriage, when on a sudden she was carried from me ; for the word was now given, that all who were pleased with their own images, should separate, and place themselves at the head of their sex.

This detachment was afterwards divided into three bodies, consisting of maids, wives, and widows: the wives being placed in the middle, with the maids on the right, and widows on the left; though it was with difficulty that these two last bodies were hindered from falling into the center.   This separation of those, who

liked their real selves, not having lessened the number
of the main body so considerably as it might have been
wished, the goddess, after having drawn up her mirror,
thought fit to make new distinctions among those who
did not like the figure which they saw in it. She made
several wholesome edicts, which are slipped out of my
mind; but there were two which dwelt upon me, as
being very extraordinary in their kind and executed
with great severity. Their design was, to make an example of two extremes in the female world; of those
who are very severe on the conduct of others, and of
those who are very regardless of their own. The first
sentence, therefore, the goddess pronounced, was, "That
all females addicted to censoriousness and detraction,
should lose the use of speech;" a punishment which
would be the most grievous to the offender, and (what
should be the end of all punishments) effectual for root-
ing out the crime. Upon this edict, which was as soon
executed as published, the noise of the assembly very
considerably abated. It was a melancholy spectacle,
to see so many who had the reputation of rigid virtue
struck dumb. A lady who stood by me, and saw my
concern, told me, she wondered how I could be concerned for such a pack of ——. I found, by the shak-
ing of her head, she was going to give me their characters; but by her saying no more, I perceived she had
lost the command of her tongue. This calamity fell
very heavy upon that part of women who are distinguished by the name of Prudes, a courtly word for
female hypocrites, who have a short way to being
virtuous, by showing that others are vicious. The
second sentence was then pronounced against the loose
part of the sex, "That all should immediately be preg-
nant, who in any part of their lives had ran the hazard

of it." This produced a very goodly appearance, and revealed so many misconducts, that made those who were lately struck dumb, repine more than ever at their want of utterance, though at the same time (as afflictions seldom come single) many of the mutes were also seized with this new calamity.

This vision lasted till my usual hour of waking, which I did with some surprise, to find myself alone, after having been engaged almost a whole night in so prodigious a multitude. I could not but reflect with wonder at the partiality and extravagance of my vision ; which, according to my thoughts, has not done justice to the sex. If virtue in men is more venerable, it is in women more lovely ; which Milton has very finely expressed in his Paradise Lost, where Adam, speaking of Eve, after having asserted his own pre-eminence, as being first in creation and internal faculties, breaks out into the following rapture :

—Yet when 1 approach
Her loveliness, so absolute she seems,
And in herself complete, so well to know
Her own, that what she wills to do, or say,
Seems wisest, virtuousest, discreetest, best.
All higher knowledge in her presence falls
Degraded. Wisdom, in discourse with her,
Loses, discountenanced, and like folly shows.
Authority and reason on her wait,
As one intended first, not after made
Occasionally : and, to consummate all,
Greatness of mind, and nobleness, their seat
Build in her loveliest, and create an awe
About her, as a guard angelic placed.

THE COURT OF HONOR.

INSTITUTION OF THE COURT.

I LAST winter erected a court of justice for the correcting of several enormities in dress and behavior, which are not cognizable in any other courts of this realm. The vintner's case, which I there tried, is still fresh in every man's memory. That of the petticoat gave also a general satisfaction, not to mention the more important points of the cane and perspective; in which, if I did not give judgments and decrees according to the strictest rules of equity and justice, I can safely say, I acted according to the best of my understanding. But as for the proceedings of that court, I shall refer my reader to an account of them, written by my secretary, which is now in the press, and will shortly be published under the title of " Lillie's Reports."

As I last year presided over a court of justice, it is my intention this year to set myself at the head of a Court of Honor. There is no court of this nature anywhere at present, except in France, where, according to the best of my intelligence, it consists of such only as are Marshals of that kingdom. I am likewise informed, that there is not one of that honorable board at present who has not been driven out of the field by the Duke of Marlborough: but whether this be only an accidental, or a necessary qualification, I must confess I am not able to determine.

As for the Court of Honor of which I am here speaking, I intend to sit myself in it as president,

with several men of honor on my right hand, and
women of virtue on my left, as my assistants. The
first place of the bench I have given to an old Tan-
gereen captain with a wooden leg. The second is a
gentleman of a long twisted periwig without a curl in
it, a muff with very little hair upon it, and a thread-
bare coat with new buttons, being a person of great
worth, and second brother to a man of quality. The
third is a gentleman usher, extremely well read in
romances, and grandson to one of the greatest wits in
Germany, who was some time master of the ceremonies to the Duke of Wolfembuttel.

As for those who sit further on my right hand, as it
is usual in public courts, they are such as will fill up
the number of faces upon the bench, and serve rather
for ornament than use.

The chief upon my left hand are, an old maiden
lady, that preserves some of the best blood of England
in her veins.

A Welsh woman of a little stature, but high spirit.

An old prude that has censured every marriage for
these thirty years, and is lately wedded to a young
rake.

Having thus furnished my bench, I shall establish
correspondencies with the Horse-guards, and the vete-
rans of Chelsea College; the former to furnish me
with twelve men of honor, as often as I shall have
occasion for a grand jury, and the latter with as many
good men and true for a petty jury.

As for the women of virtue, it will not be difficult for
me to find them about midnight at crimp and basset.

Having given this public notice of my court, I must
further add, that I intend to open it on this day seven-
night, being Monday the twentieth instant; and do

hereby invite all such as have suffered injuries and affronts, that are not to be redressed by the common laws of this land, whether they be short bows, cold salutations, supercilious looks, unreturned smiles, distant behavior, or forced familiarity; as also all such as have been aggrieved by any ambiguous expression, accidental justle, or unkind repartee; likewise all such as have been defrauded of their right to the wall, tricked out of the upper end of the table, or have been suffered to place themselves in their own wrong on the back-seat of the coach: these, and all of these, I do, as is above-said, invite to bring in their several cases and complaints, in which they shall be relieved with all imaginable expedition.

I am very sensible, that the office I have now taken upon me will engage me in the disquisition of many weighty points that daily perplex the youth of the British nation, and therefore I have already discussed several of them for my future use; as, How far a man may brandish his cane in the telling a story, without insulting his hearer? What degree of contradiction amounts to the lie? How a man should resent another's staring and cocking a hat in his face? If asking pardon is an atonement for treading upon one's toes? Whether a man may put up a box on the ear received from a stranger in the dark? Or, whether a man of honor may take a blow of his wife? with several other subtilties of the like nature.

For my direction in the duties of my office, I have furnished myself with a certain astrological pair of scales which I have contrived for this purpose. In one of them I lay the injuries, in the other the reparations. The first are represented by little weights made of a metal resembling iron, and the other in

14

gold. These are not only lighter than the weights
made use of in Avoirdupois, but also than such as are
used in Troy weight. The heaviest of those that represent the injuries, amount to but a scruple; and de-
crease by so many sub-divisions, that there are several
imperceptible weights which cannot be seen without
the help of a very fine microscope. I might acquaint
my reader, that these scales were made under the influence of the sun when he was in *Libra*, and describe
many signatures on the weights both of injury and
reparation: but as this would look rather to proceed
from an ostentation of my own art than any care for
the public I shall pass it over in silence.

CHARGE TO THE JURY.

Extract of the Journal of the Court of Honor, 1710.

Diæ Lunæ vicesimo Novembris, horá noná antemeridiana.

THE court being sat, an oath prepared by the Censor was administered to the assistants on his right hand, who were all sworn upon their honor. The women on his left hand took the same oath upon their reputation. Twelve gentlemen of the Horse-guards were impaneled, having unanimously chosen Mr. Alexander Truncheon, who is their right-hand man in the troop, for their foreman in the jury. Mr Truncheon immediately drew his sword, and holding. it with the point towards his own body, presented it to the Censor. Mr. Bickerstaffe received it, and after having surveyed the breadth of the blade, and the sharpness of the point, with more than ordinary attention, returned it to the foreman, in a very graceful manner. The rest of the jury, upon the delivery of the sword to their foreman, drew all of them together as one man, and saluted the bench with such an air, as signified the most resigned submission to those who commanded them, and the greatest magnanimity to execute what they should command.

Mr. Bickerstaffe, after having received the compliments on his right hand, cast his eye upon the left, where the whole female jury paid their respects by a low curtsy, and by laying their hands upon their mouths. Their fore-woman was a professed Platonist, that had spent much of her time in exhorting the sex to set a just value upon their persons, and to make the men know themselves.

There followed a profound silence, when at length, after some recollection, the Censor, who continued hitherto uncovered, put on his hat with great dignity; and after having composed the brims of it in a manner suitable to the gravity of his character, he gave the following charge, which was received with silence and attention, that being the only applause which he admits of, or is ever given in his presence.

" The nature of my office, and the solemnity of this occasion, requiring that I should open my first session with a speech, I shall cast what I have to say under two principal heads:

" Under the first, I shall endeavor to show the necessity and usefulness of this new-erected court; and under the second, I shall give a word of advice and instruction to every constituent part of it.

" As for the first, it is well observed by Phædrus, an heathen poet,

Nisi utile est quod facimus, frustra est gloria.

Which is the same, ladies, as if I should say, 'It would be of no reputation for me to be president of a court which is of no benefit to the public.' Now the advantages that may arise to the weal public from this institution will more plainly appear, if we consider what it suffers for the want of it. Are not our streets daily filled with wild pieces of justice and random penalties? Are not crimes undetermined, and reparations disproportioned? How often have we seen the

lie punished by death, and the liar himself deciding
his own cause; nay, not only acting the judge, but
the executioner! Have we not known a box on the
ear more severely accounted for than manslaughter?
In these extra-judicial proceedings of mankind, an
unmannerly jest is frequently as capital as a pre-
meditated murder.

" But the most pernicious circumstance in this case
is, that the man who suffers the injury must put himself upon the same foot of danger with him that gave
it, before he can have his just revenge; so that the
punishment is altogether accidental, and may fall as
well upon the innocent as the guilty. I shall only
mention a case which happens frequently among the
more polite nations of the world, and which I the
rather mention, because both sexes are concerned in it,
and which therefore, you gentlemen and you ladies of
the jury, will the rather take notice of; I mean that
great and known case of cuckoldom. Supposing the
person who has suffered insults in his dearer and better
half; supposing, I say, this person should resent the
injuries done to his tender wife; what is the reparation he may expect? Why, to be used worse than
his poor lady, run through the body, and left breath-
less upon the bed of honor? What then, will you on
my right hand say, must the man do that is affronted?
Must our sides be elbowed, our shins broken? Must
the wall, or perhaps our mistress, be taken from us?
May a man knit his forehead into a frown, toss up his
arm, or pish at what we say; and must the villain live
after it? Is there no redress for injured honor? Yes,
gentlemen, that is the design of the judicature we have
here established.

" A court of conscience, we very well know, was first

instituted for the determining of several points of property that were too little and trivial for the cognizance of higher courts of justice. In the same manner, our court of honor is appointed for the examination of several niceties and punctilios that do not pass for wrongs in the eye of our common laws. But, notwithstanding no legislators of any nation have taken into consideration these little circumstances, they are such as often lead to crimes big enough for their inspection, though they come before them too late for their redress.

" Besides, I appeal to you, ladies, [here Mr. Bickerstaffe turned to his left hand,] if these are not the little stings and thorns in life that make it more uneasy than its most substantial evils ? Confess ingenuously, did you never lose a morning's devotions, because you could not offer them up from the highest place of the pew ? Have you not been in pain, even at a ball, because another has been taken out to dance before you ? Do you love any of your friends so much as those that are below you ? Or have you any favorites that walk on your right hand ? You have answered me in your looks, I ask no more.

" I come now to the second part of my discourse, which obliges me to address myself in particular to the respective members of the court, in which I shall be very brief.

" As for you, gentlemen and ladies, my assistants and grand juries, I have made choice of you on my right hand, because I know you very jealous of your honor ; and you on my left, because I know you very much concerned for the reputation of others ; for which reason I expect great exactness and impartiality in your verdicts and judgments.

"I must in the next place address myself to you, gentlemen of the council: you all know, that I have not chosen you for your knowledge in the litigious parts of the law, but because you have all of you formerly fought duels, of which I have reason to think you have repented, as being now settled in the peaceable state of benchers. My advice to you is, only, that in your pleadings you are short and expressive; to which end you are to banish out of your discourses all synonymous terms, and unnecessary multiplications of verbs and nouns. I do moreover forbid you the use of the words *also* and *likewise;* and must further declare, that if I catch any one among you, upon any pretense whatsoever, using the particle *or*, I shall instantly order him to be stripped of his gown, and thrown over the bar."

TRIAL OF PUNCTILIOS.

The proceedings of the Court of Honor, held in Sheer Lane, on Monday, the 20th of November, 1710, before Isaac Bickerstaffe, Esq., Censor of Great Britain.

PETER PLUMB, of London, merchant, was indicted by the Honorable Mr. Thomas Gules, of Gule Hall, in the county of Salop, for that the said Peter Plumb did in Lombard Street, London, between the hours of two and three in the afternoon, meet the said Mr. Thomas Gules, and after a short salutation, put on his hat, value five pence, while the Honorable Mr. Gules stood bare-headed for the space of two seconds. It was further urged against the criminal, that, during his discourse with the prosecutor, he feloniously stole the wall of him, having clapped his back against it in such a manner that it was impossible for Mr. Gules to recover it again at his taking leave of him. The prosecutor alleged, that he was the cadet of a very ancient family, and that, according to the principles of all the younger brothers of the said family, he had never sullied himself with business, but had chosen rather to starve like a man of honor, than do anything beneath his quality. He produced several witnesses, that he had never employed himself beyond the twisting of a whip, or the making of a pair of nutcrackers, in which he only worked for his diversion, in order to make a present now and then to his friends. The prisoner being asked what he could say for himself, cast several

216

reflections upon the Honorable Mr. Gules: as, that he was not worth a groat; that nobody in the city would trust him for a half-penny; that he owed him money which he had promised to pay him several times, but never kept his word: and in short, that he was an idle, beggarly fellow, and of no use to the public. This sort of language was very severely reprimanded by the Censor, who told the criminal, that he spoke in contempt of the court, and that he should be proceeded against for contumacy, if he did not change his style. The prisoner, therefore, desired to be heard by his counsel, who urged in his defense, "That he put on his hat through ignorance, and took the wall by accident." They likewise produced several witnesses, that he made several motions with his hat in his hand, which are generally understood as an invitation to the person we talk with to be covered; and that the gentleman not taking the hint, he was forced to put on his hat, as being troubled with a cold. There was likewise an Irishman who deposed, that he had heard him cough three and twenty times that morning. And as for the wall, it was alleged, that he had taken it inadvertently, to save himself from a shower of rain which was then falling. The Censor having consulted the men of honor who sat at his right hand on the bench, found they were of opinion, that the defense made by the prisoner's counsel did rather aggravate than extenuate his crime; that the motions and intimations of the hat were a token of superiority in conversation, and therefore not to be used by the criminal to a man of the prosecutor's quality, who was likewise vested with a double title to the wall at the time of their conversation, both as it was the upper hand, and as it was a shelter from the weather. The evidence being very full and clear, the jury, without going out of court, declared their opinion unanimously by the mouth of their foreman, that the prosecutor was bound in honor to make the sun shine through the criminal, or, as they afterwards explained themselves, to whip him through the lungs.

The Censor knitting his brows into a frown, and looking very sternly upon the jury, after a little pause, gave them to know, that this court was erected for the finding out of penalties suitable to offenses, and to restrain the outrages of private justice ; and that he expected they should moderate their verdict.   The jury, therefore, retired, and being willing to comply with the advices of the Censor, after an hour's consultation, declared their opinion as follows :

" That in consideration this was Peter Plumb's first offense, and that there did not appear any 'malice prepense' in it, as also that he lived in good reputation among his neighbors, and that his taking the wall was only *se defendendo*, the prosecutor should let him escape with life, and content himself with the slitting of his nose, and the cutting off both his ears." Mr. Bickerstaffe, smiling upon the court, told them, that he thought the punishment, even under its present mitigation, too severe ; and that such penalties might be of ill consequence in a trading nation.   He therefore pronounced sentence against the criminal in the following manner : " That his hat, which was the instrument of offense, should be forfeited to the court ; that the criminal should go to the warehouse from whence he came, and thence, as occasion should require, proceed to the Exchange, or Garraway's coffee-house, in what manner he pleased ; but that neither he, nor any of the family of the Plumbs, should hereafter appear in the streets of London out of their coaches, that so the foot-way might be left open and undisturbed for their betters."

Dathan, a peddling Jew, and T. R—, a Welshman, were indicted by the keeper of an alehouse in Westminster, for breaking the peace and two earthen mugs, in a dispute about the antiquity of their families, to the great detriment of the house, and disturbance of the whole neighborhood. Dathan said for himself, that he was provoked to it by the Welshman, who pretended that the Welsh were an ancienter people than the Jews; "Whereas, (says he,) I can show by this genealogy in my hand, that I am the son of Mesheck, that was the son of Naboth, that was the son of Shalem, that was the son of—" The Welshman here interrupted him, and told him, "That he could produce shennalogy as well as himself; for that he was John ap Rice, ap Shenkin, ap Shones." He then turned himself to the Censor, and told him in the same broken accent, and with much warmth, "That the Jew would needs uphold, that King Cadwallader was younger than Issachar." Mr. Bickerstaffe seemed very much inclined to give sentence against Dathan, as being a Jew, but finding reasons, by some expressions which the Welshman let fall in asserting the antiquity of his family, to suspect that the said Welshman was a Præ-Adamite, he suffered the jury to go out, without any previous admonition. After some time they returned, and gave their verdict, that it appearing the persons at the bar did neither of them wear a sword, and that consequently they had no right to quarrel upon a point of honor; to prevent such frivolous appeals for the future, they should both of them be tossed in the same blanket, and there adjust the superiority as they could agree it between themselves. The Censor confirmed the verdict.

Richard Newman was indicted by Major Punto, for having used the words "Perhaps it may be so," in a dispute with the said major. The major urged, that the word "Perhaps" was questioning his veracity, and that it was an indirect manner of giving him the lie. Richard Newman had nothing more to say for himself, than that he intended no such thing, and threw himself upon the mercy of the court. The jury brought in their verdict special.

Mr. Bickerstaffe stood up, and after having cast his eyes over the whole assembly, hemmed thrice. He then acquainted them, that he had laid down a rule to himself, which he was resolved never to depart from, and which, as he conceived, would very much conduce to the shortening the business of the court; I mean, says he, never to allow of the lie being given by construction, implication, or induction, but by the sole use of the word itself. He then proceeded to show the great mischiefs that had arisen to the English nation from that pernicious monosyllable ; that it had bred the most fatal quarrels between the dearest friends ; that it had frequently thinned the guards, and made great havoc in the army ; that it had sometimes weakened the city trained-bands; and, in a word, had destroyed many of the bravest men in the isle of Great Britain. For the prevention of which evils for the future, he instructed the jury to "present" the word itself as a nuisance in the English tongue ; and further promised them, that he would upon such their presentment, publish an edict of the court for the entire banishment and exclusion of it out of the discourses and conversation of all civil societies.

CASES OF FALSE DELICACY.

A Continuation of the Journal of the Court of Honor, held in Sheer Lane, on Monday, the 27th of November, before Isaac Bickerstaffe, Esq., Censor of Great Britain.

ELIZABETH MAKEBATE, of the parish of St. Catherine's, spinster, was indicted for surreptitiously taking away the hassoc from under the Lady Grave-Airs, between the hours of four and five, on Sunday the 26th of November. The prosecutor deposed, that as she stood up to make a curtsey to a person of quality in a neighboring pew, the criminal conveyed away the hassoc by stealth, insomuch that the prosecutor was obliged to sit all the whole while she was at church, or to say her prayers in a posture that did not become a woman of her quality. The prisoner pleaded inadvertency; and the jury were going to bring it in chance-medley, had not several witnesses been produced against the said Elizabeth Makebate, that she was an old offender, and a woman of a bad reputation. It appeared in particular, that on the Sunday before she had detracted from a new petticoat of Mrs. Mary Doelittle, having said in the hearing of several credible witnesses, that the said petticoat was scowered, to the great grief and detriment of the said Mary Doelittle. There were likewise many evidences produced against the criminal, that though she never failed to come to church on Sunday, she was a most notorious sabbath-breaker, and that she spent her whole time, during divine service, in disparaging other people's clothes, and whispering to those who sat next her. Upon the whole, she was found guilty of the indictment, and received sentence to ask pardon of the prosecutor upon her bare knees, without either cushion or hassoc under her, in the face of the court.

N. B. As soon as the sentence was executed on the criminal, which was done in open court with the utmost severity, the first lady of the bench on Mr. Bickerstaffe's right hand stood up, and made a motion to the court, that whereas it was impossible for women of fashion to dress themselves before the church was half done, and whereas many confusions and inconveniences did arise thereupon, it might be lawful for them to send a footman, in order to keep their places, as was usual in other polite and well-regulated assemblies. The motion was ordered to be entered in the books, and considered at a more convenient time.

Charles Cambrick, Linen-draper, in the city of Westminster, was indicted for speaking obscenely to the Lady Penelope Touchwood. It appeared, that the prosecutor and her woman going in a stage-coach from London to Brentford, where they were to be met by the lady's own chariot, the criminal and another of his acquaintance traveled with them in the same coach, at which time the prisoner talked bawdy for the space of three miles and a half. The prosecutor alleged, " That over against the Old Fox at Knightsbridge, he mentioned the word linen; that at the further end of Kensington he made use of the term smock; and that before he came to Hammersmith, he talked almost a quarter of an hour upon wedding-shifts." The prose-

cutor's woman confirmed what her lady had said, and
added further, " that she had never seen her lady in so
great confusion, and in such a taking, as she was during the whole discourse of the criminal." The prisoner
had little to say for himself, but that he talked only in
his own trade, and meant no hurt by what he said.
The jury, however, found him guilty, and represented
by their forewoman, that such discourses were apt to
sully the imagination, and that by a concatenation of
ideas, the word linen implied many things that were
not proper to be stirred up in the mind of a woman
who was of the prosecutor's quality, and therefore
gave it as their verdict, that the linen-draper should lose
his tongue. Mr. Bickerstaffe said, " He thought the
prosecutor's ears were as much to blame as the prisoner's tongue, and therefore gave sentence as follows :
That they should both be placed over against one another in the midst of the court, there to remain for the
space of one quarter of an hour, during which time,
the linen-draper was to be gagged, and the lady to
hold her hands close upon both her ears ;" which was
executed accordingly.

Edward Callicoat was indicted as an accomplice to
Charles Cambrick, for that he the said Edward Callicoat did, by his silence and his smiles, seem to approve
and abet the said Charles Cambrick in everything he
said. It appeared, that the prisoner was foreman of
the shop to the aforesaid Charles Cambrick, and by
his post obliged to smile at everything that the other
should be pleased to say : upon which he was acquitted.

Josias Shallow was indicted in the name of Dame
Winifred, sole relict of Richard Dainty, Esq., for having said several times in company, and in the hearing

of several persons there present, that he was extremely
obliged to the widow Dainty, and that he should never
be able sufficiently to express his gratitude. The prosecutor urged, that this might blast her reputation,
and that it was in effect a boasting of favors which he
had never received. The prisoner seemed to be much
astonished at the construction which was put upon his
words, and said, "That he meant nothing by them,
but that the widow had befriended him in a lease, and
was very kind to his younger sister." The jury finding him a little weak in his understanding, without
going out of the court, brought in their verdict, *igno-
ramus.*

Ursula Goodenough was accused by the Lady Betty
Wou'dbe, for having said, that she the Lady Betty
Wou'dbe was painted. The prisoner brought several
persons of good credit to witness to her reputation, and
proved by undeniable evidences, that she was never at
the place where the words were said to have been
uttered. The Censor observing the behavior of the
prosecutor, found reason to believe that she had indicted the prisoner for no other reason but to make
her complexion be taken notice of, which indeed was
very fresh and beautiful; he therefore asked the
offender with a very stern voice, how she could presume to spread so groundless a report? And whether
she saw any colors in the Lady Wou'dbe's face that
could procure credit to such a falsehood? "Do you
see (says he) any lilies or roses in her cheeks, any
bloom, any probability?"—The prosecutor, not able
to bear such language any longer, told him, that he
talked like a blind old fool, and that she was ashamed
to have entertained any opinion of his wisdom: but
she was put to silence, and sentenced to wear her

mask for five months, and not presume to show her face till the town should be empty.

Benjamin Buzzard, Esq., was indicted for having told the Lady Everbloom at a public ball, that she looked very well for a woman of her years. The prisoner not denying the fact, and persisting before the court that he looked upon it as a compliment, the jury brought him in *non compos mentis*.

TRIAL OF LADIES' QUARRELS.

TIMOTHY TREATALL, Gent., was indicted by several
ladies of his sister's acquaintance for a very rude
affront offered to them at an entertainment, to which
he had invited them on Tuesday the 7th of November
last past, between the hours of eight and nine in the
evening. The indictment set forth that the said Mr.
Treatall, upon the serving up of the supper, desired
the ladies to take their places according to their different age and seniority, for that it was the way always
at his table to pay respect to years. The indictment added, that this produced an unspeakable confusion in the company; for that the ladies, who before
had pressed together for a place at the upper end of
the table, immediately crowded with the same disorder
towards the end that was quite opposite; that Mrs.
Frontly had the insolence to clap herself down at the
very lowest place of the table; that the widow Part-
lett seated herself on the right hand of Mrs. Frontly,
alleging for her excuse, that no ceremony was to be
used at a round table; that Mrs. Fidget and Mrs.
Fescue disputed above half an hour for the same chair,
and that the latter would not give up the cause till it
was decided by the parish register, which happened to
be kept hard by. The indictment further said, that
the rest of the company who sat down did it with a
reserve to their right, which they were at liberty to
assert on another occasion; and that Mrs. Mary Pippe,

an old maid, was placed by the unanimous vote of the whole company at the upper end of the table, from whence she had the confusion to behold several mothers of families among her inferiors. The criminal alleged in his defense, that what he had done was to raise mirth and avoid ceremony, and that the ladies did not complain of his rudeness till the next morning, having eaten up what he had provided for them with great readiness and alacrity. The Censor, frowning upon him, told him, that he ought not to discover so much levity in matters of a serious nature, and (upon the jury's bringing him in guilty) sentenced him to treat the whole assembly of ladies over again, and to take care that he did it with the decorum which was due to persons of their quality.

Rebecca Shapely, spinster, was indicted by Mrs. Sarah Smack, for speaking many words reflecting upon her reputation, and the heels of her silk slippers, which the prisoner had maliciously suggested to be two inches higher than they really were. The prosecutor urged, as an aggravation of her guilt, that the prisoner was herself guilty of the same kind of forgery which she had laid to the prosecutor's charge, for that she the said Rebecca Shapely did always wear a pair of steel bodice, and a false rump. The Censor ordered the slippers to be produced in open court, where the heels were adjudged to be of the statutable size. He then ordered the grand jury to search the criminal, who, after some time spent therein, acquitted her of the bodice, but found her guilty of the rump ; upon which she received sentence as is usual in such cases.

William Trippitt, Esq., of the Middle Temple, brought his action against the Lady Elizabeth Prudely, for having refused him her hand as he offered to lead

her to her coach from the opera. The plaintiff set
forth, that he had entered himself into the list of those
volunteers who officiate every night behind the boxes
as gentlemen-ushers of the play-house: that he had
been at a considerable charge in white gloves, peri-
wigs, and snuff-boxes, in order to qualify himself for
that employment, and in hopes of making his fortune
by it. The counsel for the defendant replied, that the
plaintiff had given out that he was within a month of
wedding their client, and that she had refused her
hand to him in ceremony lest he should interpret it as
a promise that she would give it him in marriage. As
soon as their pleadings on both sides were finished, the
Censor ordered the plaintiff to be cashiered from his
office of gentleman-usher to the play-house, since it was
too plain that he had undertaken it with an ill design;
and at the time ordered the defendant either to marry
the said plaintiff, or to pay him half-a-crown for the
new pair of gloves and coach-hire that he was at the
expense of in her service.

The Lady Townly brought an action of debt against
Mrs. Flambeau, for that Mrs. Flambeau had not been
to see the said Lady Townly, and wish her joy, since
her marriage with Sir Ralph, notwithstanding she the
said Lady Townly had paid Mrs. Flambeau a visit
upon her first coming to town. It was urged in the
behalf of the defendant, that the plaintiff had never
given her any regular notice of her being in town;
that the visit she alleged had been made on a Monday,
which she knew was a day on which Mrs. Flambeau
was always abroad, having set aside that only day in
the week to mind the affairs of her family; that the
servant who inquired whether she was at home, did
not give the visiting knock; that it was not between

the hours of five and eight in the evening; that there
were no candles lighted up; that it was not on Mrs.
Flambeau's day; and, in short, that there was not one
of the essential points observed that constitute a visit.
She further proved by her porter's book, which was
produced in court, that she had paid the Lady Townly
a visit on the twenty-fourth day of March, just before
her leaving the town, in the year 1709–10, for which
she was still creditor to the said Lady Townly.   To
this the plaintiff only replied, that she was now only
under covert, and not liable to any debts contracted
when she was a single woman.   Mr. Bickerstaffe finding the cause to be very intricate, and that several
points of honor were likely to arise in it, he deferred
giving judgment upon it till the next session day, at
which time he ordered the ladies on his left hand to
present to the court a table of all the laws relating to
visits.

Winifred Leer brought her action against Richard
Sly, for having broken a marriage contract, and wedded another woman, after he had engaged himself to
marry the said Winifred Leer.   She alleged, that he
had ogled her twice at an opera, thrice in St. James's
church, and once at Powel's puppet-show, at which
time he promised her marriage by a side-glance, as her
friend could testify that sat by her.   Mr. Bickerstaffe
finding that the defendant had made no further overture of love or marriage, but by looks and ocular en-
gagement; yet at the same time considering how very
apt such impudent seducers are to lead the ladies'
hearts astray, ordered the criminal to stand upon the
stage in the Haymarket, between each act of the next
opera, there to be exposed to public view as a false
ogler.

Upon the rising of the court, Mr. Bickerstaffe having taken one of these counterfeits in the very fact, as he was ogling a lady of the grand jury, ordered him to be seized, and prosecuted upon the statute of ogling. He likewise directed the clerk of the court to draw up an edict against these common cheats, that make women believe they are distracted for them by staring them out of countenance, and often blast a lady's reputation whom they never spoke to, by saucy looks and distant familiarities.

TRIAL OF FALSE AFFRONTS.

As soon as the court was sat, the ladies of the bench presented, according to order, a table of all the laws now in force, relating to visits and visiting days, methodically digested under their respective heads, which the Censor ordered to be laid upon the table, and afterwards proceeded upon the business of the day.

Henry Heedless, Esq., was indicted by Colonel Touchy, of her Majesty's trained bands, upon an action of assault and battery; for that he the said Mr. Heedless, having espied a feather upon the shoulder of the said colonel, struck it off gently with the end of a walking staff, value three-pence. It appeared, that the prosecutor did not think himself injured till a few days after the aforesaid blow was given him; but that having ruminated with himself for several days, and conferred upon it with other officers of the militia, he concluded, that he had in effect been cudgeled by Mr. Heedless, and that he ought to resent it accordingly. The counsel for the prosecutor alleged, that the shoulder was the tenderest part in a man of honor; that it had a natural antipathy to a stick, and that every touch of it, with anything made in the fashion of a cane, was to be interpreted as a wound in that part, and a violation of the person's honor who received it. Mr. Heedless replied, that what he had done was out of kindness to the prosecutor, as not thinking it proper for him to appear at the head of the trained bands with a feather upon his shoulder; and further added, that the stick he made use of on this occasion was so very small, that the prosecutor could not have felt it, had he broken it on his shoulders. The Censor hereupon directed the jury to examine into the nature of the staff, for that a great deal would depend upon that particular. Upon which he explained to them the different degrees of offense that might be given by the touch of crab-tree from that of cane, and by the touch of cane from that of a plain hazel stick. The jury, after a short perusal of the staff, declared their opinion by the mouth of their foreman, that the substance of the staff was British oak. The Censor then observing that there was some dust on the skirts of the criminal's coat, ordered the prosecutor to beat it off with his aforesaid oaken plant; "And thus, (said the Censor,) I shall decide this cause by the law of retaliation: if Mr. Heedless did the colonel a good office, the colonel will, by this means, return it in kind; but if Mr. Heedless should at any time boast that he had cudgeled the colonel, or laid his staff over his shoulders, the colonel might boast in his turn, that he has brushed Mr. Heedless's jacket, or (to use the phrase of an ingenious author) that he has rubbed him down with an oaken towel."

Benjamin Busy, of London, merchant, was indicted by Jasper Tattle, Esq., for having pulled out his watch, and looked upon it thrice, while the said Esquire Tattle was giving him an account of the funeral of the said Esquire Tattle's first wife. The prisoner alleged in his defense, that he was going to buy stocks at the time when he met the prosecutor; and that, during the story of the prosecutor, the said stocks rose above two per cent., to the great detriment of the prisoner. The prisoner further brought several witnesses, that the

said Jasper Tattle, Esq., was a most notorious story-
teller; that before he met the prisoner, he had hindered
one of the prisoner's acquaintance from the pursuit of
his lawful business, with the account of his second
marriage; and that he had detained another by the
button of his coat that very morning, till he had heard
several witty sayings and contrivances of the prosecutor's eldest son, who was a boy of about five years of
age.   Upon the whole matter, Mr. Bickerstaffe dismissed the accusation as frivolous, and sentenced the
prosecutor to pay damages to the prisoner for what the
prisoner had lost by giving him so long and patient an
hearing. He further reprimanded the prosecutor very
severely, and told him, that if he proceeded in his usual
manner to interrupt the business of mankind, he would
set a fine upon him for every quarter of an hour's impertinence, and regulate the said fine according as the
time of the person so injured should appear to be more
or less precious.

Sir Paul Swash, Kt., was indicted by Peter Double,
Gent., for not returning the bow which he received of
the said Peter Double, on Wednesday the sixth instant,
at the play-house in the Haymarket. The prisoner
denied the receipt of any such bow, and alleged in his
defense, that the prosecutor would oftentimes look full
in his face, but that when he bowed to the said prosecutor, he would take no notice of it, or bow to somebody else that sat quite on the other side of him. He
likewise alleged, that several ladies had complained of
the prosecutor, who, after ogling them a quarter of an
hour, upon their making a curtsey to him, would not
return the civility of a bow. The Censor observing
several glances of the prosecutor's eye, and perceiving,
that when he talked to the court he looked upon the

jury, found reason to suspect that there was a wrong cast in his sight, which upon examination proved true. The Censor therefore ordered the prisoner (that he might not produce any more confusions in public assemblies) never to bow to anybody whom he did not at the same time call to by his name.

Oliver Bluff, and Benjamin Browbeat, were indicted for going to fight a duel since the erection of the Court of Honor. It appeared, that they were both taken up in the street as they passed by the court, in their way to the fields behind Montague House. The criminals would answer nothing for themselves, but that they were going to execute a challenge which had been made above a week before the Court of Honor was erected. The Censor finding some reasons to suspect, (by the sturdiness of their behavior,) that they were not so very brave as they would have the court believe them, ordered them both to be searched by the grand jury, who found a breast-plate upon the one, and two quires of paper upon the other. The breast-plate was immediately ordered to be hung upon a peg over Mr. Bickerstaffe's tribunal, and the paper to be laid upon the table for the use of his clerk. He then ordered the criminals to button up their bosoms, and, if they pleased, proceed to their duel. Upon which they both went very quietly out of the court, and retired to their respective lodgings.

COUNTRY HUMORS.

THE TORY FOXHUNTER.

For the honor of his Majesty, and the safety of his government, we cannot but observe, that those who have appeared the greatest enemies to both, are of that rank of men, who are commonly distinguished by the title of Fox-hunters. As several of these have had no part of their education in cities, camps, or courts, it is doubtful whether they are of greater ornament or use to the nation in which they live. It would be an everlasting reproach to politics, should such men be able to overturn an establishment which has been formed by the wisest laws, and is supported by the ablest heads. The wrong notions and prejudices which cleave to many of these country gentlemen, who have always lived out of the way of being better informed, are not easy to be conceived by a person who has never conversed with them.

That I may give my readers an image of these rural statesmen, I shall, without further preface, set down an account of a discourse I chanced to have with one of them some time ago. I was traveling towards one of the remote parts of England, when about three o'clock in the afternoon, seeing a country gentleman trotting before me with a spaniel by his horse's side, I made up to him. Our conversation opened, as usual, upon the weather; in which we were very unanimous; having both agreed that it was too dry for the season of the year. My fellow-traveler, upon this, observed to me, that there had been no good weather since the Revolution. I was a little startled at so extraordinary a remark, but would not interrupt him till he proceeded to tell me of the fine weather they used to have in King Charles the Second's reign. I only answered that I did not see how the badness of the weather could be the king's fault; and, without waiting for his reply, asked him whose house it was we saw upon the rising ground at a little distance from us. He told me it belonged to an old fanatical cur, Mr. Such-a-one. "You must have heard of him," says he, "he's one of the Rump." I knew the gentle-man's character upon hearing his name, but assured him, that to my knowledge he was a good churchman: "Ay!" says he, with a kind of surprise, "We were told in the country, that he spoke twice, in the queen's time, against taking off the duties upon French claret." This naturally led us in the proceedings of late par-liaments, upon which occasion he affirmed roundly, that there had not been one good law passed since King William's accession to the throne, except the act for preserving the game. I had a mind to see him out, and therefore did not care for contradicting him. "Is it not hard," says he, "that honest gentlemen should be taken into custody of messengers to prevent them from acting according to their consciences? But," says he, "what can we expect when a parcel of factious sons of whores——" He was going on in great passion, but chanced to miss his dog, who was amusing himself about a bush, that grew at some distance behind us. We stood still till he had whistled him up; when he fell into a long panegyric upon his spaniel, who seemed, indeed, excellent in his kind: but I found the most remarkable adventure of his life was, that he had once like to have worried a dissenting teacher. The master could hardly sit on his horse for laughing all the while he was giving me the particulars of his story, which I found had mightily endeared his dog to him, and as he himself told me, had made him a great favorite among all the honest gentlemen of the country. We were at length diverted from this piece of mirth by a post-boy, who winding his horn at us, my companion gave him two or three curses, and left the way clear for him. "I fancy," said I, "that post brings news from Scotland. I shall long to see the next Gazette." " Sir," says he, " I make it a rule never to believe any of your printed news. We never see, sir, how things go, except now and then in Dyer's Letter, and I read that more for the style than the news. The man has a clever pen, it must be owned. But is it not strange that we should be making war upon Church of England men with Dutch and Swiss soldiers, men of antimonarchical principles? these foreigners will never be loved in England, sir; they have not that wit and good-breeding that we have." I must confess I did not expect to hear my new acquaintance value himself upon these qualifications, but finding him such a critic upon foreigners, I asked him if he had ever traveled; he told me, he did not know what traveling was good for, but to teach a man to ride the great horse, to jabber French, and to talk against passive obedience: to which he added, that he scarce ever knew a traveler in his life who had not forsook his principles, and lost his hunting-seat. "For my part," says he, "I and my father before me have always been for passive obedience, and shall be always for opposing a prince who makes use of ministers that are of another opinion.

But where do you intend to inn to-night? (for we were now come in sight of the next town ;) I can help you to a very good landlord if you will go along with me. He is a lusty, jolly fellow, that lives well, at least three yards in the girt, and the best Church of England man upon the road." I had a curiosity to see this high-church inn-keeper, as well as to enjoy more of the conversation of my fellow-traveler, and therefore readily consented to set our horses together for that night. As we rode side by side through the town, I was let into the characters of all the principal inhabitants whom we met in our way. One was a dog, another a whelp, another a cur, and another the son of a bitch, under which several denominations were comprehended all that voted on the Whig side, in the last election of burgesses. As for those of his own party, he distinguished them by a nod of his head, and asking them how they did by their Christian names. Upon our arrival at the inn, my companion fetched out the jolly landlord, who knew him by his whistle. Many endearments and private whispers passed between them; though it was easy to see by the landlord's scratching his head that things did not go to their wishes. The landlord had swelled his body to a prodigious size, and worked up his complexion to a standing crimson by his zeal for the prosperity of the church, which he expressed every hour of the day, as his customers dropt in, by repeated bumpers. He had not time to go to church himself, but, as my friend told me in my ear, had headed a mob at the pulling down of two or three meeting-houses. While supper was preparing, he enlarged upon the happiness of the neighboring shire; " For," says he, " there is scarce a Presbyterian in the whole county, except the bishop." In short, I found by his discourse that he had learned a great deal of politics, but not one word of religion, from the parson of his parish; and, indeed, that he had scarce any other notion of religion, but that it consisted in hating Presbyterians. I had a remarkable instance of his notions in this particular. Upon seeing a poor decrepit old woman pass under the window where we sat, he desired me to take notice of her; and afterwards informed me, that she was generally reputed a witch by the country people, but that, for his part, he was apt to believe she was a Presbyterian.

Supper was no sooner served in, than he took occasion from a shoulder of mutton that lay before us, to cry up the plenty of England, which would be the happiest country in the world, provided we would live within ourselves. Upon which, he expatiated on the inconveniences of trade, that carried from us the commodities of our country, and made a parcel of upstarts as rich as men of the most ancient families of England. He then declared frankly, that he had always been against all treaties and alliances with foreigners: "Our wooden walls," says he, "are our security, and we may bid defiance to the whole world, especially if they should attack us when the militia is out." I ventured to reply, that I had as great an opinion of the English fleet as he had; but I could not see how they could be paid, and manned, and fitted out, unless we encouraged trade and navigation. He replied, with some vehemence, that he would undertake to prove trade would be the ruin of the English nation. I would fain have put him upon it; but he contented himself with affirming it more eagerly, to which he added two or three curses upon the London mer-

16

chants, not forgetting the directors of the bank. After supper he asked me if I was an admirer of punch; and immediately called for a sneaker. I took this occasion to insinuate the advantages of trade, by observing to him, that water was the only native of England that could be made use of on this occasion: but that the lemons, the brandy, the sugar, and the nutmeg, were all foreigners. This put him into some confusion; but the landlord, who overheard me, brought him off, by affirming, that for constant use, there was no liquor like a cup of English water, provided it had malt enough in it. My squire laughed heartily at the conceit, and made the landlord sit down with us. We sat pretty late over our punch; and, amidst a great deal of improving discourse, drank the healths of several persons in the country, whom I had never heard of, that, they both assured me, were the ablest statesmen in the nation; and of some Londoners, whom they extolled to the skies for their wit, and who, I knew, passed in town for silly fellows. It being now midnight, and my friend perceiving by his almanack that the moon was up, he called for his horses, and took a sudden resolution to go to his house, which was at three miles' distance from the town, after having bethought himself that he never slept well out of his own bed. He shook me very heartily by the hand at parting, and discovered a great air of satisfaction in his looks, that he had met with an opportunity of showing his parts, and left me a much wiser man than he found me.

THE FOXHUNTER AT A MASQUERADE.

As I was last Friday taking a walk in the park, I saw a country gentleman at the side of Rosamond's pond, pulling a handful of oats out of his pocket, and with a great deal of pleasure, gathering the ducks about him. Upon my coming up to him, who should it be but my friend the foxhunter, whom I gave some account of in my former paper! I immediately joined him, and partook of his diversion, till he had not an oat left in his pocket. We then made the tour of the park together, when, after having entertained me with the description of a decoy-pond that lay near his seat in the country, and of a meeting-house that was going to be rebuilt in a neighboring market-town, he gave me an account of some very odd adventures which he had met with that morning; and which I shall lay together in a short and faithful history, as well as my memory will give me leave.

My friend, who has a natural aversion to London, would never have come up, had not he been subpœnaed to it, as he told me, in order to give his testimony for one of the rebels, whom he knew to be a very fair sportsman. Having traveled all night to avoid the inconveniences of dust and heat, he arrived with his guide, a little after break of day, at Charing-cross ; where, to his great surprise, he saw a running footman carried in a chair, followed by a waterman in the same kind of vehicle. He was wondering at the extravagance of their masters, that furnished them with such dresses and accommodations, when, on a sudden, he beheld a chimney-sweeper conveyed after the same manner, with three footmen running before him. During his progress through the Strand, he met with several other figures no less wonderful and surprising. Seeing a great many in rich morning-gowns, he was amazed to find that persons of quality were up so early; and was no less astonished to see many lawyers in their bar-gowns, when he knew by his almanack the term was ended. As he was extremely puzzled and confounded in himself what all this should mean, a hackney-coach chancing to pass by him, four batts popped out their heads all at once, which very much frighted both him and his horse. My friend, who always takes care to cure his horse of such starting fits, spurred him up to the very side of the coach, to the no small diversion of the batts; who, seeing him with his long whip, horse-hair periwig, jockey belt, and coat without sleeves, fancied him to be one of the masqueraders on horseback, and received him with a loud peal of laughter. His mind being full of idle stories, which are spread up and down the nation by the disaffected, he immediately concluded that all the persons he saw in these strange habits were foreigners, and conceived a great indignation against them, for pretending to laugh at an English country-gentleman. But he soon recovered out of his error, by hearing the voices of several of them, and particularly of a shepherdess quarreling with her coachman, and threatening to break his bones, in very intelligible English, though with a masculine tone. His astonishment still increased upon him, to see a continued procession of harlequins, scaramouches, punchinellos, and a thousand other merry dresses, by which people of quality distinguish their wit from that of the vulgar.

Being now advanced as far as Somerset House, and observing it to be the great hive whence these chimeras issued forth from time to time, my friend took his station among a cluster of mob, who were making themselves merry with their betters. The first that came out was a very venerable matron, with a nose and chin that were within a very little of touching one another. My friend, at the first view fancying her to be an old woman of quality, out of his good breeding put off his hat to her, when the person, pulling off her mask, to his great surprise, appeared a smock-faced young fellow. His attention was soon taken off from this object, and turned to another that had very hollow eyes and a wrinkled face, which flourished in all the bloom of fifteen. The whiteness of the lily was blended in it with the blush of the rose. He mistook it for a very whimsical kind of mask; but, upon a nearer view, he found that she held her vizard in her hand, and that what he saw was only her natural countenance, touched up with the usual improvements of an aged coquette.

The next who showed herself was a female quaker, so very pretty, that he could not forbear licking his lips, and saying to the mob about him, " It is ten thousand pities she is not a church-woman." The quaker was followed by half a dozen nuns, who filed off one after another up Catherine Street, to their respective convents in Drury Lane.

The squire, observing the preciseness of their dress, began now to imagine, after all, that this was a nest of sectaries; for he had often heard that the town was full of them. He was confirmed in this opinion upon seeing a conjurer, whom he guessed to be the holder-forth. However, to satisfy himself, he asked a porter, who stood next him, what religion these people were of? The porter replied, "They are of no religion; it is a masquerade." "Upon that, (says my friend,) I began to smoke that they were a parcel of mummers;" and being himself one of the quorum in his own county, could not but wonder that none of the Middlesex justices took care to lay some of them by the heels. He was the more provoked in the spirit of magistracy, upon discovering two very unseemly objects: the first was a judge, who rapped out a great oath at his footman; and the other a big-bellied woman, who, upon taking a leap into the coach, miscarried of a cushion. What still gave him greater offense, was a drunken bishop, who reeled from one side of the court to the other, and was very sweet upon an Indian queen. But his worship, in the midst of his austerity, was mollified at the sight of a very lovely milk-maid, whom he began to regard with an eye of mercy, and conceived a particular affection for her, until he found, to his great amazement, that the standers-by suspected her to be a duchess.

I must not conclude this narrative, without mentioning one disaster which happened to my friend on this occasion. Having for his better convenience dis-mounted, and mixed among the crowd, he found, upon his arrival at the inn, that he had lost his purse and his almanack. And though it is no wonder such a trick should be played him by some of the curious spectators, he cannot beat it out of his head, but that it was a cardinal who picked his pocket, and that this cardinal was a Presbyterian in disguise.

CONVERSION OF THE FOXHUNTER.

I QUESTION not but most of my readers will be very well pleased to hear, that my friend the foxhunter, of whose arrival in town I gave notice in my last paper, is become a convert to the present establishment, and a good subject to King George. The motives to his conversion shall be the subject of this paper, as they may be of use to other persons who labor under those prejudices and prepossessions, which hung so long upon the mind of my worthy friend. These I had an opportunity of learning the other day, when, at his request, we took a ramble together, to see the curiosities of this great town.

The first circumstance, as he ingenuously confessed to me, (while we were in the coach together,) which helped to disabuse him, was seeing King Charles I. on horseback, at Charing Cross; for he was sure that prince could never have kept his seat there, had the stories been true he had heard in the country, that forty-one was come about again.

He owned to me that he looked with horror on the new church that is half built in the Strand, as taking it, at first sight, to be half demolished : but upon inquiring of the workmen, was agreeably surprised to find, that instead of pulling it down, they were building it up ; and that fifty more were raising in other parts of the town.

To these I must add a third circumstance, which I

find had no small share in my friend's conversion. Since his coming to town, he chanced to look into the church of St. Paul, about the middle of sermon-time, where, having first examined the dome, to see if it stood safe, (for the screw-plot still ran in his head,) he observed, that the lord mayor, aldermen, and city sword, were a part of the congregation. This sight had the more weight with him, as, by good luck, not above two of that venerable body were fallen asleep.

This discourse held us till we came to the Tower; for our first visit was to the lions. My friend, who had a great deal of talk with their keeper, inquired very much after their health, and whether none of them had fallen sick upon the taking of Perth, and the flight of the Pretender? and hearing they were never better in their lives, I found he was extremely startled: for he had learned from his cradle, that the lions in the Tower were the best judges of the title of our British kings, and always sympathized with our sovereigns.

After having here satiated our curiosity, we repaired to the Monument, where my fellow-traveler, being a well-breathed man, mounted the ascent with much speed and activity. I was forced to halt so often in this perpendicular march, that, upon my joining him on the top of the pillar, I found he had counted all the steeples and towers which were discernible from this advantageous situation, and was endeavoring to compute the number of acres they stood upon. We were both of us very well pleased with this part of the prospect; but I found he cast an evil eye upon several warehouses, and other buildings, that looked like barns, and seemed capable of receiving great multitudes of people. His heart misgave him that these were so many meeting-houses, but, upon communicating his suspicions to me, I soon made him easy in this particular.

We then turned our eyes upon the river, which gave me an occasion to inspire him with some favorable thoughts of trade and merchandise, that had filled the Thames with such crowds of ships, and covered the shore with such swarms of people.

We descended very leisurely, my friend being careful to count the steps, which he registered in a blank leaf of his new almanack. Upon our coming to the bottom, observing an English inscription upon the basis, he read it over several times, and told me he could scarce believe his own eyes, for that he had often heard from an old attorney, who lived near him in the country, that it was the Presbyterians who burned down the city; whereas, says he, this pillar positively affirms in so many words, that "the burning of this ancient city was begun and carried on by the treachery and malice of the Popish faction, in order to the carrying on their horrid plot for extirpating the Protestant religion and old English liberty, and introducing Popery and slavery." This account, which he looked upon to be more authentic than if it had been in print, I found, made a very great impression upon him.

We now took coach again, and made the best of our way for the Royal Exchange, though I found he did not much care to venture himself into the throng of that place; for he told me he had heard they were, generally speaking, republicans, and was afraid of having his pocket picked amongst them. But he soon conceived a better opinion of them, when he spied the statue of King Charles II. standing up in the middle of the crowd, and most of the kings in Baker's Chronicle ranged in order over their heads; from whence he very justly concluded, that an antimonarchical assembly could never choose such a place to meet in once a day.

To continue this good disposition in my friend, after a short stay at Stocks Market, we drove away directly for the Mews, where he was not a little edified with the sight of those fine sets of horses which have been brought over from Hanover, and with the care that is taken of them. He made many good remarks upon this occasion, and was so pleased with his company, that I had much ado to get him out of the stable.

In our progress to St. James's Park (for that was the end of our journey) he took notice, with great satisfaction, that, contrary to his intelligence in the country, the shops were all open and full of business; that the soldiers walked civilly in the streets; that clergymen, instead of being affronted, had generally the wall given them; and that he had heard the bells ring to prayers from morning to night in some part of the town or another.

As he was full of these honest reflections, it happened very luckily for us, that one of the king's coaches passed by with the three young princesses in it, whom by an accidental stop we had an opportunity of surveying for some time; my friend was ravished with the beauty, innocence, and sweetness that appeared in all their faces. He declared several times, that they were the finest children he had ever seen in all his life; and assured me that, before this sight, if any one had told him it had been possible for three such pretty children to have been born out of England, he should never have believed them.

We were now walking together in the Park, and as

it is usual for men who are naturally warm and heady, to be transported with the greatest flush of good nature when they are once sweetened ; he owned to me very frankly, he had been much imposed upon by those false accounts of things he had heard in the country ; and that he would make it his business, upon his return thither, to set his neighbors right, and give them a more just notion of the present state of affairs.

What confirmed my friend in this excellent temper of mind, and gave him an inexpressible satisfaction, was a message he received, as we were walking together, from the prisoner for whom he had given his testimony in his late trial. This person having been condemned for his part in the late rebellion, sent him word that his Majesty had been graciously pleased to reprieve him, with several of his friends, in order, as it was thought, to give them their lives ; and that he hoped before he went out of town they should have a cheerful meeting, and drink health and prosperity to King George.

COUNTRY MANNERS.

THE first and most obvious reflections which arise in a man who changes the city for the country, are upon the different manners of the people whom he meets with in those two different scenes of life. By manners I do not mean morals, but behavior and good breeding, as they show themselves in the town and in the country.

And here, in the first place, I must observe a very great revolution that has happened in this article of good-breeding. Several obliging deferences, condescensions, and submissions, with many outward forms and ceremonies that accompany them, were first of all brought up among the politer part of mankind, who lived in courts and cities, and distinguished themselves from the rustic part of the species (who on all occasions acted bluntly and naturally) by such a mutual complaisance and intercourse of civilities. These forms of conversation by degrees multiplied, and grew troublesome; the modish world found too great a constraint in them, and have therefore thrown most of them aside. Conversation, like the Romish religion, was so encumbered with show and ceremony, that it stood in need of a reformation to retrench its superfluities, and restore its natural good sense and beauty. At present, therefore, an unconstrained carriage, and a certain openness of behavior, are the height of good-breeding. The fashionable world is grown free and easy; our manners sit more loose upon us; nothing is so modish as an agreeable negligence. In a word, good-breeding shows itself most, where to an ordinary eye it appears the least.

If after this we look on the people of mode in the country, we find in them the manners of the last age. They have no sooner fetched themselves up to the fashion of a polite world, but the town has dropped them, and are nearer to the first stage of nature, than to those refinements which formerly reigned in the court, and still prevail in the country. One may now know a man that never conversed in the world by his excess of good-breeding. A polite country squire shall make you as many bows in half an hour, as would serve a courtier for a week. There is infinitely more to do about place and precedency in a meeting of justices' wives, than in an assembly of duchesses.

This rural politeness is very troublesome to a man of my temper, who generally takes the chair that is next me, and walks first or last, in the front or in the rear, as chance directs. I have known my friend Sir Roger's dinner almost cold before the company could adjust the ceremonial, and be prevailed upon to sit down; and have heartily pitied my old friend, when I have seen him forced to pick and cull his guests, as they sat at the several parts of his table, that he might drink their healths according to their respective ranks and qualities. Honest Will. Wimble, who I should have thought had been altogether uninfected with ceremony, gives me abundance of trouble in this particular. Though he has been fishing all the morning, he will not help himself at dinner till I am served. When we are going out of the hall, he runs behind me; and last night, as we were walking in the fields, stopped short at a stile till I came up to it, and upon my making signs to him to get over, told me, with a serious smile, that sure I believed they had no manners in the country.

There has happened another revolution in the point of good-breeding, which relates to the conversation among men of mode, and which I cannot but look upon as very extraordinary. It was certainly one of the first distinctions of a well-bred man, to express everything that had the most remote appearance of being obscene in modest terms and distant phrases; whilst the clown, who had no such delicacy of conception and expression, clothed his ideas in those plain homely terms that are the most obvious and natural. This kind of good manners was perhaps carried to an excess, so as to make conversation too stiff, formal, and precise; for which reason (as hypocrisy in one age is generally succeeded by atheism in another) conversation is in a great measure relapsed into the first extreme; so that at present several of our men of the town, and particularly those who have been polished in France, make use of the most coarse, uncivilized words in our language, and utter themselves often in such a manner as a clown would blush to hear.

This infamous piece of good-breeding, which reigns among the coxcombs of the town, has not yet made its way into the country; and as it is impossible for such an irrational way of conversation to last long among a people that makes any profession of religion, or show of modesty, if the country gentlemen get into it they will certainly be left in the lurch. Their good-breeding will come too late to them, and they will be thought a parcel of lewd clowns, while they fancy themselves talking together like men of wit and pleasure.

As the two points of good-breeding, which I have hitherto insisted upon, regard behavior and conversation, there is a third which turns upon dress. In this too the country are very much behindhand. The rural beaus are not yet got out of the fashion that took place at the time of the Revolution, but ride about the country in red coats and laced hats ; while the women in many parts are still trying to outvie one another in the height of their head-dresses.

But a friend of mine, who is now upon the western circuit, having promised to give me an account of the several modes and fashions that prevail in the different parts of the nation through which he passes, I shall defer the enlarging upon this last topic till I have received a letter from him, which I expect every post.

COUNTRY FASHIONS.

GREAT masters in painting never care for drawing people in the fashion; as very well knowing that the head-dress, or periwig, that now prevails, and gives a grace to their portraitures at present, will make a very odd figure, and perhaps look monstrous in the eyes of posterity. For this reason they often represent an illustrious person in a Roman habit, or in some other dress that never varies. I could wish, for the sake of my country friends, that there was such a kind of everlasting drapery to be made use of by all who live at a certain distance from the town, and that they would agree upon such fashions as should never be liable to changes and innovations. For want of this standing dress, a man who takes a journey into the country, is as much surprised as one who walks in a gallery of old family pictures; and finds as great a variety of garbs and habits in the persons he converses with. Did they keep to one constant dress, they would sometimes be in the fashion, which they never are as matters are managed at present. If instead of running after the mode, they would continue fixed in one certain habit, the mode would some time or other overtake them, as a clock that stands still is sure to point right once in twelve hours: in this case, there-fore, I would advise them, as a gentleman did his friend who was hunting about the whole town after a rambling fellow: If you follow him, you will never find him; but if you plant yourself at the corner of

256

any one street, I'll engage it will not be long before you see him.

I have already touched upon this subject, in a speculation which shows how cruelly the country are led astray in following the town ; and equipped in a ridiculous habit, when they fancy themselves in the height of the mode. Since that speculation, I have received a letter (which I there hinted at) from a gentleman who is now in the western circuit.

"MR. SPECTATOR,

"Being a lawyer of the Middle Temple, a Cornish man by birth, I generally ride the western circuit for my health, and as I am not interrupted by clients, have leisure to make many observations that escape the notice of my fellow-travelers.

"One of the most fashionable women I met with in all the circuit, was my landlady at Staines, where I chanced to be on a holiday. Her commode was not half a foot high, and her petticoat within some yards of a modish circumference. In the same place I observed a young fellow with a tolerable periwig, had it not been covered with a hat that was shaped in the Ramillie cock. As I proceeded on my journey, I observed the petticoat grew scantier and scantier, and about three-score miles from London was so very unfashionable, that a woman might walk in it without any manner of inconvenience.

"Not far from Salisbury I took notice of a justice of peace's lady, who was at least ten years behind-hand in her dress, but at the same time as fine as hands could make her. She was flounced and furbelowed from head to foot ; every ribbon was wrinkled, and every part of her garments in curl, so that she looked like one of those animals which in the country we call a Friezeland hen.

"Not many miles beyond this place I was informed, that

17

one of the last year's little muffs had by some means or other straggled into those parts, and that all the women of fashion were cutting their old muffs in two, or retrenching them according to the little model which was got among them. I cannot believe the report they have there, that it was sent down franked by a parliament-man in a little packet; but probably by next winter this fashion will be at the height in the country, when it is quite out at London.

"The greatest beau at our next county-sessions was dressed in a most monstrous flaxen periwig, that was made in King William's reign. The wearer of it goes, it seems, in his own hair, when he is at home, and lets his wig lie in buckle for a whole half-year, that he may put it on upon occasion to meet the judges in it.

"I must not here omit an adventure which happened to us in a country church upon the frontiers of Cornwall. As we were in the midst of the service, a lady who is the chief woman of the place, and had passed the winter at London with her husband, entered the congregation in a little head-dress, and a hooped petticoat. The people, who were wonderfully startled at such a sight, all of them rose up. Some stared at the prodigious bottom, and some at the little top of this strange dress. In the mean time the lady of the manor filled the area of the church, and walked up to her pew with an unspeakable satisfaction, amidst the whispers, conjectures, and astonishments of the whole congregation.

"Upon my way from hence we saw a young fellow riding towards us full gallop, with a bob-wig and a black silken bag tied to it. He stop short at the coach, to ask us how far the judges were behind us. His stay was so very short, that we had only time to observe his new silk waistcoat, which was unbuttoned in several places to let us see that he had a clean shirt on, which was ruffled down to his middle.

" From this place, during our progress through the most western parts of the kingdom, we fancied ourselves in King Charles the Second's reign, the people having made very little variations in their dress since that time. The smartest of the country squires appear still in the Monmouth cock, and when they go a wooing (whether they have any post in the militia or not) they generally put on a red coat. We were, indeed, very much surprised at the place we lay at last night, to meet with a gentleman that had accoutered himself in a night-cap wig, a coat with long pockets and slit sleeves, and a pair of shoes with high scollop tops ; but we soon found by his conversation that he was a person who laughed at the ignorance and rusticity of the country people, and was resolved to live and die in the mode.

" Sir, if you think this account of my travels may be of any advantage to the public, I will next year trouble you with such occurrences as I shall meet with in other parts of England. For I am informed there are greater curiosities in the northern circuit than in the western ; and that a fashion makes its progress much slower into Cumberland than into Cornwall. I have heard in particular, that the Steenkirk arrived but two months ago at Newcastle, and that there are several commodes in those parts which are worth taking a journey thither to see."—C.

COUNTRY ETIQUETTE.

When I came home last night, my servant delivered me the following letter:

"Sir,   *Oct.* 24.

I have orders from Sir Harry Quickset, of Staffordshire, Bart, to acquaint you, that his honor Sir Harry himself, Sir Giles Wheelbarrow, Knt., Thomas Rentfree, Esq., justice of the *quorum*, Andrew Windmill, Esq., and Mr. Nicholas Doubt of the Inner Temple, Sir Harry's grandson, will wait upon you at the hour of nine to-morrow morning, being Tuesday the 25th of October, upon business which Sir Harry will impart to you by word of mouth. I thought it proper to acquaint you before-hand so many persons of quality came, that you might not be surprised therewith. Which concludes, though by many years' absence since I saw you at Stafford, unknown,

"Sir, your most humble servant,
"John Thrifty."

I received this message with less surprise than I believe Mr. Thrifty imagined; for I knew the good company too well to feel any palpitations at their approach: but I was in very great concern how I should adjust the ceremonial, and demean myself to all these great men, who perhaps had not seen anything above themselves for these twenty years last past. I am sure that is the case of Sir Harry. Besides which, I was sensible that there was a great point in adjusting my behavior to the simple squire,

260

so as to give him satisfaction, and not disoblige the
justice of the *quorum.*

The hour of nine was come this morning, and I had
no sooner set chairs (by the stewards' letter) and fixed
my tea equipage, but I heard a knock at my door,
which was opened, but no one entered; after which
followed a long silence, which was broke at last by,
" Sir, I beg your pardon ; I think I know better : " and
another voice, " Nay, good Sir Giles—" I looked out
from my window, and saw the good company all with
their hats off, and arms spread, offering the door to
each other. After many offers, they entered with
much solemnity, in the order Mr. Thrifty was so kind
as to name them to me. But they are now got to my
chamber door, and I saw my old friend Sir Harry
enter. I met him with all the respect due to so rev-
erend a vegetable ; for you are to know, that is my
sense of a person who remains idle in the same place
for half a century. I got him with great success into
his chair by the fire, without throwing down any of
my cups. The knight-bachelor told me, he had a
great respect for my whole family, and would, with
my leave, place himself next to Sir Harry, at whose
right hand he had sat at every quarter-sessions this
thirty years, unless he was sick. The steward in the
rear whispered the young Templar, " That is true to
my knowledge." I had the misfortune, as they stood
cheek by jole, to desire the squire to sit down before
the justice of the *quorum,* to the no small satisfaction
of the former, and resentment of the latter : but I saw
my error too late, and got them as soon as I could
into their seats. " Well, (said I,) gentlemen, after I
have told you how glad I am of this great honor, I
am to desire you to drink a dish of tea." They an-

swered, one and all, that "They never drank tea in a morning." "Not in a morning!" said I, staring round me. Upon which the pert jackanapes Nick Doubt tipped me the wink, and put out his tongue at his grandfather. Here followed a profound silence, when the steward in his boots and whip proposed that we should adjourn to some public-house, where everybody might call for what they pleased, and enter upon the business. We all stood up in an instant, and Sir Harry filed off from the left very discreetly, counter-marching behind the chairs towards the door: after him, Sir Giles in the same manner. The simple squire made a sudden start to follow; but the justice of the *quorum* whipped between upon the stand of the stairs. A maid going up with coals made us halt, and put us into such confusion, that we stood all in a heap, without any visible possibility of recovering our order: for the young jackanapes seemed to make a jest of this matter, and had so contrived, by pressing amongst us under pretense of making way, that his grandfather was got into the middle, and he knew nobody was of quality to stir a step, till Sir Harry moved first. We were fixed in this perplexity for some time, till we heard a very loud noise in the street; and Sir Harry asking what it was, I, to make them move, said it was fire. Upon this, all run down as fast as they could, without order or ceremony, till we got into the street, where we drew up in very good order, and filed off down Sheer Lane, the impertinent Templar driving us before him, as in a string, and pointing to his acquaintance who passed by.

I must confess, I love to use people according to their own sense of good breeding, and therefore whipped in between the justice and the simple squire.

He could not properly take this ill; but I overheard him whisper the steward, "That he thought it hard that a common conjurer should take place of him, though an elder squire." In this order we marched down Sheer Lane, at the upper end of which I lodge. When we came to Temple Bar, Sir Harry and Sir Giles got over; but a run of coaches kept the rest of us on this side the street : however, we all at last landed, and drew up in very good order before Ben. Tooke's shop, who favored our rallying with great humanity. From hence we proceeded again, till we came to Dick's Coffee-house, where I designed to carry them. Here we were at our old difficulty, and took up the street upon the same ceremony. We proceeded through the entry, and were so necessarily kept in order by the situation, that we were now got into the coffee-house itself, where, as soon as we arrived, we repeated our civilities to each other ; after which, we marched up to the high table, which has an ascent to it enclosed in the middle of the room. The whole house was alarmed at this entry, made up of persons of so much state and rusticity. Sir Harry called for a mug of ale, and Dyer's Letter. The boy brought the ale in an instant : but said, they did not take in the Letter. "No! (says Sir Harry,) then take back your mug; we are like indeed to have good liquor at this house." Here the Templar tipped me a second wink, and if I had not looked very grave upon him, I found he was disposed to be very familiar with me. In short, I observed after a long pause, that the gentlemen did not care to enter upon business till after their morning draught, for which reason I called for a bottle of mum; and finding that had no effect upon them, I ordered a second, and a third: after which,

Sir Harry reached over to me, and told me in a low voice, that the place was too public for business; but he would call upon me again to-morrow morning at my own lodgings, and bring some more friends with him.

THE GRINNING MATCH.

IN a late paper I mentioned the project of an ingenious author for the erecting of several handicraft
prizes to be contended for by our British artisans, and
the influence they might have towards the improvement of our several manufactures. I have since that
been very much surprised by the following advertisement which I find in the Post-boy of the 11th instant,
and again repeated in the Post-boy of the 15th.

"ON the 9th of October next will be run for upon
Coleshill Heath, in Warwickshire, a plate of six guineas
value, three heats, by any horse, mare, or gelding, that
hath not won above the value of 5l., the winning horse to
be sold for 10l., to carry ten stone weight, if fourteen
hands high ; if above or under, to carry or be allowed
weight for inches, and to be entered Friday the 15th
at the Swan in Coleshill, before six in the evening. Also
a plate of less value to be run for by asses. The same day
a gold ring to be grinned for by men."

The first of these diversions, that is to be exhibited
by the 10l. race-horses, may probably have its use;
but the two last, in which the asses and men are concerned, seem to me altogether extraordinary and unaccountable. Why they should keep running asses
at Coleshill, or how making mouths turns to account
in Warwickshire, more than in any other parts of
England, I cannot comprehend. I have looked over

all the Olympic games, and do not find anything in them like an ass-race, or a match at grinning. However it be, I am informed, that several asses are now kept in body-clothes, and sweated every morning upon the heath; and that all the country-fellows within ten miles of the Swan grin an hour or two in their glasses every morning, in order to qualify themselves for the 9th of October. The prize which is proposed to be grinned for, has raised such an ambition among the common people of out-grinning one another, that many very discerning persons are afraid it should spoil most of the faces in the county; and that a Warwickshire man will be known by his grin, as Roman Catholics imagine a Kentish man is by his tail. The gold ring which is made the prize of deformity, is just the reverse of the golden apple that was formerly made the prize of beauty, and should carry for its posie the old motto inverted,

Detur tetriori.

Or, to accommodate it to the capacity of the combatants,

The frightfull'st grinner
Be the winner.

In the mean while I would advise a Dutch painter to be present at this great controversy of faces, in order to make a collection of the most remarkable grins that shall be there exhibited.

I must not here omit an account which I lately received of one of these grinning matches from a gentleman, who, upon reading the above-mentioned advertisement, entertained a coffee-house with the following narrative. Upon the taking of Namur, among other public rejoicings made on that occasion, there was a gold ring given by a Whig justice of the peace to be grinned for. The first competitor that entered the lists, was a black, swarthy Frenchman, who accidentally passed that way, and being a man naturally of a withered look and hard features, promised himself good success. He was placed upon a table in the great point of view, and looking upon the company like Milton's death,

> Grinn'd horribly a ghastly smile.—

His muscles were so drawn together on each side of his face that he showed twenty teeth at a grin, and put the country in some pain, lest a foreigner should carry away the honor of the day; but upon a further trial they found he was master only of the merry grin.

The next that mounted the table was a Malecontent in those days, and a great master of the whole art of grinning, but particularly excelled in the angry grin. He did his part so well, that he is said to have made half a dozen women miscarry; but the justice being apprised by one who stood near him, that the fellow who grinned in his face was a Jacobite, and being unwilling that a disaffected person should win the gold ring, and be looked upon as the best grinner in the country, he ordered the oaths to be tendered unto him upon his quitting the table, which the grinner refusing, he was set aside as an unqualified person. There were several other grotesque figures that presented themselves, which it would be too tedious to describe. I must not, however, omit a plow-man, who lived in the further part of the country, and being very lucky in a pair of long lanthorn-jaws, wrung his face into such a hideous grimace, that every feature of it appeared under a different distortion. The whole company stood astonished at such a complicated grin, and were ready to assign the prize to him, had it not been proved by one of his antagonists that he had practised with verjuice for some days before, and had a crab found upon him at the very time of grinning; upon which the best judges of grinning declared it as their opinion, that he was not to be looked upon as a fair grinner, and therefore ordered him to be set aside as a cheat.

The prize, it seems, fell at length upon a cobbler, Giles Gorgon by name, who produced several new grins of his own invention, having been used to cut faces for many years together over his last. At the very first grin he cast every human feature out of his countenance, at the second he became the face of a spout, at the third a baboon, at the fourth the head of a bass-viol, and at the fifth a pair of nut-crackers. The whole assembly wondered at his accomplishments, and bestowed the ring on him unanimously; but, what he esteemed more than all the rest, a country wench whom he had wooed in vain for above five years before, was so charmed with his grins, and the applauses which he received on all sides, that she married him the week following, and to this day wears the prize upon her finger, the cobbler having made use of it as his wedding-ring.

This paper might perhaps seem very impertinent, if it grew serious in the conclusion. I would nevertheless leave it to the consideration of those who are the patrons of this monstrous trial of skill, whether or no they are not guilty, in some measure, of an affront to their species, in treating after this manner the Human

Face Divine, and turning that part of us, which has so great an image impressed upon it, into the image of a monkey; whether the raising such silly competitions among the ignorant, proposing prizes for such useless accomplishments, filling the common people's heads with such senseless ambitions, and inspiring them with such absurd ideas of superiority and pre-eminence, has not in it something immoral as well as ridiculous.

HUMORS OF FASHION.

A BEAU'S HEAD.

I was yesterday engaged in an assembly of virtuosos, where one of them produced many curious observations which he had lately made in the anatomy of a human body. Another of the company communicated to us several wonderful discoveries, which he had also made on the same subject, by the help of very fine glasses. This gave birth to a great variety of uncommon remarks, and furnished discourse for the remaining part of the day.

The different opinions which were started on this occasion, presented to my imagination so many new ideas, that by mixing with those which were already there, they employed my fancy all the last night, and composed a very wild, extravagant dream.

I was invited, methought, to the dissection of a beau's head and of a coquette's heart, which were both of them laid on a table before us. An imaginary operator opened the first with a great deal of nicety, which, upon a cursory and superficial view, appeared like the head of another man; but upon applying our glasses to it, we made a very odd discovery, namely, that what we looked upon as brains, were not such in reality, but an heap of strange materials wound up in that shape and texture, and packed together with wonderful art in the several cavities of the skull. For, as Homer tells us, that the blood of the gods is not real blood, but only something like it; so we found that the

18   273

brain of a beau is not a real brain, but only something like it.

The pineal gland, which many of our modern philosophers suppose to be the seat of the soul, smelt very strong of essence and orange-flower water, and was encompassed with a kind of horny substance, cut into a thousand little faces or mirrors, which were imperceptible to the naked eye; insomuch, that the soul, if there had been any here, must have been always taken up in contemplating her own beauties.

We observed a large antrum or cavity in the sinciput, that was filled with ribbons, lace, and embroidery, wrought together in a most curious piece of network, the parts of which were likewise imperceptible to the naked eye. Another of these antrums or cavities was stuffed with invisible billet-doux, love-letters, pricked dances, and other trumpery of the same nature. In another we found a kind of powder, which set the whole company a sneezing, and by the scent discovered itself to be right Spanish. The several other cells were stored with commodities of the same kind, of which it would be tedious to give the reader an exact inventory.

There was a large cavity on each side of the head which I must not omit. That on the right side was filled with fictions, flatteries, and falsehoods, vows, promises, and protestations; that on the left with oaths and imprecations. There issued out a duct from each of these cells, which ran into the root of the tongue, where both joined altogether, and passed forward in one common duct to the tip of it. We discovered several little roads or canals running from the ear into the brain, and took particular care to trace them out through their several passages. One of them extended itself to a bundle of sonnets and little musical instruments. Others ended in several bladders, which were filled with wind or froth. But the large canal entered into a great cavity of the skull, from whence there went another canal into the tongue. This great cavity was filled with a kind of spongy substance, which the French anatomists call galimatias; and the English, nonsense.

The skins of the forehead were extremely tough and thick, and what very much surprised us, had not in them any single blood-vessel that we were able to discover either with or without our glasses; from whence we concluded, that the party, when alive, must have been entirely deprived of the faculty of blushing.

The *os cribriforme* was exceedingly stuffed, and in some places damaged with snuff. We could not but take notice in particular of that small muscle, which is not often discovered in dissections, and draws the nose upwards, when it expresses the contempt which the owner of it has, upon seeing anything he does not like, or hearing anything he does not understand. I need not tell my learned reader, that this is that muscle which performs the motion so often mentioned by the Latin poets, when they talk of a man's cocking his nose, or playing the rhinoceros.

We did not find anything very remarkable in the eye, saving only that the *musculi amatorii*, or, as we may translate it into English, the ogling muscles, were very much worn and decayed with use; whereas, on the contrary, the elevator, or the muscle which turns the eye towards heaven, did not appear to have been used at all.

I have only mentioned in this dissection such new discoveries as we were able to make, and have not taken any notice of those parts which are to be met with in common heads. As for the skull, the face, and indeed the whole outward shape and figure of the head, we could not discover any difference from what we observe in the heads of other men. We were informed, that the person to whom this head belonged, had passed for a man above five-and-thirty years; during which time he eat and drank like other people, dressed well, talked loud, laughed frequently, and on particular occasions had acquitted himself tolerably at a ball or an assembly; to which one of the company added, that a certain knot of ladies took him for a wit. He was cut off in the flower of his age by the blow of a paring-shovel, having been surprised by an eminent citizen as he was tendering some civilities to his wife.

When we had thoroughly examined this head with all its apartments, and its several kinds of furniture, we put up the brain, such as it was, into its proper place, and laid it aside under a broad piece of scarlet cloth, in order to be prepared, and kept in a great repository of dissections; our operator telling us, that the preparation would not be so difficult as that of another brain, for that he had observed several of the little pipes and tubes which ran through the brain were already filled with a kind of mercurial substance, which he looked upon to be true quicksilver.

He applied himself in the next place to the coquette's heart, which he likewise laid open with great dexterity. There occurred to us many particularities in this dissection; but being unwilling to burden my reader's memory too much, I shall reserve this subject for the speculation of another day.

A COQUETTE'S HEART.

HAVING already given an account of the dissection of a beau's head, with the several discoveries made on that occasion, I shall here, according to my promise, enter upon the dissection of a coquette's heart, and communicate to the public such particularities as we observed in that curious piece of anatomy.

I should, perhaps, have waived this undertaking, had not I been put in mind of my promise by several of my unknown correspondents, who are very importunate with me to make an example of the coquette, as I have already done of the beau. It is, therefore, in compliance with the request of friends, that I have looked over the minutes of my former dream, in order to give the public an exact relation of it, which I shall enter upon without further preface.

Our operator, before he engaged in this visionary dissection, told us, that there was nothing in his art more difficult, than to lay open the heart of a coquette, by reason of the many labyrinths and recesses which are to be found in it, and which do not appear in the heart of any other animal.

He desired us first of all to observe the *pericardium*, or outward case of the heart, which we did very attentively ; and, by the help of our glasses, discerned in it millions of little scars, which seemed to have been occasioned by the points of innumerable darts and arrows, that from time to time had glanced upon the outward coat; though he could not discover the smallest orifice, by which any of them had entered and pierced the inward substance.

Every smatterer in anatomy knows, that this *pericardium*, or case of the heart, contains in it a thin reddish liquor, supposed to be bred from the vapors which exhale out of the heart, and being stopped here, are condensed into this watery substance. Upon examining this liquor, we found that it had in it all the qualities of that spirit which is made use of in the thermometer, to show the change of weather.

Nor must I here omit an experiment one of the company assures us he himself had made with this liquor, which he found in great quantity about the heart of a coquette whom he had formerly dissected. He affirmed to us, that he had actually enclosed it in a small tube made after the manner of a weather-glass; but that, instead of acquainting him with the variations of the atmosphere, it showed him the qualities of those persons who entered the room where it stood. He affirmed also, that it rose at the approach of a plume of feathers, an embroidered coat, or a pair of fringed gloves; and that it fell as soon as an ill-shaped periwig, a clumsy pair of shoes, or an unfashionable coat came into his house: nay, he proceeded so far as to assure us, that, upon his laughing aloud when he stood by it, the liquor mounted very sensibly, and immediately sunk again upon his looking serious. In short, he told us, that he knew very well by this invention whenever he had a man of sense or a coxcomb in his room.

Having cleared away the *pericardium*, or the case and liquor above-mentioned, we came to the heart itself. The outward surface of it was extremely slippery, and the *mucro,* or point, so very cold withal, that upon endeavoring to take hold of it, it glided through the fingers like a smooth piece of ice.

The fibers were turned and twisted in a more intricate and perplexed manner than they are usually found in other hearts ; insomuch, that the whole heart was wound up together like a Gordian knot, and must have had very irregular and unequal motions, whilst it was employed in its vital function.

One thing we thought very observable, namely, that upon examining all the vessels which came into it, or issued out of it, we could not discover any communication that it had with the tongue.

We could not but take notice likewise, that several of those little nerves in the heart which are affected by the sentiments of love, hatred, and other passions, did not descend to this before us from the brain, but from the muscles which lie about the eye.

Upon weighing the heart in my hand, I found it to be extremely light, and consequently very hollow, which I did not wonder at, when, upon looking into the inside of it, I saw multitudes of cells and cavities running one within another, as our historians describe the apartments of Rosamond's Bower. Several of these little hollows were stuffed with innumerable sorts of trifles, which I shall forbear giving any particular account of, and shall, therefore, only take notice of what lay first and uppermost, which, upon our unfolding it, and applying our microscope to it, appeared to be a flame-colored hood.

We were informed that the lady of this heart, when living, received the addresses of several who made love to her, and did not only give each of them encouragement, but made every one she conversed with believe that she regarded him with an eye of kindness : for which reason, we expected to have seen the impression of multitudes of faces among the several plaits and foldings of the heart ; but, to our great surprise, not a single print of this nature discovered itself, till we came into the very core and center of it. We there observed a little figure, which, upon applying our glasses to it, appeared dressed in a very fantastic manner. The more I looked upon it, the more I thought I had seen the face before, but could not possibly recollect either the place or time; when at length one of the company, who had examined this figure more nicely than the rest, showed us plainly by the make of its face, and the several turns of its features, that the little idol which was thus lodged in the very middle of the heart, was the deceased beau, whose head I gave some account of in my last paper.

As soon as we had finished our dissection, we resolved to make an experiment of the heart, not being able to determine among ourselves the nature of its substance, which differed in so many particulars from that of the heart in other females. Accordingly we laid it into a pan of burning coals, when we observed in it a certain salamandrine quality, that made it capable of living in the midst of fire and flame, without being consumed, or so much as singed.

As we were admiring this strange phænomenon, and standing round the heart in the circle, it gave a most prodigious sigh, or rather crack, and dispersed all at once in smoke and vapor. This imaginary noise, which methought was louder than the burst of a cannon, produced such a violent shake in my brain, that it dissipated the fumes of sleep, and left me in an instant broad awake.

THE HOOD.

ONE of the fathers, if I am rightly informed, has defined a woman to be ζῶον φιλοκόσμον, "An animal that delights in finery." I have already treated of the sex in two or three papers, conformably to this definition, and have in particular observed, that in all ages they have been more careful than the men to adorn that part of the head, which we generally call the outside.

This observation is so very notorious, that when in ordinary discourse we say a man has a fine head, a long head, or a good head, we express ourselves metaphorically, and speak in relation to his understanding; whereas, when we say of a woman, she has a fine, a long, or a good head, we speak only in relation to her commode.

It is observed among birds, that Nature has lavished all her ornaments upon the male, who very often appears in a most beautiful head-dress; whether it be a crest, a comb, a tuft of feathers, or a natural little plume, erected like a kind of pinnacle on the very top of the head. As Nature, on the contrary, has poured out her charms in the greatest abundance upon the female part of our species, so they are very assiduous in bestowing upon themselves the finest garnitures of art. The peacock, in all his pride, does not display half the colors that appear in the garments of a British lady, when she is dressed either for a ball or a birth-day.

But to return to our female heads. The ladies have been for some time in a kind of molting season, with regard to that part of their dress, having cast great quantities of ribbon, lace, and cambric, and in some measure reduced that part of the human figure to the beautiful globular form which is natural to it. We have for a great while expected what kind of ornament would be substituted in the place of those antiquated commodes. But our female projectors were all the last summer so taken up with the improvement of their petticoats, that they had not time to attend to anything else : but having at length sufficiently adorned their lower parts, they now begin to turn their thoughts upon the other extremity, as well remembering the old kitchen proverb, That if you light a fire at both ends, the middle will shift for itself.

I am engaged in this speculation by a sight which I lately met with at the opera. As I was standing in the hinder part of the box, I took notice of a little cluster of women sitting together in the prettiest colored hoods that I ever saw. One of them was blue, another yellow, and another philomot; the fourth was of a pink color, and the fifth of a pale green. I looked with as much pleasure upon this little party-colored assembly, as upon a bed of tulips, and did not know at first whether it might not be an embassy of Indian queens; but upon my going about into the pit, and taking them in front, I was immediately undeceived, and saw so much beauty in every face, that I found them all to be English. Such eyes and lips, cheeks and foreheads, could be the growth of no other country. The complexion of their faces hindered me from observing any further the color of their hoods, though I could easily perceive by that unspeakable satisfaction which appeared in their looks, that their own thoughts were wholly taken up on those pretty ornaments they wore upon their heads.

I am informed that this fashion spreads daily, insomuch that the Whig and Tory ladies begin already to hang out different colors, and to show their principles in their head-dress. Nay, if I may believe my friend Will. Honeycomb, there is a certain old coquette of his acquaintance, who intends to appear very suddenly in a rainbow hood, like the Iris in Dryden's Virgil, not questioning but that among such a variety of colors she shall have a charm for every heart.

My friend Will., who very much values himself upon his great insights into gallantry, tells me, that he can already guess at the humor a lady is in by her hood, as the courtiers of Morocco know the disposition of their present emperor by the color of the dress which he puts on. When Melesinda wraps her head in flame color, her heart is set upon execution. When she covers it with purple, I would not, says he, advise her lover to approach her; but if she appears in white, it is peace, and he may hand her out of her box with safety.

Will. informs me likewise, that these hoods may be used as signals. Why else, says he, does Cornelia always put on a black hood when her husband is gone into the country?

Such are my friend Honeycomb's dreams of gallantry. For my own part, I impute this diversity of colors in the hoods to the diversity of complexion in the faces of my pretty country-women. Ovid, in his Art of Love, has given some precepts as to this particular, though I find they are different from those which prevail among the moderns. He recommends a red striped silk to the pale complexion, white to the brown, and dark to the fair. On the contrary, my friend Will., who pretends to be a greater master in this art than Ovid, tells me, that the palest features look the most agreeable in white sarcenet, that a face which is over-flushed appears to advantage in the deepest scarlet, and that the darkest complexion is not a little alleviated by a black hood. In short, he is for losing the color of the face in that of the hood, as a fire burns dimly, and a candle goes half out, in the light of the sun. This, says he, your Ovid himself has hinted, where he treats of these matters, when he tells us that the Blue Water-nymphs are dressed in sky-colored garments; and that Aurora, who always appears in the light of the rising sun, is robed in saffron.

Whether these his observations are justly grounded I cannot tell; but I have often known him, as we have stood together behind the ladies, praise or dispraise the complexion of a face which he never saw, from observing the color of her hood, and has been very seldom out in these his guesses.

As I have nothing more at heart than the honor and improvement of the fair sex, I cannot conclude this paper without an exhortation to the British ladies, that they would excel the women of all other nations as much in virtue and good sense, as they do in beauty; which they may certainly do, if they will be as industrious to cultivate their minds as they are to adorn their bodies: in the mean while I shall recommend to their most serious consideration the saying of an old Greek poet,

Γυναιχὶ κόσμος ὁ τρόπος, κ᾽ οὐ χρυσία

THE HEAD-DRESS.

THERE is not so variable a thing in nature as a lady's head-dress : within my own memory I have known it rise and fall above thirty degrees. About ten years ago it shot up to a very great height, insomuch that the female part of our species were much taller than the men. The women were of such an enormous stature, that "we appeared as grasshoppers before them : " at present the whole sex is in a manner dwarfed and shrunk into a race of beauties that seems almost another species. I remember several ladies, who were once very near seven foot high, that at present want some inches of five : how they came to be thus curtailed I cannot learn ; whether the whole sex be at present under any penance which we know nothing of, or whether they have cast their head-dresses in order to surprise us with something in that kind which shall be entirely new ; or whether some of the tallest of the sex, being too cunning for the rest, have contrived this method to make themselves appear sizeable, is still a secret ; though I find most are of opinion, they are at present like trees new lopped and pruned, that will certainly sprout up and flourish with greater heads than before. For my own part, as I do not love to be insulted by women who are taller than myself, I admire the sex much more in their present humiliation, which has reduced them to their natural dimensions, than when they had extended their persons, and lengthened

themselves out into formidable and gigantic figures.
I am not for adding to the beautiful edifice of nature,
nor for raising any whimsical superstructure upon her
plans : I must, therefore, repeat it, that I am highly
pleased with the coiffure now in fashion, and think it
shows the good sense which at present very much
reigns among the valuable part of the sex. One may
observe, that women in all ages have taken more pains
than men to adorn the outside of their heads; and,
indeed, I very much admire, that those female archi-
tects, who raise such wonderful structures out of ribbons, lace, and wire, have not been recorded for their
respective inventions. It is certain there have been as
many orders in these kinds of building, as in those
which have been made of marble: sometimes they rise
in the shape of a pyramid, sometimes like a tower, and
sometimes like a steeple. In Juvenal's time the building grew by several orders and stories, as he has very
humorously described it.

> Tot premit ordinibus, tot adhuc compagibus altum
> Ædificat caput : Andromachen a fronte videbis;
> Post minor est : aliam credas.—Juv.

But I do not remember, in any part of my reading,
that the head-dress aspired to so great an extravagance as in the fourteenth century ; when it was built
up in a couple of cones or spires, which stood so excessively high on each side of the head, that a woman
who was but a Pigmy without her head-dress, appeared
like a Colossus upon putting it on. Monsieur Paradin
says, " That these old-fashioned frontanges rose an ell
above the head ; that they were pointed like steeples,
and had long loose pieces of crape fastened to the tops

of them, which are curiously fringed, and hung down their backs like streamers."

The women might possibly have carried this Gothic building much higher, had not a famous monk, Thomas Connecte by name, attacked it with great zeal and resolution. This holy man traveled from place to place to preach down this monstrous commode ; and succeeded so well in it, that as the magicians sacrificed their books to the flames upon the preaching of an apostle, many of the women threw down their head-dresses in the middle of his sermon, and made a bonfire of them within sight of the pulpit. He was so re-nowned, as well for the sanctity of his life as his manner of preaching, that he had often a congregation of twenty thousand people ; the men placing them-selves on the one side of his pulpit, and the women on the other, that appeared (to use the similitude of an ingenious writer) like a forest of cedars with their heads reaching to the clouds. He so warmed and animated the people against this monstrous ornament, that it lay under a kind of persecution ; and whenever it ap-peared in public, was pelted down by the rabble, who flung stones at the persons that wore it. But notwith-standing this prodigy vanished while the preacher was among them, it began to appear again some months after his departure ; or, to tell it in Monsieur Para-din's own words, " The women, that, like snails in a fright, had drawn in their horns, shot them out again as soon as the danger was over." This extrava-gance of the women's head-dresses in that age is taken notice of by Monsieur D'Argentre in his History of Bretagne, and by other historians as well as the person I have here quoted.

It is usually observed, that a good reign is the only

time for the making of laws against the exorbitance of power; in the same manner, an excessive head-dress may be attacked the most effectually when the fashion is against it. I do, therefore, recommend this paper to my female readers by way of prevention.

I would desire the fair sex to consider how impossible it is for them to add anything that can be ornamental to what is already the master-piece of nature. The head has the most beautiful appearance, as well as the highest station, in a human figure. Nature has laid out all her art in beautifying the face: she has touched it with vermilion, planted in it a double row of ivory, made it the seat of smiles and blushes, lighted it up and enlivened it with the brightness of the eyes, hung it on each side with curious organs of sense, given it airs and graces that cannot be described, and surrounded it with such a flowing shade of hair as sets all its beauties in the most agreeable light; in short, she seems to have designed the head as the cupola to the most glorious of her works; and when we load it with such a pile of supernumerary ornaments, we destroy the symmetry of the human figure, and foolishly contrive to call off the eye from great and real beauties, to childish gew-gaws, ribbons, and bone-lace.

THE FAN EXERCISE.

I DO not know whether to call the following letter a satire upon coquettes, or a representation of their several fantastical accomplishments, or what other title to give it; but as it is I shall communicate it to the public. It will sufficiently explain its own intentions, so that I shall give it my reader at length, without either preface or postscript.

"MR. SPECTATOR,

"Women are armed with fans as men with swords, and sometimes do more execution with them. To the end, therefore, that ladies may be entire mistresses of the weapon which they bear, I have erected an Academy for the training up of young women in the Exercise of the Fan, according to the most fashionable airs and motions that are now practised at court. The ladies who carry fans under me are drawn up twice a day in my great hall, where they are instructed in the use of their arms, and exercised by the following words of command :

> *Handle your Fans,*
> *Unfurl your Fans,*
> *Discharge your Fans,*
> *Ground your Fans,*
> *Recover your Fans,*
> *Flutter your Fans.*

By the right observation of these few plain words of command, a woman of a tolerable genius who will apply herself diligently to her exercise for the space of one half year, shall be able to give her fan all the graces that can possibly enter into that little modish machine.

" But to the end that my readers may form to themselves a right notion of this exercise, I beg leave to explain it to them in all its parts. When my female regiment is drawn up in array, with every one her weapon in her hand, upon my giving the word to Handle their Fans, each of them shakes her fan at me with a smile, then gives her right-hand woman a tap upon the shoulder, then presses her lips with the extremity of her fan, then lets her arms fall in an easy motion, and stands in readiness to receive the next word of command. All this is done with a close fan, and is generally learned in the first week.

" The next motion is that of Unfurling the Fan, in which are comprehended several little flirts and vibrations, as also gradual and deliberate openings, with many voluntary fallings asunder in the fan itself, that are seldom learned under a month's practise. This part of the exercise pleases the spectators more than any other, as it discovers on a sudden an infinite number of Cupids, garlands, altars, birds, beasts, rainbows, and the like agreeable figures, that display themselves to view, whilst every one in the regiment holds a picture in her hand.

" Upon my giving the word to Discharge their Fans, they give one general crack, that may be heard at a considerable distance when the wind sits fair. This is one of the most difficult parts of the exercise ; but I have several ladies with me, who at their first entrance could not give a pop loud enough to be heard at the further end of a room, who can now Discharge a Fan in such a manner, that it shall make a report like a pocket-pistol. I have likewise taken care (in order to hinder young women from letting off their fans in wrong places or unsuitable occasions) to show upon what subject the crack of a fan may come in properly. I have likewise invented a fan, with which a girl of sixteen, by the help of a little wind which is enclosed about one of the largest sticks, can make as loud a crack as a woman of fifty with an ordinary fan.

" When the fans are thus discharged, the word of command in course is to Ground their Fans. This teaches a lady to quit her fan gracefully when she throws it aside, in order to take up a pack of cards, adjust a curl of hair, replace a fallen pin, or apply herself to any other matter of importance. This part of the exercise, as it only consists in tossing a fan with an air upon a long table (which stands by for that purpose) may be learnt in two days' time as well as in a twelvemonth.

" When my female regiment is thus disarmed, I generally let them walk about the room for some time ; when on a sudden (like ladies that look upon their watches after a long visit) they all of them hasten to their arms, catch them up in a hurry, and place themselves in their proper stations upon my calling out Recover your Fans. This part of the exercise is not difficult, provided a woman applies her thoughts to it.

" The Fluttering of the Fan is the last, and, indeed, the master-piece of the whole exercise ; but if a lady does not misspend her time, she may make herself mistress of it in three months. I generally lay aside the dog-days and the hot time of the summer for the teaching of this part of the exercise ; for as soon as ever I pronounce Flutter your Fans, the place is filled with so many zephyrs and gentle breezes as are very refreshing in that season of the year, though they might be dangerous to ladies of a tender constitution in any other.

" There is an infinite variety of motions to be made use of in the Flutter of a Fan : there is the angry flutter, the modest flutter, the timorous flutter, the confused flutter, the merry flutter, and the amorous flutter. Not to be tedious, there is scarce any emotion in the mind which does not produce a suitable agitation in the fan ; insomuch, that if I only see the fan of a disciplined lady, I know very well whether she laughs, frowns, or blushes. I have seen a fan so very angry, that it would have been danger-ous for the absent lover who provoked it to have come within the wind of it; and at other times so very languish-ing, that I have been glad for the lady's sake the lover was at a sufficient distance from it. I need not add, that a fan is either a prude or coquette, according to the nature of the person who bears it. To conclude my letter, I must acquaint you, that I have from my own observations com-piled a little treatise for the use of my scholars, entitled, The Passions of the Fan; which I will communicate to you, if you think it may be of use to the public. I shall have a general review on Thursday next; to which you shall be very welcome if you will honor it with your presence.

"I am," etc.

"P. S. I teach young gentlemen the whole art of gal-lanting a fan.

"N. B. I have several little plain fans made for this use, to avoid expense."

A LADY'S DIARY.

THE journal with which I presented my reader on Tuesday last, has brought me in several letters, with accounts of many private lives cast into that form. I have the Rake's Journal, the Sot's Journal, the Whoremaster's Journal, and among several others a very curious piece, entitled, "The Journal of a Mohock." By these instances I find that the intention of my last Tuesday's paper has been mistaken by many of my readers. I did not design so much to expose vice as idleness, and aimed at those persons who pass away their time rather in trifles and impertinence, than in crimes and immoralities. Offenses of this latter kind are not to be dallied with, or treated in so ludicrous a manner. In short, my journal only holds up folly to the light, and shows the disagreeableness of such actions as are indifferent in themselves, and blameable only as they proceed from creatures endowed with reason.

My following correspondent, who calls herself Clarinda, is such a journalist as I require : she seems by her letter to be placed in a modish state of indifference between vice and virtue, and to be susceptible of either, were there proper pains taken with her. Had her journal been filled with gallantries, or such occurrences as had shown her wholly divested of her natural innocence, notwithstanding it might have been more pleasing to the generality of readers, I should not have

293

published it; but as it is only the picture of a life filled with a fashionable kind of gayety and laziness, I shall set down five days of it, as I have received it from the hand of my correspondent.

"DEAR MR. SPECTATOR,

You having set your readers an exercise in one of your last week's papers, I have performed mine according to your orders, and herewith send it you enclosed. You must know, Mr. Spectator, that I am a maiden lady of a good fortune, who have had several matches offered me for these ten years last past, and have at present warm applications made to me by a very pretty fellow. As I am at my own disposal, I come up to town every winter, and pass my time in it after the manner you will find in the following journal, which I began to write upon the very day after your Spectator upon that subject.

TUESDAY *night*.   Could not go to sleep till one in the morning for thinking of my journal.

WEDNESDAY.   *From eight to ten.*   Drank two dishes of chocolate in bed, and fell asleep after them.
From ten to eleven.   Eat a slice of bread and butter, drank a dish of bohea, read the Spectator.
From eleven to one.   At my toilette, tried a new head. Gave orders for Veny to be combed and washed.   Mem. I look best in blue.
From one till half an hour after two.   Drove to the 'Change.   Cheapened a couple of fans.
Till four.   At dinner.   Mem. Mr. Froth passed by in his new liveries.
From four to six.   Dressed, paid a visit to old Lady Blithe and her sister, having before heard they were gone out of town that day.

From six to eleven. At basset. Mem. Never set again upon the ace of diamonds.

THURSDAY. *From eleven at night to eight in the morning.* Dreamed that I punted to Mr. Froth.

From eight to ten. Chocolate. Read two acts in Aurenzebe a-bed.

From ten to eleven. Tea-table. Sent to borrow Lady Faddle's Cupid for Veny. Read the play-bills. Received a letter from Mr. Froth. Mem. Locked it up in my strong box.

Rest of the morning. Fontange, the tire-woman, her account of Lady Blithe's wash. Broke a tooth in my little tortoise-shell comb. Sent Frank to know how my Lady Hectick rested after her monkey's leaping out at the window. Looked pale. Fontange tells me my glass is not true. Dressed by three.

From three to four. Dinner cold before I sat down.

From four to eleven. Saw company. Mr. Froth's opinion of Milton. His account of the Mohocks. His fancy for a pin-cushion. Picture in the lid of his snuff-box. Old Lady Faddle promises me her woman to out my hair. Lost five guineas at crimp.

Twelve o'clock at night. Went to bed.

FRIDAY. *Eight in the morning.* A-bed. Read over all Mr. Froth's letters. Cupid and Veny.

Ten o'clock. Stayed within all day, not at home.

From ten to twelve. In conference with my mantua-maker. Sorted a suit of ribbons. Broke my blue china cup.

From twelve to one. Shut myself up in my chamber, practised Lady Betty Modely's skuttle.

One in the afternoon. Called for my flowered handkerchief. Worked half a violet leaf in it. Eyes ached and head out of order.   Threw by my work, and read over the remaining part of Aurenzebe.

From three to four.   Dined.

From four to twelve.   Changed my mind, dressed, went abroad, and played at crimp till midnight.   Found Mrs. Spitely at home.   Conversation : Mrs. Brilliant's necklace false stones.   Old Lady Loveday going to be married to a young fellow that is not worth a groat.   Miss Prue gone into the country.   Tom Townley has red hair.   Mem. Mrs. Spitely whispered in my ear that she had something to tell me about Mr. Froth, I am sure it is not true.

Between twelve and one.   Dreamed that Mr. Froth lay at my feet, and called me Indamora.

SATURDAY.   Rose at eight o'clock in the morning.   Sat down to my toilette.

From eight to nine.   Shifted a patch for half an hour before I could determine it.   Fixed it above my left eyebrow.

From nine to twelve.   Drank my tea, and dressed.

From twelve to two.   At chapel.   A great deal of good company.   Mem.   The third air in the new opera.   Lady Blithe dressed frightfully.

From three to four.   Dined.   Mrs. Kitty called upon me to go to the opera before I was risen from table.

From dinner to six.   Drank tea.   Turned off a footman for being rude to Veny.

Six o'clock.   Went to the opera.   I did not see Mr. Froth till the beginning of the second act.   Mr. Froth talked to a gentleman in a black wig.   Bowed to a lady in the front box.   Mr. Froth and his friend clapped Nicolini in the third act.   Mr. Froth cried out Ancora. Mr. Froth led me to my chair.   I think he squeezed my hand.

Eleven at night.   Went to bed.   Melancholy dreams. Methought Nicolini said he was Mr. Froth.

SUNDAY. Indisposed.

MONDAY. *Eight o'clock.* Waked by Miss Kitty. Aurenzebe lay upon the chair by me. Kitty repeated without book the eight best lines in the play. Went in our mobs to the dumb man, according to appointment. Told me that my lover's name began with a G. Mem. The conjurer was within a letter of Mr. Froth's name, &c.

"Upon my looking back into this my journal, I find that I am at a loss to know whether I pass my time well or ill ; and indeed never thought of considering how I did it, before I perused your speculation upon that subject. I scarce find a single action in these five days that I can thoroughly approve of, except the working upon the violet leaf, which I am resolved to finish the first day I am at leisure. As for Mr. Froth and Veny, I did not think they took up so much of my time and thoughts, as I find they do upon my journal. The latter of whom I will turn off if you insist upon it ; and if Mr. Froth does not bring matters to a conclusion very suddenly, I will not let my life run away in a dream.

" Your humble servant,

" CLARINDA."

To resume one of the morals of my first paper, and to confirm Clarinda in her good inclinations, I would have her consider what a pretty figure she would make among posterity, were the history of her whole life published like these five days of it. I shall con- clude my paper with an epitaph written by an uncertain author on Sir Philip Sidney's sister, a lady who seems to have been of a temper very much different from that of Clarinda. The last thought of it is so very noble, that I dare say my reader will pardon the quotation.

On the Countess Dowager of PEMBROKE.

Underneath this marble hearse
Lies the subject of all verse,
Sidney's sister, Pembroke's mother ;
Death, ere thou hast killed another,
Fair, and learned, and good as she,
Time shall throw a dart at thee.

FASHIONS FROM FRANCE.

THERE is nothing which I more desire than a safe and honorable peace, though at the same time I am very apprehensive of many ill consequences that may attend it. I do not mean in regard to our politics, but to our manners. What an inundation of ribbons and brocades will break in upon us! what peals of laughter and impertinence shall we be exposed to! For the prevention of these great evils, I could heartily wish that there was an act of parliament for prohibiting the importation of French fopperies.

The female inhabitants of our island have already received very strong impressions from this ludicrous nation, though by the length of the war (as there is no evil which has not some good attending it) they are pretty well worn out and forgotten. I remember the time when some of our well-bred country-women kept their *valet de chambre*, because, forsooth, a man was much more handy about them than one of their own sex. I myself have seen one of these male Abigails tripping about the room with a looking-glass in his hand, and combing his lady's hair a whole morning together. Whether or no there was any truth in the story of a lady's being got with child by one of these her handmaids, I cannot tell; but I think at present the whole race of them is extinct in our own country.

About the time that several of our sex were taken into this kind of service, the ladies likewise brought up the fashion of receiving visits in their beds. It was then looked upon as a piece of ill-breeding for a woman to refuse to see a man because she was not stirring; and a porter would have been thought unfit for his place, that could have made so awkward an excuse. As I love to see everything that is new, I once prevailed upon my friend Will. Honeycomb to carry me along with him to one of these traveled ladies, desiring him, at the same time, to present me as a foreigner who could not speak English, that so I might not be obliged to bear a part in the discourse. The lady, though willing to appear undrest, had put on her best looks, and painted herself for our reception. Her hair appeared in a very nice disorder, as the night-gown which was thrown upon her shoulders was ruffled with great care. For my part, I am so shocked with everything which looks immodest in the fair sex, that I could not forbear taking off my eye from her when she moved in her bed, and was in the greatest confusion imaginable every time she stirred a leg or an arm. As the coquets, who introduced this custom, grew old, they left it off by degrees; well knowing that a woman of threescore may kick and tumble her heart out, without making any impressions.

Sempronia is at present the most profest admirer of the French nation, but is so modest as to admit her visitants no further than her toilet. It is a very odd sight that beautiful creature makes, when she is talking politics with her tresses flowing about her shoulders, and examining that face in the glass, which does such execution upon all the male standers-by. How prettily does she divide her discourse between her woman and her visitants! What sprightly transitions does she make from an opera or a sermon, to an ivory comb or a pincushion! How have I been pleased to see her interrupted in an account of her travels by a message to her footman! and holding her tongue in the midst of a moral reflection by applying the tip of it to a patch!

There is nothing which exposes a woman to greater dangers, than that gayety and airiness of temper, which are natural to most of the sex. It should be therefore the concern of every wise and virtuous woman, to keep this sprightliness from degenerating into levity. On the contrary, the whole discourse and behavior of the French is to make the sex more fantastical, or (as they are pleased to term it) more awakened, than is consistent either with virtue or discretion. To speak loud in public assemblies, to let every one hear you talk of things that should only be mentioned in private, or in whisper, are looked upon as parts of a refined education. At the same time, a blush is unfashionable, and silence more ill-bred than anything that can be spoken. In short, discretion and modesty, which in all other ages and countries have been regarded as the greatest ornaments of the fair sex, are considered as the ingredients of narrow conversation and family behavior.

Some years ago I was at the tragedy of Macbeth, and unfortunately placed myself under a woman of quality that is since dead; who, as I found by the noise she made, was newly returned from France. A little before the rising of the curtain, she broke out into a loud soliloquy, "When will the dear witches enter?" and immediately upon their first appearance, asked a lady that sat three boxes from her, on her right hand, if those witches were not charming creatures. A little after, as Betterton was in one of the finest speeches of the play, she shook her fan at another lady, who sat as far on the left hand, and told her with a whisper, that might be heard all over the pit, we must not expect to see Balloon to-night. Not long after, calling out to a young baronet by his name, who sat three seats before me, she asked him whether Macbeth's wife was still alive; and before he could give an answer, fell a talking of the ghost of Banquo. She had by this time formed a little audience to herself, and fixed the attention of all about her. But as I had a mind to hear the play, I got out of the sphere of her impertinence, and planted myself in one of the remotest corners of the pit.

This pretty childishness of behavior is one of the most refined parts of coquetry, and is not to be attained in perfection by ladies that do not travel for their improvement. A natural and unconstrained behavior has something in it so agreeable, that it is no wonder to see people endeavoring after it. But at the same time, it is so very hard to hit, when it is not born with us, that people often make themselves ridiculous in attempting it.

A very ingenious French author tells us, that the ladies of the court of France, in his time, thought it ill-breeding, and a kind of female pedantry, to pronounce an hard word right; for which reason they took frequent occasion to use hard words, that they might show a politeness in murdering them. He further adds, that a lady of some quality at court, having accidentally made use of an hard word in a proper place, and pronounced it right, the whole assembly was out of countenance for her.

I must, however, be so just to own, that there are many ladies who have traveled several thousands of miles without being the worse for it, and have brought home with them all the modesty, discretion, and good sense, that they went abroad with. As, on the contrary, there are great numbers of traveled ladies, who have lived all their days within the smoke of London. I have known a woman that never was out of the parish of St. James's betray as many foreign fopperies in her carriage, as she could have gleaned up in half the countries of Europe.

WOMAN ON HORSEBACK.

MOST of the papers I give the public are written on subjects that never vary, but are for ever fixt and immutable. Of this kind are all my more serious essays and discourses; but there is another sort of speculations, which I consider as occasional papers, that take their rise from the folly, extravagance, and caprice of the present age. For I look upon myself as one set to watch the manners and behavior of my countrymen and contemporaries, and to mark down every absurd fashion, ridiculous custom, or affected form of speech, that makes its appearance in the world, during the course of these my speculations. The petticoat no sooner begun to swell, but I observed its motions. The party-patches had not time to muster themselves before I detected them. I had intelligence of the colored hood the very first time it appeared in a public assembly. I might here mention several other the like contingent subjects, upon which I have bestowed distinct papers. By this means I have so effectually quashed those irregularities which gave occasion to them, that I am afraid posterity will scarce have sufficient idea of them to relish those discourses which were in no little vogue at the time when they were written. They will be apt to think that the fashions and customs I attacked were some fantastic conceits of my own, and that their great-grandmothers could not be so whimsical as I have represented them. For this

reason, when I think on the figure my several volumes
of speculations will make about a hundred years hence,
I consider them as so many pieces of old plate, where
the weight will be regarded, but the fashion lost.

Among the several female extravagances I have
already taken notice of, there is one which still keeps
its ground. I mean that of the ladies who dress themselves in a hat and feather, a riding-coat and a periwig; or at least tie up their hair in a bag or ribbon,
in imitation of the smart part of the opposite sex. I
have already shown my dislike of this immodest custom
more than once; but in contempt of everything I have
hitherto said, I am informed that the highways about
this great city are still very much infested with these
female cavaliers.

I remember when I was at my friend Sir Roger de
Coverley's about this time twelvemonth, an equestrian
lady of this order appeared upon the plains which lay
at a distance from his house. I was at that time
walking in the fields with my old friend; and as his tenants ran out on every side to see so strange a sight, Sir
Roger asked one of them who came by us, what it
was? To which the country fellow replied, "'Tis a
gentlewoman, saving your worship's presence, in a
coat and hat." This produced a great deal of mirth
at the knight's house, where we had a story at the
same time of another of his tenants, who meeting this
gentleman-like lady on the highway, was asked by
her whether that was Coverley Hall; the honest man
seeing only the male part of the querist, replied, "Yes,
sir;" but upon the second question, "whether Sir
Roger de Coverley was a married man," having
dropped his eye upon the petticoat, he changed his
note into "No, madam."

20

Had one of these hermaphrodites appeared in Juvenal's day, with what an indignation should we have seen her described by that excellent satirist. He would have represented her in her riding habit, as a greater monster than the Centaur. He would have called for sacrifices, or purifying waters, to expiate the appearance of such a prodigy. He would have invoked the shades of Portia or Lucretia, to see into what the Roman ladies had transformed themselves.

For my own part, I am for treating the sex with greater tenderness, and have all along made use of the most gentle methods to bring them off from any little extravagance into which they are sometimes unwarily fallen: I think it however absolutely necessary to keep up the partition between the two sexes, and to take notice of the smallest encroachments which the one makes upon the other. I hope, therefore, that I shall not hear any more complaints on this subject. I am sure my she-disciples who peruse these my daily lectures, have profited but little by them, if they are capable of giving into such an amphibious dress. This I should not have mentioned, had not I lately met one of these my female readers in Hyde Park, who looked upon me with a masculine assurance, and cocked her hat full in my face.

For my part, I have one general key to the behavior of the fair sex. When I see them singular in any part of their dress, I conclude it is not without some evil intention; and therefore question not but the design of this strange fashion is to smite more effectually their male beholders. Now to set them right in this particular, I would fain have them consider with themselves whether we are not more likely to be struck by a figure entirely female, than with such an one as we may see every day in our glasses : or, if they please, let them reflect upon their own hearts, and think how they would be affected should they meet a man on horseback in his breeches and jack-boots, and at the same time dressed up in a commode and a night-rail.

I must observe that this fashion was first of all brought to us from France, a country which has in-fected all the nations in Europe with its levity. I speak not this in derogation of a whole people, having more than once found fault with those general reflec-tions which strike at kingdoms or commonwealths in the gross ; a piece of cruelty, which an ingenious writer of our own compares to that of Caligula, who wished the Roman people had all but one neck, that he might behead them at a blow. I shall therefore only remark, that as liveliness and assurance are in a peculiar manner the qualifications of the French nation, the same habits and customs will not give the same offense to that people, which they produce among those of our own country. Modesty is our distinguish-ing character, as vivacity is theirs ; and when this our national virtue appears in that family beauty, for which our British ladies are celebrated above all others in the universe, it makes up the most amiable object that the eye of man can possibly behold.

VARIOUS ESSAYS.

OMENS.

Going yesterday to dine with an old acquaintance, I had the misfortune to find his whole family very much dejected. Upon asking him the occasion of it, he told me that his wife had dreamt a strange dream the night before, which they were afraid portended some misfortune to themselves or to their children. At her coming into the room, I observed a settled melancholy in her countenance, which I should have been troubled for, had I not heard from whence it proceeded. We were no sooner sat down, but, after having looked upon me a little while, "My dear," says she, turning to her husband, " you may now see the stranger that was in the candle last night." Soon after this, as they began to talk of family affairs, a little boy at the lower end of the table told her, that he was to go into join-hand on Thursday. "Thursday!" says she. "No, child, if it please God, you shall not begin upon Childermas-day : tell your writing master that Friday will be soon enough." I was reflecting with myself on the oddness of her fancy, and wondering that anybody would establish it as a rule to lose a day in every week. In the midst of these my musings, she desired me to reach her a little salt upon the point of my knife, which I did in such a trepidation and hurry of obedience, that I let it drop by the way; at which she immediately startled, and said it fell towards her. Upon this I looked very blank; and observing the

311

concern of the whole table, began to consider myself, with some confusion, as a person that had brought a disaster upon the family. The lady, however, recovering herself, after a little space, said to her husband, with a sigh, " My dear, misfortunes never come single." My friend, I found, acted but an under part at his table, and being a man of more good-nature than understanding, thinks himself obliged to fall in with all the passions and humors of his yoke-fellow. "Do not you remember, child," says she, " that the pigeon-house fell the very afternoon that our careless wench spilt the salt upon the table ? " " Yes," says he, " my dear ; and the next post brought us an account of the battle of Almanza." The reader may guess at the figure I made, after having done all this mischief. I despatched my dinner as soon as I could, with my usual taciturnity ; when, to my utter confusion, the lady seeing me quitting my knife and fork, and laying them across one another upon my plate, desired me that I would humor her so far as to take them out of that figure, and place them side by side. What the absurdity was which I had committed I did not know, but I suppose there was some traditionary superstition in it; and therefore in obedience to the lady of the house, I disposed of my knife and fork in two parallel lines, which is the figure I shall always lay them in for the future, though I do not know any reason for it.

It is not difficult for a man to see that a person has conceived an aversion to him. For my own part, I quickly found, by the lady's looks, that she regarded me as a very odd kind of fellow, with an unfortunate aspect. For which reason I took my leave immediately after dinner, and withdrew to my own lodgings. Upon my return home, I fell into a profound contemplation of the evils that attend these superstitious follies of mankind; how they subject us to imaginary afflictions, and additional sorrows, that do not properly come within our lot. As if the natural calamities of life were not sufficient for it, we turn the most indifferent circumstances into misfortunes, and suffer as much from trifling accidents as from real evils. I have known the shooting of a star spoil a night's rest; and have seen a man in love grow pale, and lose his appetite, upon the plucking of a merrythought. A screech-owl at midnight has alarmed a family more than a band of robbers: nay, the voice of a cricket hath struck more terror than the roaring of a lion. There is nothing so inconsiderable, which may not appear dreadful to an imagination that is filled with omens and prognostics. A rusty nail, or a crooked pin, shoot up into prodigies.

I remember I was once in a mixt assembly, that was full of noise and mirth, when on a sudden an old woman unluckily observed there were thirteen of us in company. This remark struck a panic terror into several who were present, insomuch that one or two of the ladies were going to leave the room; but a friend of mine taking notice that one of our female companions was big with child, affirmed, there were fourteen in the room, and that, instead of portending one of the company should die, it plainly foretold one of them should be born. Had not my friend found this expedient to break the omen, I question not but half the women in the company would have fallen sick that very night.

An old maid, that is troubled with the vapors, produces infinite disturbances of this kind among her friends and neighbors. I know a maiden aunt of a great family, who is one of these antiquated Sibyls, that forebodes and prophesies from one end of the year to the other. She is always seeing apparitions and hearing death-watches; and was the other day almost frighted out of her wits by the great house-dog, that howled in the stable at a time when she lay ill of the toothache. Such an extravagant cast of mind engages multitudes of people, not only in impertinent terrors, but in supernumerary duties of life; and arises from that fear and ignorance which are natural to the soul of man. The horror with which we entertain the thoughts of death, (or indeed of any future evil,) and the uncertainty of its approach, fill a melancholy mind with innumerable apprehensions and suspicions, and consequently dispose it to the observation of such groundless prodigies and pre-dictions. For as it is the chief concern of wise men to retrench the evils of life by the reasonings of phi-losophy, it is the employment of fools to multiply them by the sentiments of superstition.

For my own part, I should be very much troubled were I endowed with this divining quality, though it should inform me truly of everything that can befall me. I would not anticipate the relish of any hap-piness, nor feel the weight of any misery, before it actually arrives.

I know but one way of fortifying my soul against these gloomy presages and terrors of mind, and that is, by securing to myself the friendship and protection of that Being who disposes of events, and governs futurity. He sees at one view the whole thread of my existence; not only that part of it which I have already passed through, but that which runs forward into all the depths of eternity. When I lay me down to sleep, I recommend myself to his care; when I awake, I give myself up to his direction. Amidst all the evils that threaten me, I will look up to him for help, and question not but he will either avert them, or turn them to my advantage. Though I know neither the time nor the manner of the death I am to die, I am not at all solicitous about it; because I am sure that he knows them both, and that he will not fail to comfort and support me under them.

LADY ORATORS.

We are told by some ancient authors, that Socrates was instructed in eloquence by a woman, whose name, if I am not mistaken, was Aspasia. I have, indeed, very often looked upon that art as the most proper for the female sex, and I think the universities would do well to consider whether they should not fill their rhetoric chairs with she-professors.

It has been said in the praise of some men, that they could talk whole hours together upon anything; but it must be owned to the honor of the other sex, that there are many among them who can talk whole hours together upon nothing. I have known a woman branch out into a long extempore dissertation upon the edging of a petticoat, and chide her servant for breaking a china cup in all the figures of rhetoric.

Were women admitted to plead in courts of judicature, I am persuaded they would carry the eloquence of the bar to greater heights than it has yet arrived at. If any one doubts this, let him but be present at those debates which frequently arise among the ladies of the British fishery.

The first kind, therefore, of female orators which I shall take notice of, are those who are employed in stirring up the passions, a part of rhetoric in which Socrates his wife had perhaps made a greater proficiency than his above-mentioned teacher.

The second kind of female orators are those who

316

deal in invectives, and who are commonly known by the name of the censorious. The imagination and elocution of this set of rhetoricians is wonderful. With what a fluency of invention, and copiousness of expression, will they enlarge upon every little slip in the behavior of another! With how many different circumstances, and with what variety of phrases, will they tell over the same story! I have known an old lady make an unhappy marriage the subject of a month's conversation. She blamed the bride in one place; pitied her in another; laughed at her in a third; wondered at her in a fourth; was angry with her in a fifth; and in short, wore out a pair of coach-horses in expressing her concern for her. At length, after having quite exhausted the subject on this side, she made a visit to the new-married pair, praised the wife for the prudent choice she had made, told her the unreasonable reflections which some malicious people had cast upon her, and desired that they might be better acquainted. The censure and approbation of this kind of women are therefore only to be considered as helps to discourse.

A third kind of female orators may be comprehended under the word Gossips. Mrs. Fiddle Faddle is perfectly accomplished in this sort of eloquence; she launches out into descriptions of christenings, runs divisions upon an head-dress, knows every dish of meat that is served up in her neighborhood, and entertains her company a whole afternoon together with the wit of her little boy, before he is able to speak.

The coquette may be looked upon as a fourth kind of female orator. To give herself the larger field for discourse, she hates and loves in the same breath, talks to her lap-dog or parrot, is uneasy in all kinds of weather, and in every part of the room : she has false quarrels and feigned obligations to all the men of her acquaintance ; sighs when she is not sad, and laughs when she is not merry. The coquette is in particular a great mistress of that part of oratory which is called action, and indeed seems to speak for no other purpose, but as it gives her an opportunity of stirring a limb, or varying a feature, of glancing her eyes, or playing with her fan.

As for news-mongers, politicians, mimics, story-tellers, with other characters of that nature, which give birth to loquacity, they are as commonly found among the men as the women; for which reason I shall pass them over in silence.

I have been often puzzled to assign a cause why women should have this talent of a ready utterance in so much greater perfection than men. I have sometimes fancied that they have not a retentive power, the faculty of suppressing their thoughts, as men have, but that they are necessitated to speak everything they think ; and if so, it would perhaps furnish a very strong argument to the Cartesians, for the supporting of their doctrine, that the soul always thinks. But as several are of opinion that the fair sex are not altogether strangers to the arts of dissembling, and concealing their thoughts, I have been forced to relinquish that opinion, and have, therefore, endeavored to seek after some better reason. In order to it, a friend of mine, who is an excellent anatomist, has promised me by the first opportunity to dissect a woman's tongue, and to examine whether there may not be in it certain juices which render it so wonderfully voluble or flippant, or whether the fibers of it may not be made up of a finer or more pliant thread, or whether there are not in it some particular muscles, which dart it up and down by such sudden glances and vibrations; or whether, in the last place, there may not be certain undiscovered channels running from the head and the heart, to this little instrument of loquacity, and conveying into it a perpetual affluence of animal spirits. Nor must I omit the reason which Hudibras has given, why those who can talk on trifles speak with the greatest fluency; namely, that the tongue is like a race-horse, which runs the faster the lesser weight it carries.

Which of these reasons soever may be looked upon as the most probable, I think the Irishman's thought was very natural, who, after some hours' conversation with a female orator, told her, that he believed her tongue was very glad when she was asleep, for that it had not a moment's rest all the while she was awake.

That excellent old ballad of the " Wanton Wife of Bath " has the following remarkable lines:

> I think, quoth Thomas, women's tongues
> Of aspen leaves are made.

And Ovid, though in the description of a very barbarous circumstance, tells us, that when the tongue of a beautiful female was cut out, and thrown upon the ground, it could not forbear muttering even in that posture:

> —Comprehensam forcipe linguam
> Abstulit ense fero. Radix micat ultima linguæ
> Ipsa jacet, terraquæ tremens immurmurat atræ;
> Utque salire solet mutilatæ cauda colubræ,
> Palpitat.

If a tongue would be talking without a mouth, what could it have done when it had all its organs of speech, and accomplices of sound, about it? I might here mention the story of the pippin-woman, had not I some reason to look upon it as fabulous.

I must confess I am so wonderfully charmed with the music of this little instrument, that I would by no means discourage it. All that I aim at by this dissertation is, to cure it of several disagreeable notes, and in particular of those little jarrings and dissonances which arise from anger, censoriousness, gossiping, and coquetry. In short, I would have it always tuned by good-nature, truth, discretion, and sincerity.

ADVENTURES OF A SHILLING.

I was last night visited by a friend of mine, who has an inexhaustible fund of discourse, and never fails to entertain his company with a variety of thoughts and hints that are altogether new and uncommon. Whether it were in complaisance to my way of living, or his real opinion, he advanced the following paradox, "That it required much greater talents to fill up and become a retired life, than a life of business." Upon this occasion he rallied very agreeably the busy men of the age, who only valued themselves for being in motion, and passing through a series of trifling and insignificant actions. In the heat of his discourse, seeing a piece of money lying on my table, "I defy (says he) any of these active persons to produce half the adventures that this twelvepenny piece has been engaged in, were it possible for him to give us an account of his life."

My friend's talk made so odd an impression upon my mind, that soon after I was a-bed I fell insensibly into a most unaccountable reverie, that had neither moral nor design in it, and cannot be so properly called a dream as a delirium.

Methoughts the shilling that lay upon the table reared itself upon its edge, and turning the face towards me, opened its mouth, and in a soft silver sound, gave me the following account of his life and adventures:

" I was born (says he) on the side of a mountain, near
a little village of Peru, and made a voyage to England
in an ingot, under the convoy of Sir Francis Drake.
I was, soon after my arrival, taken out of my Indian
habit, refined, naturalized, and put into the British
mode, with the face of Queen Elizabeth on one side,
and the arms of the country on the other. Being thus
equipped, I found in me a wonderful inclination to
ramble, and visit all parts of the new world into
which I was brought. The people very much favored
my natural disposition, and shifted me so fast from
hand to hand, that before I was five years old, I had
traveled into almost every corner of the nation. But
in the beginning of my sixth year, to my unspeakable
grief, I fell into the hands of a miserable old fellow,
who clapped me into an iron chest, where I found five
hundred more of my own quality who lay under the
same confinement. The only relief we had, was to be
taken out and counted over in the fresh air every
morning and evening. After an imprisonment of
several years, we heard somebody knocking at our
chest, and breaking it open with a hammer. This we
found was the old man's heir, who, as his father lay a
dying, was so good as to come to our release: he
separated us that very day. What was the fate of my
companions I know not: as for myself, I was sent to
the apothecary's shop for a pint of sack. The apothecary gave me to an herb-woman, the herb-woman
to a butcher, the butcher to a brewer, and the brewer
to his wife, who made a present of me to a noncon-
formist preacher. After this manner I made my way
merrily through the world ; for, as I told you before,
we shillings love nothing so much as traveling. I
sometimes fetched in a shoulder of mutton, sometimes

a play-book, and often had the satisfaction to treat a
Templar at a twelvepenny ordinary, or carry him, with
three friends, to Westminster Hall.

"In the midst of this pleasant progress which I made
from place to place, I was arrested by a superstitious
old woman, who shut me up in a greasy purse, in pur-
suance of a foolish saying, 'That while she kept a
Queen Elizabeth's shilling about her, she should never
be without money.' I continued here a close prisoner
for many months, till at last I was exchanged for eight
and forty farthings.

"I thus rambled from pocket to pocket till the beginning of the civil wars, when, to my shame be it
spoken, I was employed in raising soldiers against the
king: for being of a very tempting breadth, a sergeant
made use of me to inveigle country fellows, and list
them in the service of the parliament.

"As soon as he had made one man sure, his way
was to oblige him to take a shilling of a more homely
figure, and then practise the same trick upon another.
Thus I continued doing great mischief to the crown
till my officer, chancing one morning to walk abroad
earlier than ordinary, sacrificed me to his pleasures,
and made use of me to seduce a milk-maid. This
wench bent me, and gave me to her sweetheart,
applying more properly than she intended the usual
form of, 'To my love and from my love.' This un-
generous gallant marrying her within a few days after,
pawned me for a dram of brandy, and drinking me out
next day, I was beaten flat with a hammer, and again
set a running.

"After many adventures, which it would be tedious
to relate, I was sent to a young spendthrift, in company with the will of his deceased father. The young

fellow, who I found was very extravagant, gave great demonstrations of joy at the receiving of the will: but opening it, he found himself disinherited and cut off from the possession of a fair estate, by virtue of my being made a present to him. This put him into such a passion, that after having taking me in his hand, and cursed me, he squirred me away from him as far as he could fling me. I chanced to light in an unfrequented place under a dead wall, where I lay undiscovered and useless, during the usurpation of Oliver Cromwell.

" About a year after the king's return, a poor cavalier that was walking there about dinner-time, fortunately cast his eye upon me, and, to the great joy of us both, carried me to a cook's shop, where he dined upon me, and drank the king's health. When I came again into the world, I found that I had been happier in my retirement than I thought, having probably, by that means, escaped wearing a monstrous pair of breeches.

"Being now of great credit and antiquity, I was rather looked upon as a medal than an ordinary coin; for which reason a gamester laid hold of me, and converted me to a counter, having got together some dozens of us for that use. We led a melancholy life in his possession, being busy at those hours wherein current coin is at rest, and partaking the fate of our master, being in a few moments valued at a crown, a pound, or a sixpence, according to the situation in which the fortune of the cards placed us. I had at length the good luck to see my master break, by which means I was again sent abroad under my primitive denomination of a shilling.

" I shall pass over many other accidents of less moment, and hasten to that fatal catastrophe, when I fell into the hands of an artist, who conveyed me under ground, and with an unmerciful pair of shears, cut off my titles, clipped my brims, retrenched my shape, rubbed me to my inmost ring, and, in short, so spoiled and pillaged me, that he did not leave me worth a groat. You may think what a confusion I was in, to see myself thus curtailed and disfigured. I should have been ashamed to have shown my head, had not all my old acquaintance been reduced to the same shameful figure, excepting some few that were punched through the belly. In the midst of this general calamity, when everybody thought our misfortune irretrievable, and our case desperate, we were thrown into the furnace together, and (as it often happens with cities rising out of a fire) appeared with greater beauty and luster than we could ever boast of before. What has happened to me since this change of sex which you now see, I shall take some other opportunity to relate. In the mean time, I shall only repeat two adventures, as being very extraordinary, and neither of them having ever happened to me above once in my life. The first was, my being in a poet's pocket, who was so taken with the brightness and novelty of my appearance, that it gave occasion to the finest burlesque poem in the British language, entitled from me, 'The Splendid Shilling.' The second adventure,. which I must not omit, happened to me in the year 1703, when I was given away in charity to a blind man; but indeed this was by a mistake, the person who gave me having heedlessly thrown me into the hat among a pennyworth of farthings."

HUSBANDS AND WIVES.

My friend Will. Honeycomb has told me, for above this half year, that he had a great mind to try his hand at a Spectator, and that he would fain have one of his writing in my works. This morning I received from him the following letter, which, after having rectified some little orthographical mistakes, I shall make a present of to the public.

"DEAR SPEC.,

I was, about two nights ago, in company with very agreeable young people of both sexes, where talking of some of your papers which are written on conjugal love, there arose a dispute among us, whether there were not more bad husbands in the world than bad wives. A gentleman, who was advocate for the ladies, took this occasion to tell us the story of a famous siege in Germany, which I have since found related in my historical dictionary, after the following manner. When the emperor Conrade the Third had besieged Guelphus, duke of Bavaria, in the city of Hensberg, the women, finding that the town could not hold out long, petitioned the emperor that they might depart out of it, with so much as each of them could carry. The emperor, knowing they could not convey away many of their effects, granted them their petition ; when the women, to his great surprise, came out of the place with every one her husband upon her back. The emperor was so moved at the sight, that he burst into tears, and after having very much extolled the women for their

326

conjugal affection, gave the men to their wives, and received the duke into his favor.

" The ladies did not a little triumph at this story, asking us at the same time, whether in our consciences we believed that the men of any town in Great Britain would, upon the same offer, and at the same conjuncture, have loaden themselves with their wives; or rather, whether they would not have been glad of such an opportunity to get rid of them ? To this, my very good friend Tom Dapperwit, who took upon him to be the mouth of our sex, replied, that they would be very much to blame, if they would not do the same good office for the women, considering that their strength would be greater, and their burdens lighter. As we were amusing ourselves with discourses of this nature, in order to pass away the evening, which now begins to grow tedious, we fell into that laudable and primitive diversion of questions and commands. I was no sooner vested with the regal authority, but I enjoined all the ladies, under pain of my displeasure, to tell the company ingenuously, in case they had been in the siege above-mentioned, and had the same offers made them as the good women of that place, what every one of them would have brought off with her, and have thought most worth the saving ? There were several merry answers made to my question, which entertained us till bed-time. This filled my mind with such a huddle of ideas, that upon my going to sleep, I fell into the following dream.

" I saw a town of this island, which shall be nameless, invested on every side, and the inhabitants of it so straitened as to cry for quarter. The general refused any other terms than those granted to the above-mentioned town of Hensberg, namely, that the married women might come out with what they could bring along with them. Immediately the gate flew open, and a female procession appeared, multitudes of the sex following one another in a row, and staggering under their respective burdens. I took my stand upon an eminence in the enemy's camp, which was appointed for the general rendezvous of these female carriers, being very desirous to look into their several ladings. The first of them had a huge sack upon her shoulders, which she set down with great care : upon the opening of it, when I expected to have seen her husband shoot out of it, I found it was filled with china ware. The next appeared in a more decent figure, carrying a handsome young fellow upon her back : I could not forbear commending the young woman for her conjugal affection, when, to my great surprise, I found that she had left the good man at home, and brought away her gallant. I saw the third, at some distance, with a little withered face peeping over her shoulder, whom I could not suspect for any but her spouse, till upon her setting him down I heard her call him dear Pug, and found him to be her favorite monkey. A fourth brought a huge bale of cards along with her ; and the fifth a Bolonia lap-dog : for her husband, it seems, being a very burly man, she thought it would be less trouble for her to bring away little Cupid. The next was the wife of a rich usurer, loaden with a bag of gold ; she told us that her spouse was very old, and by the course of nature, could not expect to live long ; and that to show her tender regards for him, she had saved that which the poor man loved better than his life. The next came towards us with her son upon her back, who, we were told, was the greatest rake in the place, but so much the mother's darling, that she left her husband behind, with a large family of hopeful sons and daughters, for the sake of this graceless youth.

" It would be endless to mention the several persons, with their several loads, that appeared to me in this strange vision. All the place about me was covered with packs of ribbon, brocades, embroidery, and ten thousand other materials, sufficient to have furnished a whole street of toy-shops. One of the women having a husband that was none of the heaviest, was bringing him off upon her shoulders, at the same time that she carried a great bundle of Flanders lace under her arm ; but finding herself so over-loaden, that she could not save both of them, she dropped the good man, and brought away the bundle. In short, I found but one husband among this great mountain of baggage, who was a lively cobbler, and kicked and spurred all the while his wife was carrying him on, and, as it was said, had scarce passed a day in his life without giving her the discipline of the strap.

"I cannot conclude my letter, dear Spec., without telling thee one very odd whim in this my dream. I saw, methought, a dozen women employed in bringing off one man ; I could not guess who it should be, till upon his nearer approach I discovered thy short phiz. The women all declared that it was for the sake of thy works, and not thy person, that they brought thee off, and that it was on condition that thou shouldst continue the Spectator. If thou thinkest this dream will make a tolerable one, it is at thy service, from,

"DEAR SPEC., thine, sleeping and waking,

"WILL. HONEYCOMB."

The ladies will see by this letter, what I have often told them, that WILL. is one of those old-fashioned men of wit and pleasure of the town, that shows his parts by raillery on marriage, and one who has often tried his fortune that way without success. I cannot, however, dismiss his letter, without observing, that the true story on which it is built, does honor to the sex, and that, in order to abuse them, the writer is obliged to have recourse to dream and fiction.

RELIGIONS IN WAXWORK.

EVERY nation is distinguished by productions that are peculiar to it. Great Britain is particularly fruitful in religions, that shoot up and flourish in this climate more than in any other. We are so famous abroad for our great variety of sects and opinions, that an ingenious friend of mine, who is lately returned from his travels, assures me, there is a show at this time carried up and down in Germany, which represents all the religions in Great Britain in wax-work. Notwithstanding that the pliancy of the matter in which the images are wrought, makes it capable of being molded into all shapes and figures, my friend tells me, that he did not think it possible for it to be twisted and tortured into so many screwed faces and wry features as appeared in several of the figures that composed the show. I was, indeed, so pleased with the design of the German artist, that I begged my friend to give me an account of it in all its particulars, which he did after the following manner:

"I have often," says he, "been present at a show of elephants, camels, dromedaries, and other strange creatures, but I never saw so great an assembly of spectators as were met together at the opening of this great piece of wax-work. We were all placed in a large hall, according to the price that we had paid for our seats. The curtain that hung before the show was made by a master of tapestry, who had woven it in the figure of a monstrous hydra that had several heads, which bran-
330

dished out their tongues, and seemed to hiss at each other. Some of these heads were large and entire; and where any of them had been lopped away, there sprouted up several in the room of them; insomuch that for one head cut off, a man might see ten, twenty, or an hundred of a smaller size, creeping through the wound. In short, the whole picture was nothing but confusion and bloodshed. On a sudden," says my friend, " I was startled with a flourish of many musical instruments that I had never heard before, which was followed by a short tune (if it might be so called) wholly made up of jars and discords. Among the rest, there was an organ, a bagpipe, a groaning-board, stentorophonic trumpet, with several wind instruments of a most disagreeable sound, which I do not so much as know the names of. After a short flourish, the curtain was drawn up, and we were presented with the most extraordinary assembly of figures that ever entered into a man's imagination. The design of the workman was so well expressed in the dumb show before us, that it was not hard for an Englishman to comprehend the meaning of it.

" The principal figures were placed in a row, consisting of seven persons. The middle figure, which immediately attracted the eyes of the whole company, and was much bigger than the rest, was formed like a matron, dressed in the habit of an elderly woman of quality in Queen Elizabeth's days. The most remarkable parts of her dress, were the beaver with the steeple crown, the scarf that was darker than sable, and the lawn apron that was whiter than ermine. Her gown was of the richest black velvet and just upon her heart studded with large diamonds of an inestimable value, disposed in the form of a cross. She bore an inex-

pressible cheerfulness and dignity in her aspect; and
though she seemed in years, appeared with so much
spirit and vivacity, as gave her at the same time an air
of old age and immortality. I found my heart touched
with so much love and reverence at the sight of her,
that the tears ran down my face as I looked upon her;
and still the more I looked upon her, the more my heart
was melted with the sentiments of filial tenderness and
duty. I discovered every moment something so charming in this figure, that I could scarce take my eyes off
it. On its right hand there sat the figure of a woman
so covered with ornaments, that her face, her body,
and her hands, were almost entirely hid under them.
The little you could see of her face was painted; and
what I thought very odd, had something in it like artificial wrinkles; but I was the less surprised at it, when
I saw upon her forehead an old-fashioned tower of gray
hairs. Her head-dress rose very high by three several stories or degrees; her garments had a thousand
colors in them, and were embroidered with crosses in
gold, silver, and silk: she had nothing on, so much as
a glove or a slipper, which was not marked with this
figure; nay, so superstitiously fond did she appear of
it, that she sat cross-legged. I was quickly sick of this
tawdry composition of ribbons, silks, and jewels, and
therefore cast my eye on a dame which was just the
reverse of it. I need not tell my reader, that the lady
before described was Popery, or that she I am now
going to describe is Presbytery. She sat on the left
hand of the venerable matron, and so much resembled
her in the features of her countenance, that she seemed
her sister; but at the same time that one observed a
likeness in her beauty, one could not but take notice,
that there was something in it sickly and splenetic.

Her face had enough to discover the relation, but it was drawn up into a peevish figure, soured with discontent, and overcast with melancholy. She seemed offended at the matron for the shape of her hat, as too much resembling the triple coronet of the person who sat by her. One might see, likewise, that she dissented from the white apron and the cross ; for which reasons she had made herself a plain homely dowdy, and turned her face towards the sectaries that sat on the left hand, as being afraid of looking upon the matron, lest she should see the harlot by her.

" On the right hand of Popery sat Judaism, represented by an old man embroidered with phylacteries, and distinguished by many typical figures, which I had not skill enough to unriddle. He was placed among the rubbish of a temple; but instead of weeping over it, (which I should have expected from him,) he was counting out a bag of money upon the ruins of it.

" On his right hand was Deism, or Natural Religion. This was a figure of a half-naked awkward country wench, who with proper ornaments and education would have made an agreeable and beautiful appearance; but for want of those advantages, was such a spectacle as a man would blush to look upon.

" I have now," continued my friend, "given you an account of those who were placed on the right hand of the matron, and who, according to the order in which they sat, were Deism, Judaism, and Popery. On the left hand, as I told you, appeared Presbytery. The next to her was a figure which somewhat puzzled me : it was that of a man looking, with horror in his eyes, upon a silver bason filled with water. Observing something in his countenance that looked like lunacy,

I fancied at first that he was to express that kind of distraction which the physicians call the Hydrophobia : but considering what the intention of the show was, I immediately recollected myself, and concluded it to be Anabaptism.

" The next figure was a man that sat under a most profound composure of mind : he wore an hat whose brims were exactly parallel to the horizon: his garment had neither sleeve nor skirt, nor so much as a superfluous button. What he called his cravat, was a little piece of white linen quilled with great exactness, and hanging below his chin about two inches. Seeing a book in his hand, I asked our artist what it was, who told me it was the Quaker's religion; upon which I desired a sight of it. Upon perusal, I found it to be nothing but a new-fashioned grammar, or an art of abridging ordinary discourse. The nouns were reduced to a very small number, as the *light*, *friend*, *Babylon*. The principal of his pronouns was *thou ;* and as for *you, ye,* and *yours*, I found they were not looked upon as parts of speech in this grammar. All the verbs wanted the second person plural ; the participles ending all in *ing* or *ed,* which were marked with a particular accent. There were no adverbs besides *yea* and *nay*. The same thrift was observed in the prepositions. The conjunctions were only *hem !* and *ha !* and the interjections brought under the three heads of sighing, sobbing, and groaning. There was at the end of the grammar a little nomenclature, called ' The Christian Man's Vocabulary,' which gave new appellations, or (if you will) Christian names to almost everything in life. I replaced the book in the hand of the figure, not without admiring the simplicity of its garb, speech, and behavior.

" Just opposite to this row of religions, there was a statue dressed in a fool's coat, with a cap of bells upon his head, laughing and pointing at the figures that stood before him. This idiot is supposed to say in his heart what David's fool did some thousands of years ago, and was therefore designed as a proper representative of those among us who are called atheists and infidels by others, and free-thinkers by themselves.

" There were many other groups of figures which I did not know the meaning of ; but seeing a collection of both sexes turning their backs upon the company, and laying their heads very close together, I inquired after their religion, and found that they called themselves the Philadelphians, or the family of love.

" In the opposite corner there sat another little congregation of strange figures, opening their mouths as wide as they could gape, and distinguished by the title of ' The sweet Singers of Israel.'

" I must not omit, that in this assembly of wax there were several pieces that moved by clock-work, and gave great satisfaction to the spectators. Behind the matron there stood one of these figures, and behind Popery, another, which, as the artist told us, were each of them the genius of the person they attended. That behind Popery represented Persecution, and the other Moderation. The first of these moved by secret springs towards a great heap of dead bodies that lay piled upon one another at a considerable distance behind the principal figures. There were written on the foreheads of these dead men several hard words, as Prae-Adamites, Sabbatarians, Cameronians, Muggletonians, Brownists, Independents, Masonites, Camisars, and the like. At the approach of Persecution, it was so contrived, that as she held up her bloody flag, the whole assembly of dead men, like those in the Rehearsal, started up and drew their swords. This was followed by great clashings and noise, when, in the midst of the tumult, the figure of Moderation moved gently towards this new army, which, upon her holding up a paper in her hand, inscribed, ' Liberty of Conscience,' immediately fell into a heap of carcasses, remaining in the same quiet posture that they lay at first."

A FRIEND OF MANKIND.

CHARITY is a virtue of the heart, and not of the hands, says an old writer. Gifts and alms are the expressions, not the essence, of this virtue. A man may bestow great sums on the poor and indigent, without being charitable, and may be charitable when he is not able to bestow anything. Charity is therefore a habit of good will, or benevolence, in the soul, which disposes us to the love, assistance, and relief of mankind, especially of those who stand in need of it. The poor man who has this excellent frame of mind, is no less entitled to the reward of this virtue, than the man who founds a college. For my own part, I am charitable to an extravagance this way. I never saw an indigent person in my life without reaching out to him some of this imaginary relief. I cannot but sympathize with every one I meet that is in affliction; and if my abilities were equal to my wishes, there should be neither pain nor poverty in the world.

To give my reader a right notion of myself in this particular, I shall present him with the secret history of one of the most remarkable parts of my life.

I was once engaged in search of the philosopher's stone. It is frequently observed of men who have been busied in this pursuit, that though they have failed in their principal design, they have, however, made such discoveries in their way to it, as have sufficiently recompensed their inquiries. In the same manner, though I cannot boast of my success in that affair, I do not repent of my engaging in it, because it produced in my mind such an habitual exercise of charity, as made it much better than perhaps it would have been, had I never been lost in so pleasing a delusion.

As I did not question but I should soon have a new Indies in my possession, I was perpetually taken up in considering how to turn it to the benefit of mankind. In order to it I employed a whole day in walking about this great city, to find out proper places for the erection of hospitals. I had likewise entertained that project, which had since succeeded in another place, of building churches at the court end of the town, with this only difference, that instead of fifty, I intended to have built a hundred, and to have seen them all finished in less than one year.

I had with great pains and application got together a list of all the French Protestants ; and by the best accounts I could come at, had calculated the value of all those estates and effects which every one of them had left in his own country for the sake of his religion, being fully determined to make it up to him, and return some of them the double of what they had lost.

As I was one day in my laboratory, my operator, who was to fill my coffers for me, and used to foot it from the other end of the town every morning, complained of a sprain in his leg, that he had met with over against St. Clement's church. This so affected me, that, as a standing mark of my gratitude to him, and out of compassion to the rest of my fellow-citizens, I resolved to new pave every street within the liberties, and entered a memorandum in my pocket-book accordingly. About the same time I entertained some thoughts of mending all the highways on this side the Tweed, and of making all the rivers in England navigable.

But the project I had most at heart, was the settling upon every man in Great Britain three pounds a year, (in which sum may be comprised, according to Sir William Pettit's observations, all the necessities of life,) leaving to them whatever else they could get by their own industry, to lay out on superfluities.

I was above a week debating in myself what I should do in the matter of Impropriations; but at length came to a resolution to buy them all up, and restore them to the church.

As I was one day walking near St. Paul's, I took some time to survey that structure, and not being entirely satisfied with it, though I could not tell why, I had some thoughts of pulling it down, and building it up anew at my own expense.

For my own part, as I have no pride in me, I intended to take up with a coach and six, half a dozen footmen, and live like a private gentleman.

It happened about this time that public matters looked very gloomy, taxes came hard, the war went on heavily, people complained of the great burdens that were laid upon them; this made me resolve to set aside one morning, to consider seriously the state of the nation. I was the more ready to enter on it, because I was obliged, whether I would or no, to sit at home in my morning gown, having, after a most incredible expense, pawned a new suit of clothes, and a full-bottomed wig, for a sum of money which my operator assured me was the last he should want to bring all matters to bear.

After having considered many projects, I at length resolved to beat the common enemy at his own weapons, and laid a scheme which would have blown him up in a quarter of a year, had things succeeded to my wishes. As I was in this golden dream, somebody knocked at my door. I opened it, and found it was a messenger that brought me a letter from the laboratory. The fellow looked so miserably poor, that I was resolved to make his fortune before he delivered his message; but seeing he brought a letter from my operator, I concluded I was bound to it in honor, as much as a prince is to give a reward to one that brings him the first news of a victory. I knew this was the long-expected hour of projection, and which I had waited for, with great impatience, above half a year before. In short, I broke open my letter in a transport of joy, and found it as follows.

" SIR,

After having got out of you everything you can conveniently spare, I scorn to trespass upon your generous nature, and, therefore, must ingenuously confess to you, that I know no more of the philosopher's stone than you do. I shall only tell you for your comfort, that I never yet could bubble a blockhead out of his money. They must be men of wit and parts who are for my purpose. This made me apply myself to a person of your wealth and ingenuity. How I have succeeded, you yourself can best tell.

" Your humble servant to command,

THOMAS WHITE."

"I have locked up the laboratory, and laid the key under the door."

I was very much shocked at the unworthy treatment of this man, and not a little mortified at my disappointment, though not so much for what I myself, as what the public, suffered by it. I think, however, I ought to let the world know what I designed for them, and hope that such of my readers who find they had a share in my good intentions, will accept the will for the deed.

ADVICE IN LOVE.

It is an old observation, which has been made of politicians who would rather ingratiate themselves with their sovereign, than promote his real service, that they accommodate their counsels to his inclinations, and advise him to such actions only as his heart is naturally set upon. The privy-counselor of one in love must observe the same conduct, unless he would forfeit the friendship of the person who desires his advice. I have known several odd cases of this nature. Hipparchus was going to marry a common woman, but being resolved to do nothing without the advice of his friend Philander, he consulted him upon the occasion. Philander told him his mind freely, and represented his mistress to him in such strong colors, that the next morning he received a challenge for his pains, and before twelve o'clock was run through the body by the man who had asked his advice. Celia was more prudent on the like occasion; she desired Leonilla to give her opinion freely upon a young fellow who made his addresses to her. Leonilla, to oblige her, told her with great frankness, that she looked upon him as one of the most worthless —— Celia, foreseeing what a character she was to expect, begged her not to go on, for that she had been privately married to him above a fortnight. The truth of it is, a woman seldom asks advice before she has bought her wedding-clothes. When she has made her own choice, for form's sake she sends a *congé d'elire* to her friends.

If we look into the secret springs and motives that set people at work on these occasions, and put them upon asking advice, which they never intend to take; I look upon it to be none of the least, that they are incapable of keeping a secret which is so very pleasing to them. A girl longs to tell her confidant, that she hopes to be married in a little time, and, in order to talk of the pretty fellow that dwells so much in her thoughts, asks her very gravely, what she would advise her to in a case of so much difficulty. Why else should Melissa, who had not a thousand pounds in the world, go into every quarter of the town to ask her acquaintance whether they would advise her to take Tom Townly, that made his addresses to her with an estate of five thousand a year? 'Tis very pleasant on this occasion, to hear the lady propose her doubts, and to see the pains she is at to get over them.

I must not here omit a practise that is in use among the vainer part of our own sex, who will often ask a friend's advice, in relation to a fortune whom they are never likely to come at. Will. Honeycomb, who is now on the verge of threescore, took me aside not long since, and asked me in his most serious look, whether I would advise him to marry my Lady Betty Single, who, by the way, is one of the greatest fortunes about town. I stared him full in the face upon so strange a question; upon which he immediately gave me an inventory of her jewels and estate, adding, that he was resolved to do nothing in a matter of such consequence without my approbation. Finding he would have an answer, I told him, if he could get the lady's consent, he had mine. This is about the tenth match which, to my knowledge, Will. has consulted his friends upon, without ever opening his mind to the party herself.

I have been engaged in this subject by the following letter, which comes to me from some notable young female scribe, who, by the contents of it, seems to have carried matters so far, that she is ripe for asking advice; but as I would not lose her good-will, nor forfeit the reputation which I have with her for wisdom, I shall only communicate the letter to the public, without returning any answer to it.

" MR. SPECTATOR,

Now, sir, the thing is this : Mr. Shapely is the prettiest gentleman about town. He is very tall, but not too tall neither. He dances like an angel. His mouth is made I do not know how, but it is the prettiest that I ever saw in my life. He is always laughing, for he has an infinite deal of wit. If you did but see how he rolls his stockings ! He has a thousand pretty fancies, and I am sure, if you saw him, you would like him. He is a very good scholar, and can talk Latin as fast as English. I wish you could but see him dance. Now you must understand poor Mr. Shapely has no estate; but how can he help that, you know? and yet my friends are so unreasonable as to be always teasing me about him, because he has no estate: but I am sure he has that that is better than an estate ; for he is a good-natured, ingenious, modest, civil, tall, well-bred, handsome man, and I am obliged to him for his civilities ever since I saw him. I forgot to tell you that he has black eyes, and looks upon me now and then as if he had tears in them. And yet my friends are so unreasonable, that they would have me be uncivil to him. I have a good portion which they cannot hinder me of, and I shall be fourteen on the 29th day of August next, and am therefore willing to settle in the world as soon as I can, and so is Mr. Shapely. But everybody I advise with here is poor Mr. Shapely's enemy. I desire, therefore, you will give me your advice, for I know you are a wise man; and if you advise me well, I am resolved to follow it. I heartily wish you could see him dance, and am,

" Sir, your most humble servant,

B. D.

" He loves your Spectators mightily."

THOUGHTS IN WESTMINSTER ABBEY.

WHEN I am in a serious humor, I very often walk by myself in Westminster Abbey ; where the gloominess of the place, and the use to which it is applied, with the solemnity of the building, and the condition of the people who lie in it, are apt to fill the mind with a kind of melancholy, or rather thoughtfulness, that is not disagreeable. I yesterday passed a whole afternoon in the churchyard, the cloisters, and the church, amusing myself with the tombstones and inscriptions that I met with in those several regions of the dead. Most of them recorded nothing else of the buried person, but that he was born upon one day, and died upon another : the whole history of his life being comprehended in those two circumstances, that are common to all mankind. I could not but look upon these registers of existence, whether of brass or marble, as a kind of satire upon the departed persons ; who had left no other memorial of them, but that they were born and that they died. They put me in mind of several persons mentioned in the battles of heroic poems, who have sounding names given them, for no other reason but that they may be killed, and are celebrated for nothing but being knocked on the head. The life of these men is finely described in holy writ by " the path of an arrow," which is immediately closed up and lost.

Upon my going into the church, I entertained myself with the digging of a grave; and saw in every shovelful of it that was thrown up, the fragment of a bone or skull intermixt with a kind of fresh moldering earth, that some time or other had a place in the composition of a human body. Upon this I began to consider with myself what innumerable multitudes of people lay confused together under the pavement of that ancient cathedral; how men and women, friends and enemies, priests and soldiers, monks and prebendaries, were crumbled amongst one another, and blended together in the same common mass; how beauty, strength, and youth, with old age, weakness, and deformity, lay undistinguished in the same promiscuous heap of matter.

After having thus surveyed this great magazine of mortality, as it were, in the lump; I examined it more particularly by the accounts which I found on several of the monuments which are raised in every quarter of that ancient fabric. Some of them were covered with such extravagant epitaphs, that, if it were possible for the dead person to be acquainted with them, he would blush at the praises which his friends have bestowed upon him. There are others so excessively modest, that they deliver the character of the person departed in Greek or Hebrew, and by that means are not understood once in a twelvemonth. In the poetical quarter, I found there were poets who had no monuments, and monuments which had no poets. I observed, indeed, that the present war had filled the church with many of these uninhabited monuments, which had been erected to the memory of persons whose bodies were perhaps buried in the plains of Blenheim, or in the bosom of the ocean.

I could not but be very much delighted with several

modern epitaphs, which are written with great elegance of expression and justness of thought, and therefore do honor to the living as well as to the dead. As a foreigner is very apt to conceive an idea of the ignorance or politeness of a nation, from the turn of their public monuments and inscriptions, they should be submitted to the perusal of men of learning and genius, before they are put in execution. Sir Cloudesly Shovel's monument has very often given me great offense: instead of the brave rough English Admiral, which was the distinguishing character of that plain gallant man, he is represented on his tomb by the figure of a beau, dressed in a long periwig, and reposing himself upon velvet cushions under a canopy of state. The inscription is answerable to the monument; for instead of celebrating the many remarkable actions he had performed in the service of his country, it acquaints us only with the manner of his death, in which it was impossible for him to reap any honor. The Dutch, whom we are apt to despise for want of genius, show an infinitely greater taste of antiquity and politeness in their buildings and works of this nature, than what we meet with in those of our own country. The monuments of their admirals, which have been erected at the public expense, represent them like themselves; and are adorned with rostral crowns and naval ornaments, with beautiful festoons of seaweed, shells, and coral.

But to return to our subject. I have left the repository of our English kings for the contemplation of another day, when I shall find my mind disposed for so serious an amusement. I know that entertainments of this nature are apt to raise dark and dismal thoughts in timorous minds and gloomy imaginations;

but for my own part, though I am always serious, I do not know what it is to be melancholy; and can therefore take a view of nature in her deep and solemn scenes, with the same pleasure as in her most gay and delightful ones. By this means I can improve myself with those objects which others consider with terror. When I look upon the tombs of the great, every emotion of envy dies in me; when I read the epitaphs of the beautiful, every inordinate desire goes out; when I meet with the grief of parents upon a tombstone, my heart melts with compassion; when I see the tomb of the parents themselves, I consider the vanity of grieving for those whom we must quickly follow: when I see kings lying by those who deposed them, when I consider rival wits placed side by side, or the holy men that divided the world with their contests and disputes, I reflect with sorrow and astonishment on the little competitions, factions, and debates of mankind. When I read the several dates of the tombs, of some that died yesterday, and some six hundred years ago, I consider that great day when we shall all of us be contemporaries, and make our appearance together.

THE END.